The Economics of Courts and Litigation

NEW HORIZONS IN LAW AND ECONOMICS

Series editors: Gerrit De Geest, *University of Ghent and University of Antwerp, Belgium and University of Utrecht, the Netherlands*; Roger Van den Bergh, *University of Rotterdam and University of Utrecht, the Netherlands*; and Thomas S. Ulen, *University of Illinois at Urbana-Champaign, USA.*

The application of economic ideas and theories to the law and the explanation of markets and public economics from a legal point of view is recognized as one of the most exciting developments in both economics and the law. This important series is designed to make a significant contribution to the development of law and economics.

The main emphasis is on the development and application of new ideas. The series provides a forum for original research in areas such as criminal law, civil law, labour law, corporate law, family law, regulation and privatization, tax, risk and insurance and competition law. International in its approach it includes some of the best theoretical and empirical work from both well-established researchers and the new generation of scholars.

Titles in the series include:

Post-Chicago Developments in Antitrust Law
Edited by Antonio Cucinotta, Robert Pardolesi and Roger Van den Burgh

From Economic to Legal Competition
New Perspectives on Law and Institutions in Europe
Edited by Alain Marciano and Jean-Michel Josselin

New Perspectives on Economic Crime
Edited by Hans Sjögren and Göran Skogh

Law, Economics and Cyberspace
The Effects of Cyberspace on the Economic Analysis of Law
Niva Elkin-Koren and Eli M. Salzberger

Games and Public Administration
The Law and Economics of Regulation and Licensing
Georg von Wangenheim

Law and the State
A Political Economy Apoproach
Edited by Alain Marciano and Jean-Michel Josselin

Democracy, Freedom and Coercion
A Law and Economics Approach
Edited by Alain Marciano and Jean-Michel Josselin

The Economics of Courts and Litigation
Francisco Cabrillo and Sean Fitzpatrick

The Economics of Courts and Litigation

Francisco Cabrillo

Professor of Economics, Complutense University, Madrid, Spain

Sean Fitzpatrick

Consultant, Economic and Social Committee, Regional Government of Madrid, Spain

NEW HORIZONS IN LAW AND ECONOMICS

Edward Elgar

Cheltenham, UK • Northampton, MA, USA

Published by
Edward Elgar Publishing Limited
Glensanda House
Montpellier Parade
Cheltenham
Glos GL50 1UA
UK

Edward Elgar Publishing, Inc.
William Pratt House
9 Dewey Court
Northampton
Massachusetts 01060
USA

A catalogue record for this book
is available from the British Library

Library of Congress Control Number: 2008927691

ISBN 978 1 84376 804 3

Typeset by Cambrian Typesetters, Camberley, Surrey
Printed and bound in Great Britain by MPG Books Ltd, Bodmin, Cornwall

Contents

Figures, tables and boxes

FIGURES

TABLES

BOXES

Acknowledgements

We would like to thank *The Lawyer* for permission to republish the Global 100 and Euro 100 surveys in the Appendix to Chapter 5.

We would like to express our gratitude to the Foundation Rafael Del Pino for their generous support of this project. Financial assistance offered by the Spanish Ministry of Education, project number SEJ2006-10041, is also gratefully acknowledged.

1. Overview

1. INTRODUCTION

The importance of an effective legal and justice system for economic development is now beyond dispute. Economists have highlighted the importance of securing property rights and the enforcement of contracts for economic development at least since the writings of Adam Smith.[1] Legal institutions do not have a complementary or incidental role in economic development but are a fundamental requisite for the functioning of a market economy.[2] This factor is now acknowledged by lawyers, economists, political scientists and members of international donor institutions alike. Failure to guarantee and enforce legal rights and norms is economically devastating. For example, where courts do not enforce contractual obligations, there is a general unwillingness to enter into anonymous (market-based) exchange, leading to a loss in productivity and seriously hindering long-term economic development. Where the judiciary is ill-functioning, firms wishing to do business in these countries must operate with scant legal protection which injects great uncertainty into activities, increases transaction costs and opens up possibilities for opportunism.[3] In such an environment it becomes impossible to secure international investment, as investors have no means to secure their capital. Any policy for attracting foreign investment – by reducing taxes or facilitating the entry and exit of capital – is of little use where investors face numerous problems in recovering debts, owing to an inadequate and inefficient judicial administration.

The relationship between justice and the economy is one of mutual dependency. Whilst a given judicial structure can facilitate or frustrate economic development, the latter may also permit the improvement of the judicial system. An economy defines the quantity of resources and technology a judicial system has at its disposal, but altering the efficiency of the judiciary can affect economic growth. History instructs us that, with the same levels of economic development, different judicial standards are feasible and that an

1 See Smith (1776 [1981]); see also North (1990).
2 Cabrillo and Pastor (2001), p. 9.
3 See Schäfer (1998).

independent, competent and efficient judiciary have all been key factors for long-term economic development.

Further, failure to provide a legal safety net has important social implications, as ineffective legal frameworks and institutions present a critical obstacle to the alleviation of poverty, institutionalizing the exclusion of the poor and marginalized from participation in development.[4] Without the protection of human and property rights and a comprehensive framework of laws no equitable development is possible. As James D. Wolfensohn, former president of the World Bank, argues,

> A government must ensure that it has an effective system of property, contract, labor, bankruptcy, commercial codes, personal rights laws and other elements of a comprehensive legal system that is effectively, impartially and cleanly administered by a well-functioning, impartial and honest judicial and legal system.[5]

For this reason, international donor institutions have exerted great efforts in legal and judicial reform since the early 1990s. To wit, the World Bank recognizes 'effective legal and justice systems' as one of the four structural pillars of development in the Comprehensive Development Framework. It seems to be agreed by most scholars and policy reformers involved in the area today that judicial reform within the larger goal of legal reform warrants increased attention. In 2002 there were over 300 World Bank financed projects dealing with, or including elements of, legal and judicial reform.[6] World Bank projects are aimed solely at increasing the economic performance of a nation, as the Bank is proscribed from interfering in the political affairs of its members.[7] Up to 2002 the World Bank, the Inter-American Development Bank and the Asian Development Bank had given over $800 million in loans directed towards judicial reform.[8] Other actors include the UNDP, the European Union and its member states and the American, Norwegian, Australian, Canadian and Japanese governments.[9]

Judicial reform is only part of a greater body of legal reform. Legal reform generally includes 'everything from writing or revising commercial codes, bankruptcy statutes, and company laws through overhauling regulatory agencies and teaching justice ministry officials how to draft legislation that fosters

4 For a discussion on the relationship between poverty and legal structures, see Wolfensohn (1999).

5 Ibid., p. 10.

6 World Bank (2002).

7 Messick (1999), p. 119.

8 Messick (2002), p. 1.

9 Ibid.

private investment.'[10] Judicial reform, on the other hand, generally refers to measures taken within the courts and the judicial branch of government. It is common for these reform efforts to address issues directly related to court capacity, such as wages, number of personnel, court infrastructure and technology. More recently, thinking has shifted towards broadening the scope of judicial reform. Emphasis is now being placed on organizational aspects, management, incentives, education and rules, and is directed at courts of all types and instances, without excluding those organs responsible for judicial power and the administration of justice.[11] Moreover, reforms should be aimed not only at increasing court capacity but also at accountability and broader issues of governance.

2. JUSTICE DELAYED

Judicial delay has been with us since the very inception of judicial systems and over the passage of time has been the lament of many scholars and judges alike. Commenting on the flood of automobile accidents in 1955, Judge Ulysses Schwart of the Illinois Appellate Court professed that:

> The law's delay in many lands and throughout history has been the subject of tragedy and comedy. Hamlet summarized the seven burdens of man and put the law's delay fifth on his list. If the meter of his verse had permitted, he would perhaps have put it first. Dickens memorialized it in *Bleak House*, Chekhov and Moliére have written tragedies based on it. Gilbert and Sullivan have satirized it in song. Thus, it is not a new problem for the profession, although we doubt that it has ever assumed the proportion which now confronts it.[12]

Recognition of the importance of timely adjudication is not new. In England, it may already be found in Magna Carta. 'To no one will we sell, to no one deny or delay right or justice.' In the Preamble to the Code Louis XIV (1667) – a precursor to modern European codification – the code, it was stated, was formulated '*de rendre l'expédition des affaires plus prompte*.'[13] It has become a constitutional right in many cases. Article 24(2) of the Spanish Constitution identifies the '*proceso sin dilaciones indebidas*' or right of everyone to a trial without undue delays, which is related to '*tutela judicial efectiva*', or the right to effective judicial protection.[14] Rule 1 of the Federal Rules

---

10 Messick (1999), p. 118.
11 Cabrillo and Pastor (2001), p. 9.
12 Carrington (2004), p. 69.
13 Storme (2004), p. iii.
14 See Velayos (2004).

of Civil Procedure in the United States governing the conduct of proceedings in civil litigation states that all other rules should 'be construed and administered to secure the just, speedy and inexpensive determination of every action.'[15] Indeed, similar written 'assertions' can be found in most legal systems.

The right to adjudication within a reasonable time is stated in Article 6 of the European Convention on Human Rights. It provides that, 'In the determination of their rights and obligations . . . everyone is entitled to a . . . hearing within a reasonable time.'[16] Though it is difficult to identify what a reasonable time is and subsequent rulings have considered this to vary substantially according to the nature of the case at hand,[17] active involvement by the European Court of Human Rights must be welcomed as a resource for putting additional pressure on national governments and their courts.

Whilst court delay has been with us since the inception of judicial systems, we argue that we are currently at an opportune moment in legal scholarship. Legal scholars have begun to move past merely highlighting the importance of proceedings without undue delay and have essentially begun to recognize the importance of the allocation of judicial resources 'proportionate to the nature of the issues involved.'[18] Legal scholarship has presented an opportunity for the application of economics as a tool to improve the courts and the administration of justice.

Economics recognizes that the task of the courts is too important to be left in the hands of any particular group of stakeholders.[19] Legal scholarship is catching up with economic analysis. Lord Woolf, in perhaps the single most influential report on civil law reform in Europe of the last thirty years, emphasized the fact that litigants and lawyers use as many of the courts' resources as desired.[20] Poorly designed procedural law in many countries (be it too

---

15 See Carrington (2004).

16 Art. 6, para. 1, in its entirety provides: 'In the determination of his civil rights and obligations or of any criminal charge against him, everyone is entitled to a fair and public hearing within a reasonable time by an independent and impartial tribunal established by law. Judgment shall be pronounced publicly but the press and public may be excluded from all or part of the trial in the interests of morals, public order or national security in a democratic society, where the interests of juveniles or the protection of the private life of the parties so require, or to the extent strictly necessary in the opinion of the court in special circumstances where publicity would prejudice the interests of justice.'

17 See Zuckerman (2003), Chapter 1.

18 See Woolf (1996).

19 Shavell (1999a).

20 Woolf (1996). Most of his recommendations were accepted by the government, and formed the basis for the Civil Procedure Rules (CPR) introduced in England in 1999. We will return to this later.

BOX 1.1 HEAVEN CAN WAIT

Heaven can wait, Italian court tells dying man

With six months to live, man told to return to court in 14 months

Tuesday, March 8, 2005 Posted: 2142 GMT (0542 HKT)

ROME, Italy (Reuters) – A man given six months to live by his doctors has been told by an Italian court to come back in 14 months to hear the outcome of his demand for insurance damages.

Carmelo Cisabella, 39, has an inoperable spine disease and is anxious to pick up some 450 000 euros ($596 300) in already-agreed damages from his insurers to help ease his final months of life, *Il Messaggero* newspaper reported on Tuesday.

In a bid to speed up the process, Cisabella turned to the Sicilian courts to put pressure on the slow-moving insurers, but was told to return next year to hear their decision.

In his frustration, he chained himself to the gates of the law courts to bring attention to his plight. *Il Messaggero* said Cisabella's woes dated back more than a decade when he was left paralysed by a motorcycle accident. Confined to a wheelchair, he subsequently developed a lethal infection of the spine.

The insurance claim dates back to the road crash.

Italian justice is notoriously slow and it takes on average 3041 days to obtain a definitive sentence in a civil case.

Source: http://edition.cnn.com/2005/LAW/03/08/italy.court.reut/index.html.

complex or too discretionary) has afforded lawyers and their clients the possibility to 'fight it out' on matters of procedure as opposed to substance, with ample room for socially wasteful strategic behaviour. Massive differences exist within Europe.[21]

[21] For instance, first instance civil proceedings last about 3.3 years on average in Italy and litigants frequently have to wait 10 years for a final judgment (see Box 1.1). (See Chiarloni 1999, p. 268.) Debt recovery on moveable goods almost does not exist. For real estate, these proceedings routinely take over four years. In Spain, small claims procedures that should last 100 days according to legally established time limits take on average 436 days. Debt enforcement proceedings take more than 250 days where a debtor does not contest a proceeding instead of the 20 days set out by law, and 550 days

A major reason for delay has been that the legal establishment has overemphasized accuracy over costs. Courts, in defence of the honourable principle of the right to a fair and impartial trial, have tended to overstate the importance of accuracy in adjudication. Often, they have done so with clear neglect for cost and delay. The value of accuracy has simply been assumed as intrinsic and courts work with procedural rules (as well as substantive law) based on the importance of increased accuracy.[22] It is easy to see why lawyers would overstate the significance of accuracy, or as Zuckerman puts it 'rectitude of decision.'[23] If cost considerations – or time – are not taken into account, there is little means to quantify the benefits of accuracy or understand when more or less accuracy is desirable.[24] Correctly applying the law to the facts of a case without heed to costs and time is a clear mismanagement of resources. An increase in accuracy is accompanied by social costs, as it necessitates a more time-consuming and higher-value legal process.

Courts must make important resource allocation decisions which are, in the words of Lord Woolf, 'proportionate to the nature of the issues involved.'[25] The socially optimal degree of accuracy is dependent on a trade-off between social value and cost.[26] Accuracy comes at a cost and beyond a certain point the marginal gains to accuracy are less than the prevailing costs incurred. The fact that Lord Woolf recognized the importance of proportionality of costs and the importance of resource allocation decisions constitutes a significant shift in traditional legal scholarship. Moreover, though his work was based on the

---

when the debtor contests the action. Judgment enforcement proceedings take on average 9.16 months (Giménez 1999, p. 395). In Germany, on the other hand, local court proceedings take on average only 4.6 months to deal with cases, which includes the time taken from filing a claim to settlement or final decision. Regional court proceedings take on average only 6.5 months for cases, from filing to settlement or final decision. The appeal rate on regional court proceedings is approximately 50 per cent, which can prolong proceedings substantially, given that the average duration of appeal proceedings in the higher regional courts is 8.7 months. Appeals on local court decisions to the regional courts take 5.3 months on average and are less common. One of the factors that place a substantial burden on appellate courts in Germany is the fact that appeals can generally be made on fact as well as law (Gottwald 1999, pp. 212–13).

22 Kaplow (1994).

23 Zuckerman (1999).

24 Zuckerman (1999), Chapter 1.

25 Woolf (1995), p. 3.

26 The social value of accuracy is discussed at greater length below. Among the benefits associated with accuracy are: the increased incentives to obey the law; increased incentives to engage in certain activities because one will not falsely be accused; better incentives to engage in optimal – not sub-optimal or excessive – precautions, and lower litigation costs because parties are better able to estimate trial outcome. For an overview, see Shavell (2004), pp. 450–56.

legal system in England and Wales, its message would appear to have spread to continental Europe and many commissions have been set up to review his recommendations.[27]

There are substantial costs to delay. First, there is a disutility associated with a remedy over time.[28] Arriving at a correct decision ten years after an incident may be of little use to an injured party, as our example with the paralysed Italian motorcyclist suggests. Second, the sheer amount of time devoted to one case by the courts means that other complaints are not given due attention. Moreover, and perhaps more importantly, other complaints will never be heard because they will never be brought to court. Third, arriving at the truth with (near) 100 per cent certitude is a very expensive endeavour. Whilst it is plausible to assume that increasing the resources invested increases the probability of arriving at a correct decision, there are good reasons to suspect that there are decreasing marginal returns to such investments. Further, it is the duty of the state to allocate its resources efficiently between numerous sectors, including health, defence and education. The latter sectors clearly suffer as a result of the endeavour to get to the truth 'at any cost', as this money could be spent differently. Fourth, there is a waste of human capital. The time spent by lawyers, judges, and all other parties could be better allocated to other activities. Lawyers, in particular, are the clearest beneficiaries of this weakness within court structures.

It is encouraging to see that responsibility for the speed of civil litigation is increasingly being placed in the hands of the courts, as the pace and nature of adjudication are too important to be left in the hands of litigants and their lawyers. The European Court of Human Rights has held that in civil litigation it is the responsibility of the courts to ensure that a litigant's entitlement to expeditious adjudication is not undermined by the delay that other parties are willing to cause. In Unión Alimentaria Sanders S.A. *v.* Spain,[29] the Court received a complaint by a Spanish litigant who argued there had been an infringement of his right to adjudication within a reasonable time. The Spanish Government argued that, given that it was a principle of Spanish civil procedure that the responsibility for progressing proceedings rested on the parties, the Spanish courts could not be held responsible for delays induced by parties. The Court rejected this argument, reiterating that 'such a principle does not absolve the courts from ensuring compliance with the requirements of Article 6 (art. 6) concerning reasonable time.'

---

27 Storme (2004).

28 Zuckerman (1999), p. 7.

29 Unión Alimentaria Sanders S.A. *v.* Spain – 11681/85 [1989] ECHR 16 (7 July 1989).

3. IS THERE AN INCENTIVE CRISIS IN THE COURTS?

The departure point for this book is an analysis of the incentive structures facing key players in the courts and litigation process. We examine the possibility of an incentive crisis in the courts. Legal inertia, bias and maladministration are the norm in many countries, with devastating social and economic repercussions. Commentators argue that civil justice is in crisis,[30] delays are rendering the courts useless,[31] the monetary costs of adjudication render using the courts all but impossible for everyone except the wealthy,[32] justices are out of touch with business,[33] formal institutions are out of sync with informal practices,[34] judges are not independent and favour the wealthy and powerful,[35] the costs of justice for the state are too high,[36] and there is a litigation explosion.[37] Undue delay discussed above is a symptom of a broader incentive crisis.

A useful exercise is to view judicial systems from the perspective of access to justice. This allows one to address fundamental questions concerning the allocation of costs and fees. For instance, who should chiefly finance the courts? Societies must decide essentially between giving this task to the taxpayer and giving it to the court users themselves.[38] Where the burden falls on the taxpayer, incentives are clearly given for citizens and firms to litigate, as they do not internalize the costs they produce. On the other hand, where the burden falls completely on court users, many users arguably may not be able to afford to go to court and be denied access to justice. What about the desirability of legal aid? When is legal aid desirable and when does it create perverse incentives? Do wealthy litigants have a strategic advantage over poorer litigants? If so, is it advisable to finance the poorer litigant to put him on equal footing? What does access to justice teach us about how lawyers should be compensated? How can we control for strategic behaviour of attorneys and their clients and how is this affected by the allocation of costs and fees?

Moreover, considering judicial systems from the standpoint of access to justice highlights the importance of other questions often considered outside

---

30 See Zuckerman (1999).
31 See Jarquín and Carrillo (1998).
32 See Yuille (2004).
33 See Cabrillo and Pastor (2001).
34 See Cooter (1996).
35 See Ramseyer (1994); Klerman (2006).
36 See Woolf (1997).
37 See Olson (1991).
38 Zuckerman (1999), p. 9.

of the domain of traditional legal analysis, such as judicial accountability and responsiveness. Too often, judicial institutions have hidden behind the notion of independence or the singular nature of the service they provide, to shield themselves from the organizational analysis that other institutions are commonly submitted to. Questions related to performance and accountability are neglected. For instance, the issue of judicial accountability was near-taboo in most countries until the last decade, as judges were hailed as divine-like figures. Whereas historically the divine model may have been important to separate the judge from powerful elements in society or environments where blood relationship and rules of reciprocity governed, it is widely accepted today that judges maximize the same things as everyone else does.[39]

4. STRUCTURE OF THE BOOK

The administration of justice is no longer a theme delegated to the peripheries of economic analysis but is recognized by many economists as an issue of fundamental importance for economic development. It is, then, not surprising that from the perspective of efficiency an expansive literature has emerged related to the diverse legal institutions of the administration of justice. Though there are substantial differences between countries, a common theme of this work is a degree of dissatisfaction with these institutions and a recognition of the need to institute reform measures.

In this literature the focus has clearly been on institutions pertaining to the common law, particularly in the United States. The reason is two-fold. First, the economic analysis of law is significantly more developed, both academically and in terms of application, than in Europe. Second, judges and the courts often exercise a more relevant role in the common law system than their counterparts in the civil law system, employed in continental Europe.

But, as we argue in Chapter 2 of this book, it would be a mistake to exaggerate the differences between the two systems. As we shall see, the objectives of the legal system are – and have been historically – similar in both models. And, the greater part of economic analysis already developed is applicable to both, though certain institutional differences do exist that create incentives in some cases for actors to behave differently. In this work we shall pay attention to both legal models, with emphasis on points in common. We do, however, offer sections on issues normally not found in the North American literature, such as the Latin notary and the selection and values of judges in civil law systems.

---

39 Posner (1993).

Chapter 2 begins with a discussion of courts as public institutions. We propose that at the heart of any analysis of the courts – and the desirability of judicial reform – is the need for institutional comparison in order to understand precisely what factors and issues courts can realistically be relied upon for the allocation of goods and services within a society. Courts must essentially be called upon when they have a comparative advantage over markets and the political process to satisfy the needs and wants of society. To borrow from the public administration literature, courts should exercise 'core functions', defined as those in which they enjoy a comparative advantage over alternatives.

Government structures are changing. Formerly, it was widely accepted that the fundamental mission of government in political economy was the management of macro-economic variables. Today, however, things have changed substantially and what we see in both developed and developing countries is a very different definition of political economy, which is related to the view taken by classical economists that efficient laws and institutions constitute a basic element for socio-economic development. One of the factors that has greatly influenced the size and nature of courts has been the rise of the welfare state and social protection, which has clearly been a factor behind increasing caseloads. But more than just increasing the business of courts, it has led to courts' involvement in a broader range of issues previously left to the political process and the market. The state now acts as guarantor not just for basic rights but also for other 'minimal conditions', such as education, health, protection against social risks, unemployment and the consequences of old age. The courts – as the ultimate guarantor of citizens' rights – have become accessible to a vastly superior number of possible claims than was previously the case.[40]

Another tendency that has clearly altered the nature and scope of court decisions has been globalization. Changes induced by shifts in social values and globalization have not been restricted by any manner of means to countries of either the common law or the civil law tradition. We will argue that the civil and common law systems have undergone parallel evolutions, searching for similar objectives and adapting themselves to the ideas and dominant values in force at historical moments in Western society. Moreover, the *Zeitgeist* and dominant values in a given society have conditioned legal evolution to a larger degree than internal structures present within a specific judicial system.

In the remainder of Chapter 2, we analyse the structure of courts and numerous procedural operations from an economic perspective. We shall provide an overview of the basic features of court structures in common law and civil law countries. Among the factors we further analyse are the notion of

---

40 See Fix-Fierro (2003), p. 14.

optimal territorial jurisdiction, specialization, appeals and streamlining procedures.

It is fundamental to understand the incentives facing judges given that they are the central actors within the courts. This is the subject of our analysis in Chapter 3. Traditional tools of public administration, such as the carrot and the stick, are generally not available to influence judges' behaviour, the obvious reason for which being judicial independence.[41] This is a riddle for economists and students of judicial administration alike. Beginning our discussion with an analysis of what judges actually do, we proceed to analyse a wide array of factors that affect judges' behaviour. It is clear, for instance, that judges, particularly in civil law countries, have similar utility functions to bureaucrats. The fact that candidates enter the judiciary at a much younger age than in common law countries, in which it is necessary to have proven experience as a lawyer before becoming a judge, stresses this similarity with other civil service professionals. Moreover, factors such as a group's social capital are arguably more important than in the common law system. Assimilation, we argue, is a primary factor that influences judges' preferences. Judicial incentives are traced in the light of factors such as accountability and independence, salary and selection and promotion. Developing better measures of judicial performance, in terms of workload or output, is a noble pursuit that is very much on the agenda in many countries. Given measurement difficulties and judicial independence concerns, however, the usefulness of performance measurement as a tool to influence judges' behaviour is probably limited in scope and most applicable as a shaming device. Performance measures are likely to be more useful as a management tool in determining the allocation of scarce resources than as a tool for holding individual judges accountable.

To understand the volume and nature of judicial proceedings, it is necessary to review the incentives of all stakeholders. Following the discussion on judges, Chapter 4 is devoted to litigants. Economic analysis has made excellent advances in the study of litigation with direct relevance for judicial scholars and reformers. In particular, it provides a strong theory – supported by empirical evidence – as to why citizens initiate lawsuits, when cases will actually go to trial and why cases settle. The economics of litigation also provides valuable insights regarding whether or not the level of litigation is too high and on the issue of who should finance the courts. In this chapter, we trace the most salient factors behind litigants' incentives for using the court. Having outlined the basic model, we proceed with a discussion of settlement. Thereafter, we address the important question of who should finance litigation and the issue of user fees, as well as legal aid and class actions.

---

41 Posner (1993), p. 2.

Chapter 5 is dedicated to assessing lawyers' incentives. The history of judicial reform teaches us that Dickens' famous observation, 'The one great principle of the English law is to make business for itself' may just as easily have been formulated for lawyers in numerous other countries. Lawyers' costs and lawyer-invoked delays are a great source of economic inefficiency and provide a serious barrier to access to justice, preventing parties in many jurisdictions with legitimate claims from taking legal action. Where injured parties do not go to court as a result of these costs, not only are legal entitlements ignored but private actors may not be deterred from engaging in socially harmful behaviour.

These costs are aggravated by four key (and interrelated) factors. First, the market for legal services is still virtually monopolized by lawyers in most countries. Second, there is a serious agency problem in lawyer–client relations. Lawyers have far more information about their actions and the nature of the legal system than their clients, and importantly the actions taken and effort exerted by a lawyer are not easily verifiable nor can it easily be assessed whether they were for the benefit of the client. Third, the manner of payment in client–lawyer relations generally does not align lawyers' interests with those of their clients. Fourth, the law is a self-regulated profession. Given the opacity of the legal market, the great group disincentives among lawyers to hold each other accountable (given that others are invariably involved in the same practices), and the disincentives to introduce real market-based conditions, lawyers are more often a cause of than a solution to the problem.

A priori it remains difficult to see how lawyers' incentives can be better aligned with socially desirable behaviour, given that the law profession is self-regulated and legislatures generally have been reluctant to tackle the issue. Nevertheless, in both common law and civil law countries recent developments in case management, particularly by shifting control over the speed of litigation away from lawyers to judges and emphasizing proportionality of the costs of litigation to the nature of the dispute involved, seem to be useful first steps in controlling the strategic behaviour of lawyers and their clients. Moreover, economic analysis teaches us that payment mechanisms as well as different groupings of lawsuits may further align lawyers' incentives with that which is socially desirable.

In Chapter 6, we address other key players in the litigation process. For those from common law countries it is often a surprise to learn of the role played by Latin notaries in the civil law system. Latin notaries write the documents they certify, guaranteeing their legality, and occupy a function in the legal system that in common law systems is exercised by judges and lawyers. Notaries offer a measure of ex ante control over the legality of documents that in common law countries is generally handled by the courts ex post, in addition to providing assistance to the parties to an agreement normally offered by lawyers in common law systems. Their role serves as a means to reduce the rate of litigation, given that it prevents many cases from entering the adjudicative system, and speeds up cases that do make it before the courts.

We then proceed to an analysis of juries, which continue to exercise an important function in the administration of justice in many countries, though substantial differences clearly exist. Unlike in civil law countries, where juries simply may not exist or are of limited importance, the jury is an institution of great importance in common law countries. This is particularly the case in the United States, where juries are not limited in use to criminal law cases but are also used in civil cases, even establishing the size of compensation in some tort cases.

Pursuant to our analysis of juries, we address alternative dispute resolution (ADR) mechanisms, which have received much attention and support in recent years, in academic as well as policy circles, in many countries. We shall argue that alternative dispute resolution mechanisms may be of some use in particular situations, but their supporters have to recognize their limitations. To understand the use of ADR processes, one must ask, compared with what?

In Chapter 7 we turn our attention to considerations for a reform agenda. Judicial reform has been with us for as long as we have had judiciaries. The need and practicability of any measure will differ from one jurisdiction to the next. Moreover, we offer an additional discussion on reform measures in developing countries, which face a series of other factors that significantly worsen their situation. What we attempt to show is a list of possible measures that may be taken, with discussion of the accompanying, foreseeable costs and benefits. Whilst suggestions are to a certain degree abstract, given that we do not focus on a specific jurisdiction, they may be locally accommodated to the circumstances prevailing in a particular jurisdiction.

2. The courts

1. INTRODUCTION

Courts should be seen as public institutions within the broader set-up of a political economy. Within this comparative framework, the judicial administration occupies a position of primary importance, serving as an alternative to other means of allocating resources within an economy. There are essentially two alternatives to the adjudication process for the allocation of economic resources within a society, the market and the political process. These alternatives do not act separately but are based on interdependency. It is not the case that as the market expands the adjudicative process loses in importance, or that when the political process wields its legislative sword allocative decisions are only taken by political bodies. Quite the contrary, fluctuations in market and political activity greatly influence the nature and scope of adjudicative decisions. Greater intervention by the political process – as in the case of the welfare state – leads to a greater workload for the courts; economic boom and economic crisis in the market similarly affect the demands upon the courts.

Within the market, societies' needs and wants are satisfied according to the laws of supply and demand. Freedom of contract, according to which individuals decide of their own accord to enter into the voluntary exchange of goods and services, is at the heart of market transactions. As discussed in greater detail below, freedom of contract has been taking a beating largely since the beginning of the 20th century. Law, supported by legal scholarship, has painted freedom of contract with an unfavourable brush, to the advantage of regulation, largely effectuated through the political and adjudicative processes.

Within the political process, there are essentially two basic activities. The first activity is that of legislator or regulator, according to which the rules of economic behaviour are defined by the state. The second sees the state as economic agent, producing goods and services, in either a direct or an indirect fashion. The state as economic agent has seen its role decline substantially in recent years. Whilst formerly it was widely accepted that the fundamental mission of government in political economy was the macro-economic management of great quantities, things have changed substantially and emphasis today has shifted greatly towards the role of the state as regulator.

In other words, the state's function is increasingly the first activity described above, as the role of the state as producer of goods and services has been substantially reduced. The primary reason for this transition is the widely held belief that the private sector is more efficient in the production of most goods and services, facing incentives that favour both cost reduction and innovation. Though this trend has been accepted by countries – both developed and less developed alike – at different rates, the sheer strength of the arguments, supported by strong empirical evidence, is leading to an inexorable decline in state activity in the direct provision of goods and services the world over. It is interesting to observe that, whilst the role of the state as economic agent has declined substantially, the role of the state – via legislation and regulation – in defining economic behaviour has actually increased. Whereas there is increasing reliance on the market for satisfying societies' needs and wants, there is increasing regulation of these activities.

Courts provide two services.[1] The first is dispute resolution – assessing whether a rule has been violated. The second function of the courts is related to the creation of rules of law as a result of the dispute settlement process. In the common law systems, the latter manifests itself as the system of precedent. Unlike systems following the common law tradition, civil law jurisdictions do not adhere to the principle of *stare decisis* in adjudication, with precedents being confined to a more 'persuasive role'.[2] Further to the doctrine of *jurisprudence constante*, a court should only take past decisions into consideration where there is sufficient uniformity in previous case law and split jurisprudence is not heeded. Courts then treat precedents as a sort of 'soft law' once uniformity has developed. The more uniform case law becomes, the greater the persuasive force it acquires.[3] Spain provides a good example of the aforementioned. Article 1(1) of the 1889 Civil Code states that the sources of law are statute (*ley*), custom and general principles of law. Article 1(6) states that 'Case law will complement the legal system with the doctrine which the Supreme Court [*Tribunal Supremo*] establishes in a repeated manner in order to interpret and apply statute, custom, and the general principles of law.' Decisions of the highest court are afforded recognition which ensures the unity of the case law, whereas decisions taken by the lower courts carry little formal

---

1 Landes and Posner (1979), p. 236.

2 Fon and Parisi (2004).

3 Ibid. Fon and Parisi (p. 1) observe that 'Civil law jurisdictions do not allow dissenting judges to attach a dissent to a majority opinion, but cases that do not conform to the dominant trend serve as a signal of dissent among the judiciary. These cases influence future decisions in varying ways in different legal traditions. Judges may also be influenced by recent jurisprudential trends and fads in case law.'

authority.[4] It is well recognized that judges are called upon to make law, admittedly, however, through interpretation.

Though most regulation of economic activities is made by the executive, the judiciary also plays an important role in establishing new regulatory rules or providing arguments for new government regulations. It is, thus, possible to have regulation through litigation. The basis for regulation through litigation is quite similar to that of government regulation: the existence of market failures and the idea that it is possible to raise the efficiency of a market with specific rules. However, regulation through litigation presents some serious problems in comparison with government regulation. First, it may threaten the principle of division of powers between the parliament and the judiciary. Second, courts may lack technical expertise, given that judges and juries are not trained to regulate markets. Third, regulation via litigation is less publicly accountable than government regulation.[5] These factors are related to the inherent structural characteristics of courts which present supply-side limitations that affect the possibilities of courts meeting the demands placed upon them.

2. STRUCTURAL CHARACTERISTICS AND LIMITATIONS OF COURTS

In essence, three defining characteristics of the adjudicative process are fundamental for understanding its uses and limitations. They form the basis for comprehending supply-side constraints that limit the ability of courts to respond to societies' demands.[6] The first characteristic is that it is very formalized and regulated. The second is the fact that substantial efforts are made to insulate judges from outside influence, particularly through the design of their terms of employment.[7] The third characteristic of the adjudicative process is that it is small in size and has limited resources at its disposal, particularly vis-à-vis the market. For numerous reasons identified below, one cannot expand the judiciary in a similar manner to other organizational structures.

2.1 The Regulated Nature of the Adjudicative Process

The adjudicative process is very formalized, with strict procedures and rigid

---

4 Nevertheless, the growing importance of local legislation has furthered the importance of the High Court of the Autonomous Regions.

5 See Viscusi (2002).

6 See Komesar (1994), Chapter 5.

7 This is analysed at length in our discussion of judges in Chapter 3.

criteria. Formal obstacles to litigating aim to control the volume and nature of cases heard by courts.[8] There are sound economic arguments for the presence of formal requisites to litigating, as societies should aim to control the volume and nature of cases that enter the adjudicative system, allowing those issues to be adjudicated that can best be dealt with by the courts, and leaving to the market and the political arena those areas that they are best suited to handle.

Among the formal regulations, a party with a complaint (plaintiff) must have the right to initiate or participate in a legal action, known as 'standing' or *locus standi*. Rules regarding jurisdiction determine which court can hear a case. Choice of law as set out in contracts may determine which state's law may be used, although courts still have discretion to apply local law (*lex fori*). Moreover, wrongs must be specific and linked to identifiable actions taken by an identifiable set of finite persons.[9] According to well-determined rules, courts then require these complaints to be put down in written form, filed and served on parties against whom suit has been initiated, and so on. Given the formalities and complex nature of the litigation process, knowledge and experience become paramount. As a solution to these expensive information problems, parties generally have to turn to a lawyer.

Though the rules of procedure which shape how litigation is conducted differ according to jurisdictions, the legally stated goal of these requirements is generally the same – to guarantee litigants evenhandedness and a fair and unbiased outcome. Procedural requirements, as we shall see in repeated examples below, however, can and indeed must promote other goals if the objective is a fair, expeditious and efficient system of judicial administration.

2.2 Insulation of Judges from External Influence

The second feature of the courts is that judges are insulated in their professional capacity from outside influence, in order to guarantee their independence. For the purposes of accurate and independent decision making, judges are more removed than either political or market actors. In contrast, for instance, to those who negotiate a contract for their own personal benefit and politicians who approve a specific law based on the interests of potential voters to remain in power, great efforts are extended to ensure judges are only swayed by issues of law and equality, without voicing personal preferences in individual cases.

There are substantial costs related to the aforementioned, designed in large part to preserve impartiality and judicial independence. One such cost is inferior

---

8 For a detailed overview, see Komesar (1994), pp. 125–6.

9 Ibid.

technical knowledge in comparison with that of professionals from certain sectors or specialized agencies. The greater the level of technical knowledge, the more likely it is that disputes will be resolved accurately. However, given vested interests, impartiality may be reduced, as well as confidence of economic groups with respect to neutrality. The problem is not merely confined to judges, as the same dilemma is occurring with the creation of generic and specialized regulatory organisms where impartiality is tested on many occasions. This is not to suggest that independence should be denounced in favour of specialization. This would be a hasty conclusion that could debilitate the entire mechanism. The solution, given a lack of qualifications, would be to increase training and give greater specialization to the courts, questions that shall be addressed later.[10]

Moreover, judicial insulation may lead to a disjunction between citizens and the courts. Studies have consistently highlighted a substantial disconnect between the business world and the administration of justice. Both seem to have a different world view and speak a separate language. This is a serious problem given that the efficiency of the administration of justice as a mechanism for allocating resources demands that courts arrive at similar results to those which parties would have agreed upon contractually in the market. It would appear necessary that judges understand not just the legal regulation of economic institutions but also how markets and business work. Where judges do not feel comfortable taking decisions in complex economic or financial issues, litigants do not feel confident in front of a court.

In some countries, there would appear to be an anti-market mentality among many judges which adds to the disconnect between business and the courts. Many judges reject freedom of contract principles in favour of principles of redistribution, by forcing transfers from one social group to another. Two interesting surveys have been conducted in Spain on this matter.[11] In both surveys, business-persons highlight court inefficiency in resolving problems common to economic life and the lack of economic training amongst judges. Moroever, they highlight an extended aversion amongst judges to business activity in general. Cabrillo and Pastor (2001) analysed court decisions in Spain, particularly those of the Supreme Court and the Constitutional Court. Their findings suggest that Spanish judges are largely against the principles of a market economy and freedom of contract.[12] It is interesting to note that this

[10] See Cabrillo and Pastor (2001), Chapter 1.

[11] Toharia (1998) and Círculo de Empresarios (2003).

[12] Some examples of rulings included the following: freedom of enterprise is a concept that is very difficult to define (STC 37/1987); in some economic activities, it is fair to discriminate in favour of persons and against legal entities because the latter are driven by 'mere mercantile interest' whereas the former are trying to 'earn a decent

attitude is not always linked to any specific political orientation of judges but rather to a specific value system which stresses considerations other than efficiency.

A clear cost of judicial insulation is that judges – in theory – do not need to consider the wishes of the majority in their decisions. In this respect, some have argued that the judiciary is less accountable than the legislature, thus issuing a warning against judge-made law.[13] Whilst there is clearly some truth in the argument, one must also realize the limits present in the alternatives. Judges per se cannot be considered less accountable to the majority of the people than legislators, as the political process itself has numerous weaknesses. Indeed, history is replete with examples of legislators yielding to the preferences of special interest groups or engaging in blatant populism, ignoring the costs and benefits of their own actions. The difficulties in aligning the incentives of political representatives with the incentives of represented citizens are well known,[14] as are the difficulties in aggregating individual preferences.[15]

2.3 The Size of the Adjudicative Process

The third factor that shapes the adjudicative process is related to its limited size and resources vis-à-vis the market and the political process.[16] The central constraint preventing the expansion of size or scale of the adjudicative process is related to the role of the judge.[17] Attempts to increase the number of judges proportional to caseload would lead to a distortion in the structure of the adjudicative process. As Posner notes,

> a judicial system that makes law, whether through common law creation or through legislative or constitutional interpretation, rather than just resolving disputes, is a pyramid with an apex of more or less fixed size, so that the base, as it expands, grows relative to the apex, implying a loss of control.[18]

---

living' (STS 12 April 1985); although the Constitution states in its Article 28-1 that 'everyone is entitled to freely join a trade union', this right is not applicable to entrepreneurs (STC 8 April 1981).

[13] See, for example, Devlin (1976).

[14] This is the basis of much work done in the tradition of Public Choice Theory. For an introduction to Public Choice, see Mueller (1979).

[15] The authoritative article on this subject is by Arrow (1950).

[16] Markets can expand and contract as the laws of supply and demand dictate. Within the political process, governments can easily set up new agencies, form commissions and groups of experts, and so on.

[17] Komesar (1994), p. 144.

[18] Posner (1996), p. 133.

There are two possible measures for increasing the size of the adjudicative process: creating new courts and increasing the number of judges within existing courts.

There are two difficulties with creating new courts. The first difficulty is related to a loss of control, as there are increasingly large monitoring costs to layers in a hierarchical structure. The second problem is related to inconsistencies in the interpretation of the law, as it is quite possible that as the number of courts grows opinions will begin to differ. Where opinions begin to differ in the courts, legal uncertainty will increase, and increased demands will be placed on higher courts to rectify the situation. This is not to suggest that there are not possible benefits to be had by increasing the number of courts, but that the aforementioned costs will clearly at some point exceed the benefits – the most obvious of which is the reduction in caseloads.[19]

There are also problems with increasing the number of judges. One is related to the costs of collective decision-making. Consider for example the case of a Supreme Court. Though increasing the number of judges in a court should theoretically reduce the caseload per judge, collective decisions become more labourious and time-consuming.[20] A second cost is political, particularly among higher courts. Fix-Fierro (2003) reports that increasing the number of judges in the Mexican Supreme Court actually weakened its 'political clout', leading to differences of opinion within the court.[21]

So, how serious are these limitations? The answer to this question will depend on the realities of any particular country. A country, for instance, of well-paid, professional, and highly educated judges will surely avail of both better judicial resources and more accurate court judgments. Courts in many developing countries, on the other hand, will not attract highly educated professional staff, nor will they avail of the latest technology or modern court infrastructure. The economic costs of attempting to upgrade court resources and man them with highly educated staff may be intangible. This has resulted in some authors arguing for a greater shift in responsibilities from the courts towards the political process in developing countries.[22] One means of doing so is by creating more precise rules (laws) within the political process and fewer general standards, a subject we shall return to in Chapter 7.

---

[19] Here we were looking at adding homogeneous courts in a judicial system; there may, however, be substantial gains to expansion through specialization, which we discuss in detail below.

[20] Komesar (1994), p. 132.

[21] Fix-Fierro (2003), pp. 104–5.

[22] Schäfer (2002).

3. THE WELFARE STATE AND SOCIAL PROTECTION

Government structures have been changing dramatically. Whilst the role of the state as economic agent has declined substantially, the role of the state – via legislation and regulation – in defining economic behaviour has significantly increased. We have seen an increasing reliance on the market for the delivery of goods and services but an accompanying increase in the regulation of these activities. In part this regulation is the natural result of governments ceasing to deliver certain goods and services, opting instead for market provision. In large part, however, this increase is due to shifts towards the welfare state and social protection. The state intervenes actively in all aspects of social life, drafting and implementing a massive supply of public policies and programmes. The state, as Fix-Fierro highlights, not only renders citizens most basic facilities, such as physical integrity and liberty, but also functions as guarantor to ensure minimal services are being met, in health, education and pension schemes, as well as protecting against numerous social risks. [23]

To some, these developments may be seen as the inevitable result of societies becoming increasingly complicated and markets developing at unprecedented levels. Conflicts, like markets, have grown in size and sophistication and societies, both through the courts and the political process, are searching for means to respond to these developments.[24] Changes have not just led to a greater caseload for the courts, but have altered the nature of adjudication; courts are now actively involved in a far greater number of areas of the law and public policy. There has been an unprecedented growth of judicial review of administrative action. Judicial supervision, though derived and administered within various constitutional traditions, quintessentially determines whether governmental bodies function within the confines afforded to them under the law.[25] Moreover, increases in the amount of statutory law have inevitably led to increases in the amount of judge-made law, given that statutory law is by its nature incomplete.[26] This is another burden that has been placed on the judges. Courts now face rising caseloads and more complex questions of law and public policy, and often risk losing their legitimacy and

---

[23] Fix-Fierro (2003), p. 14.

[24] See Cappelletti (1989).

[25] As an aside, the reader should note that the Anglo-American system is provided by ordinary courts deciding cases involving the legitimacy of governmental action, and not special, separate administrative courts dealing with administrative cases exclusively as is the case in many parts of Europe, such as France, Germany and Poland. The main requirement for the court to effectually conduct this role is that it be independent from the organs it so monitors.

[26] Cappelletti (1989), p. 4.

impartiality.[27] They have become increasingly accessible to minorities and organized groups who wish to change government policy, which has resulted in strong accusations of the politicization of courts.[28]

Judicial activism has seen decisions taken by bodies within the administration of justice which go beyond strict law enforcement, extending some legal principles to situations that were never foreseen by legislators, and in a manner in which it can reasonably be assumed the legislators would not have acted at the time the law was enacted. This role of judges as lawmakers is especially relevant in common law systems in which judges have a much greater capacity for creating law than those in civil law systems.[29] Development of this role has given rise, especially in the United States, to debate on whether the capacity of judges for creating law should focus on what is strictly 'common law' or whether it should be extended – as in fact happens in practice – to statutory law. It is easy to understand how relevant this is for the study of relations between the administration of justice and the economy by considering the wide range of statutory laws that regulate economic activity – from antitrust law to the formulation of 'positive' subjective rights with clear economic content.

In the United States, Judge Antonin Scalia, for example, insists that a state's social policy should not be established by judges but by the legislative power. And he extends this idea to the interpretation of the Constitution which, in his opinion, has been treated by North American judges as if it were common law.[30] Scalia draws attention to the problems created when 'positive' rights are extended – as they were, for example, by the North American Supreme Court under Judge Warren – and he insists on the danger of formulating a wide set of rights of this type if enforcement is to be in the hands of independent judges who cannot be held responsible for their actions. This trend towards increasing activism on the part of judges can also be seen in civil law systems in Western Europe. It has even been suggested that, since continental legal codes are less flexible in adapting to market realities, they may actually encourage judicial activism in fields such as tort law.[31]

Extensive legalization of market and social practices places a strain on the courts. Some have naturally fared better than others, being better able to adapt

---

27 Fix-Fierro (2003), p. 15.

28 Hommes (1998), p. 50.

29 It is not always easy to determine which countries really belong to the common law tradition, especially considering that a jurist of the rank of Richard Posner has stated that today's English law cannot be fully considered as being of the common law tradition.

30 Scalia (1997).

31 See, for example, Provine (1996), p. 234.

to these changing circumstances. Governments – and many judges alike – however have concentrated too much on the desirability of increasing the demand for judicial intervention without a realistic appraisal of the limits inherent in the adjudicative process.

4. COMMON LAW AND CIVIL LAW: THE ROLE OF COURTS AND LEGISLATION IN ECONOMIC DEVELOPMENT[32]

There is ample literature based on the position of demonstrating the superiority of common law over the civil law system. We shall dispute this position here. We will not offer a complete overview of this position as found in the literature, but rather analyse the role played by the law and courts in economic development, focusing on the two major areas of private law: contract law and tort law. In doing so, we shall look at some of the more interesting features in the evolution of these two branches of both common law and civil law systems.

The thesis put forward here is the following. The civil and common law systems have undergone parallel evolutions, searching for similar objectives and adapting themselves to the ideas and dominant values in force at historical moments in Western society. Moreover, the *Zeitgeist* and dominant values in a given society have conditioned legal evolution to a larger degree than internal structures present within a specific judicial system.

In accordance with this interpretation, neither the principle of freedom of contract nor the remaining legal institutions that have fostered economic development in the Western world are specific characteristics of common law. And, more importantly, a common law system does not permit a sounder defence of free market principles than civil law. Put differently, there are no sound arguments that demonstrate that judge-made law is better placed to defend a market economy than legislation passed by parliament or legislative assemblies.

4.1 Efficiency of Common Law and Civil Law

Comparative analysis of the development of the administration of justice within the common law and civil law systems received much attention in the literature after some studies argued in favour of the superiority of the common law system over its civil law counterpart.[33] There are two fundamental arguments put

---

32 This section is based on Cabrillo (2007).
33 For a good bibliography on this topic, see Rubin (2000).

forward to defend this idea. The first relates to what is considered the superiority of common law as an instrument for the defence of human rights, as a result its political implications. The second, alternatively, emphasizes the supposedly superior capacity of common law in achieving economic efficiency. Though numerous authors have advanced one or other of the two above arguments, we will look at the work of two of the more influential authors – Hayek and Posner.

Hayek's opinions concerning common law and the role of judges in the British system are interesting for various reasons. Firstly, few economists had shown any interest in the role played by judicial institutions in the development of a free and prosperous society. Indeed, few would question that Hayek was not just a great economist but also one of the leading legal philosophers of the 20th century. Secondly, Hayek himself was trained in the continental system; his enthusiasm for common law came from time spent in England and the discovery of a model of social institutions that was beyond his initial academic training. For Hayek, the foundations for superior freedom that British citizens enjoyed over their European continental counterparts were a result not of the separation of powers, as was thought by Montesquieu, but of common law. In his opinion, the English institutional system was superior because common law had not been created by political volition and furthermore was administered by judges and courts that had acquired a high degree of independence from the political branch. In this system, not only is legislative power independent from government, but it is also limited by law over which it does not have control.[34]

For Hayek, common law fitted well into his own model of 'abstract norms of behaviour'. Common law is not just a collection of loosely bound cases, although this could be the interpretation of a continental jurist reading a work such as Blackstone's *Commentaries*. Common law, rather, consists of a collection of general principles to be explained and developed by judges in their decisions. It is also interesting to note that for Hayek the role of the judge was not to find efficient solutions to particular problems in the sense of maximizing social utility, but rather to ascertain whether or not behaviour corresponded with previously established legal principles.[35]

Many lawyers and judges in the common law tradition, however, would be quite critical of Hayek's ideas. From our point of view, it is especially interesting to recall certain ideas about common law and the role of public policy formulated by Judge Oliver Wendell Holmes throughout his extensive career.

---

[34] Hayek defends the superiority of the common law in several of his works; but his most systematic analysis is in Hayek (1973–79), Vol. 1, Chapter 4.

[35] Hayek (1973), pp. 85–8.

Holmes not just made important contributions to resolving particular cases but also addressed the significance of common law per se. His interpretation of the role general principles play in common law was quite different from Hayek's. His idea that general propositions do not decide concrete cases and opinions are based on a judgment or intuition rather than a general proposition is well known.

Those of us active in law and economics enjoy citing the sentence which Holmes used to explain his view of the future of legal theory: 'For the rational study of the law the black-letter man may be the man of the present, but the man of the future is the master of statistics and the master of economics.' Does this statement have a meaning beyond the obvious necessity today to have an understanding of economics in order to understand the law, or, in Holmes's own words, that 'every lawyer ought to seek an understanding of economics'? In *The Path of the Law* (1897) Holmes established a clear relationship between the evolution of the law and the social problems that legal rules and judges should solve. He criticized judges for not recognizing their duty 'of weighting considerations of social advantage.'[36] In fact, he thought that the law is no more than a concealed, half-conscious battle on the question of legislative policy. The law, in his opinion, is open to reconsideration upon a slight change in the habit of the public mind. And some of the basic principles of social and economic life – the principle of free competition, for instance – may vary in different times and places.[37]

Richard Posner and some other scholars in the law and economics tradition also defend the superiority of common law, but their arguments are very different from Hayek's, as they are based on the idea of efficiency. In a well-known paper, Landes and Posner (1987) tried to illustrate the efficiency of common law in terms of a well-known concept of tort law, the Hand Formula. Accordingly, a person or company should be held liable for an accident if the cost of preventing it is less than the expected cost of the accident – that is, the product of the damage and the probability that an accident would result. So this rule places liability on the party better able to prevent or minimize the damage. Contract law does the same in the case of unforeseen contingencies that make the performance of a specific contract impossible. The superiority of common law would, therefore, be based on its assumed superiority in finding efficient solutions to some of the main questions involved in the development of private law.

There is, however, cause to doubt the soundness of the notion that common law is superior from an efficiency perspective. Bentham's criticisms regarding

[36] Holmes (1992), pp. 170, 174.
[37] Ibid., p. 167.

the legislative function of the courts and the stability of principles based on the system of *stare decisis* or the subjection of judges to precedent, are now two hundred years old.[38] And to cite but another example as a means of demonstrating critical opinions regarding basic aspects of common law, one need only look at Roscoe Pound when he criticized the adversarial system as having contributed to a 'sporting theory of justice', defending the idea that administrative courts would surely be more efficient than common law courts in the resolution of many types of cases (Pound 1906).

More recently it has been argued that both systems in reality have acted efficiently, allowing for the development of prosperous economies.[39] To wit, if the aim is to adopt the law to socially changing economic realities, it is not easy to say which of the two systems is superior. In support of the common law one can put forward the position that judges are continuously creating law, which permits legal principles to better adapt to changing situations. One may, however, also argue that the application of the principle of *stare decisis* can have the opposite effect. In reference to the civil law system, the principle of respect for statutes would appear to reduce the possibilities of adapting the law to a changing society; in reality, however, a statute can be modified without great difficulty in the majority of cases. As an aside, the widespread notion that within civil law systems a single word by the legislature can render entire law libraries useless appears to raise more the problem of legal stability than the difficulty of adopting laws to new situations.

It is further important to emphasize the idea that the separate and varied evolutions of the two systems is more related to different historical realities than to different views of what should be the main objectives of the law. In fact, it is not difficult to show that the evolution of both models reflects a search for efficiency in institutional design. Within both the civil and the common law systems changes are introduced in order to find solutions for situations not appropriately being dealt with. Judges in common law countries and parliaments in civil law countries have often tried throughout history to reach similar goals.

If one had to mention a single differentiating characteristic between the two systems, it is, without doubt, the different role associated to judicial precedent. In this sense, nothing better defines the model of continental civil law than the well-known Justinian maxim '*non exemplis sed legibus iudicandum est*' (courts must adjudicate on the strength of the law not the case). This consideration clearly grants a more limited role to judges in the allocation of resources in an economy. This Justinian position, however, was not a product

[38] Bentham (1776).

[39] Some examples may be found in Rubin (2000).

of real innovation, but rather the continuation of a far more ancient tradition. In Roman law, judges from the beginning were not the basic pieces in the administration of justice – this role was assigned to 'jurists'. Without understanding the influence of these jurists, it is impossible to understand the evolution of civil law systems up to the present day. These jurists were legal assessors to the parties and the judges that had to resolve a conflict. They interpreted the law and with the passage of time had their opinions put down in writing, leading to the development of authentic legal rules and influencing to a great extent the entire development of the judicial system. Some of these legal assessors acquired such importance that their opinions became binding for the courts, and had, as a result, the authentic force of the law. In comparison with the jurists, the role of the judge was of less importance. Judges were initially selected by the parties for the resolution of a specific case and needed to consult the jurists in exercising their function.

Looking from a historical perspective at the role of the judges and jurists in diverse judicial systems one can unearth a rule with few exceptions: the importance of one of the groups is inverse to that of the other. Wherever judges have formed a professional group of prestige – as was the case in England in the 13th century – the role jurists occupied has been small. In those cases, however, where judges lacked technical expertise – as was the case in the Roman Republic and Empire or in Germany prior to the 18th century the jurists were the authentic protagonists in the process of developing legal rules.

Naturally, this rule may have some exceptions and its strength is not the same in every country. In civil law countries the weight of academic doctrine in the development of law has been larger, for instance, in Germany than in France. Moreover, Sir William Blackstone, who was a key figure in the diffusion of common law in England and its extension to the colonies, was a professor at Oxford. It should be remembered, however, that Blackstone was the first professor to teach English law at a university, and his appointment did not take place until as late as 1758. The European continental tradition was markedly different, where the teaching of law acquired an important role from the beginning. Moreover, the structure of Blackstone's *Commentaries* was criticized precisely because it lacked judicial analysis – in the continental law meaning of the term. The work has, rather, very much the feeling of a practical guide, to serve as a manual to understanding the principal matters of English law for judges, lawyers, and even for persons not versed in the law.

In the Italian universities of the early Middle Ages the tradition of Latin jurists would be continued, to a large extent, by academic scholars, so-called 'glossators'. Their work would quickly spread to other universities in continental Europe, permitting the recuperation of Roman law and forming the basis of a judicial system – with contributions from canon law and new mercantile law – culminating in the process of codification in the 19th century, whose final objective was to organize and systematize in accordance with well-established rational principles. If the Roman law tradition permits the formation of a model of economic relations based on the principle of exchange with voluntarily formed contracts, the recovery of this tradition in the early Middle Ages and in the Renaissance allowed the development in this age of the Italian mercantile republics. England in the 14th, 15th, and 16th centuries was underdeveloped in comparison with Venice, Genoa or Florence. This process of development would not have been possible without a body of laws and an administration of justice that offered security to economic agents.

Later on, the idea of the existence of individual, natural rights that could be understood in a purely rational way and incorporated in legal texts helped further the belief in the necessity of codes that judges and courts should obey. Codification should assume, in principle, a clear restriction in the discretion afforded to continental judges. The old idea that the judge's principal mission was to serve as the mouthpiece of the law becomes more lucid as the law and its application become more precise. In this sense, there can be no doubt that the codes, beginning in the 19th century, offered a clear guide for the behaviour of the courts. Codification was not easy in many countries and generated internal tensions and numerous conflicts between a conservative approach in defence of local laws and a position in favour of unification of national law, which a code of general application clearly demands. Legal unity was achieved in a diverse manner and at a varied pace in different countries. The French Code Civil of 1804 became the model to be followed by all countries in the path towards codification. In Spain this process manifested itself in a languid fashion, where the power of local laws ensured that a code did not emerge until 1889, eighty-five years after French codification, and more than sixty years after the country introduced its first commercial code, which in substance related more to the practices of merchants than to local traditions.

From our perspective it is necessary to emphasize the fact that, in civil law countries, the economic development of the markets was precisely one of the principal aims of codification. It was considered that if the supremacy of the code over local law and local judges could be affirmed, a double objective could be reached. On the one hand, the creation of an authentic national market had presented itself as very difficult due to local differences, which created distortions in the economic marketplace. On the other hand, a decisive advance was to be made towards the principle of the freedom of contract, which had been troubled by the presence of local privileges of every type.

4.2 Courts, Legislation and the Principle of Freedom of Contract

One of the key features often put forward to support the view that common law is superior to civil law is the greater support it offers to the principle of the autonomy of contracting parties, or, in other words, freedom of contract. To many continental lawyers, however, this view has always appeared somewhat surprising, given that the principle of freedom of contract served as a great inspiration for the wording of civil codes in Europe in the 19th century, beginning with the French Code Civil in 1804. This position is unmistakably manifest in later codifications, such as the Spanish civil code of 1889, where Article 1255 establishes with clarity the principle of liberty of contract, stating that contracting parties may create their own agreements, clauses and conditions as the parties see fit, as long as they do not run counter to the law, morals or public order.

It is certain that if one analyses the evolution of legislation post-codification, one can bear witness to how (1) the principle of contractual freedom is losing importance, and how (2) legal scholars and judges have discredited it as a basic principle of the legal system. In reference to point (1), it makes sense to interpret a good part of the laws passed over the last century as a departure from the civil code and the principle of freedom of contract which inspired it. From laws that regulate labour relations to those that seriously limit contractual freedoms for parties entering rent contracts, they were in large part introduced as a means of redistribution in favour of certain social groups. Individual volition is to a large extent substituted by common obligations.

In reference to the second point, the evolution of legal theory and jurisprudence in a civil law country like Spain represents a situation repeated in many others. A work by J. Castán Tobeñas, *Derecho Civil Español, Común y Foral* – without doubt the most studied textbook on civil law ever in the history of Spain – may serve as an example. In his introduction to the analysis of contract law, Castán has no doubt in affirming 'it must be confessed that civil law in many points concedes excessive respect to private conventions to the detriment of equality and moral demands.'[40] Regarding what he considers to be the future of contractual agreements, he unsurprisingly suggests: 'One needs to replace the old individualist dogma of the autonomy of volition with the rule of the principle of intervention.'[41] Moreover, Federico de Castro, surely one of the most important specialists in civil law in Spain in the 20th century, argued that the principle of freedom of contract in the performance of services led to 'scandalous extremes'.[42] In his interpretation of the role played by liberal Spanish jurists dominant at the time of wording the civil code, he suggested, 'the legal dogma that has been dominant up to now attempts to dry out legal precepts, depriving them of moral sap, putting them at the service of

40 Castán Tobeñas (1967), p. 375.
41 Ibid., p. 376.
42 de Castro (1984), p. 58.

the calculative safety of traders and financiers.'[43] This position was naturally compounded with the view that there is a need to abandon the individualist view of the law and substitute it with a version that favours the notion of 'community'.

One may make a similar evaluation of the decisions handed down by courts which have recognized the loss in importance of contractual freedom. This can be seen, for example, in a sentence handed down by the Supreme Court in 1946:

> if one reviews legislation since the passing of the civil code, one soon realises that legal evolution is commandingly moving down the path towards a greater infiltration of social and ethical elements, which in both a general and absolute manner discipline private law relations, imposing upon them a public character at the expense of the principle of freedom of contract.[44]

There can be little doubt therefore that civil law systems, of which the Spanish may be considered representative, have been gradually moving away from the position where decisions taken within markets are the principal means for allocating productive resources in an economy. But is common law really different? According to Posner, 'in setting the cost of voluntary transactions . . . common law doctrines create incentives for people to channel their . . . actions through the market.'[45] One can, however, also suggest that similar developments against the principle of freedom of contract also occurred in the common law system, and that the evolution of North American legal tradition in the 20th century was quite similar to the continental experience, bar differences in institutional settings.

American law witnessed an important change regarding freedom of contract in the 20th century. For an extended period of time the Supreme Court struck down numerous economic and social laws on the grounds that they ran counter to freedoms constitutionally protected by the Fifth and Fourteenth Amendments. Later, however, the Supreme Court abandoned this process of revising statutes, which in turn would lead to a serious restriction in many economic activities based on the principle of contractual freedom. Moreover, local, state and federal authorities could now regulate economic activity without any restriction other than discrimination or arbitrariness. In the final decades of the 19th century, the Supreme Court accepted on various occasions the constitutionality of regulatory laws in economic activity. Though one could cite earlier cases, Munn *v.* Illinois [1876] is particularly representative.

---

43 Ibid., p. 40.

44 Spanish Supreme Court, Decision of 2 April 1946.

45 Posner (1998), p. 230.

Here a Chicago-based firm that refused to apply for a state licence as a warehouse owner and accept its regulation was unsuccessful in the Supreme Court on the grounds that there was a public interest in the warehouse sector.

Almost thirty years later Lochner *v*. New York [1905] constituted a reaffirmation of the principles of classical jurisprudence from the 19th century and for this reason was harshly criticized by those who considered this position to be unsustainable, given existing economic conditions and the changes that the North American economy had been experiencing. The Supreme Court in Lochner ruled that it was contrary to the constitution to limit the maximum working time in the bakery sector to 60 hours weekly and ten hours daily. Holmes's dissenting vote in Lochner, perhaps the most famous dissenting vote in the history of North American legal history, would constitute an authentic manifesto for those in favour of what became known as the progressive approach to the problem. The liberty of citizens to do as they like so long as they do not interfere with the liberty of others to do the same – wrote Holmes – is interfered with by many laws and regulations from school laws to every state or municipal institution that takes their money whether they like it or not. Cutting down the liberty of contract was, therefore, not a new principle. 'The Fourteenth amendment does not enact Mr. Herbert Spencer's Social Statics.'[46]

Judges' and law professors' positions would very much go along the same lines. Only four years after Lochner, Roscoe Pound published his famous article 'Liberty of Contract'.[47] In this article Pound attacked the application of the principle of contractual freedom in US courts from two standpoints: first, because this was not a traditional principle in US law; second, because it assigned the false impression of equality between the parties in contractual relations. In his opinion, previous legal doctrine had exaggerated the relevance of the principle of freedom of contract and had, contrarily, downplayed the importance of public interest. Individualism should, accordingly, be surmounted by a more social vision of legal relations.

The specific circumstances and legal tradition were undisputedly different from those found in civil law countries, but legal doctrines in both systems showed clear signs of convergence. Opposition to the principle of freedom of contract would accrue strength in the years following and the Supreme Court in the 1930s would, in some cases, further reel it in. In Nebbia *v.* New York in 1934, for instance, the Supreme Court endorsed a law passed by the State of New York establishing a minimum price for milk, with the aim of helping farmers who had experienced a large fall in the price of this product. Many other cases could be mentioned. In fact, one can find in either system an evolution in

---

46 Holmes (1992), pp. 305–7.
47 Pound (1909).

both law and legal theory towards the reduction of contractual freedom in favour of regulatory ideas, presented as part of the path towards progress and modernity. Principles of freedom of contract were subordinated to other principles based on ethics and moral values, thus reducing contractual freedom in favour of a redistribution of gains to the benefit of weaker contracting parties.[48]

4.3 The Role of the Courts and Legislation in Liability Rules

Throughout most of the Western world the 19th century was the century of industrialization. And in this process, an important part was played by the legal body in the way of laws and regulations. According to Coase's theory, in a world with no transaction costs and with well-defined property rights, situations of conflict would be solved efficiently by agreement between the parties. But, in a real world of confused property rights and positive transaction costs, laws and courts of justice play an important role since they exert a direct influence on the economy.

As it has been pointed out, in the analysis of economic problems such as those raised by tort law, the strict theory of market failures gives only a partial view, and often a misleading one at that. In these cases what usually happens is that the market, indeed, fails; but, at the same time, the laws of private property which are a prerequisite for the functioning of the market also fail. It is very rare that we find ourselves faced with a simple alternative between the free market and public regulation. The problem is, rather, the option between two forms of control, both proceeding from public authority: private law and administrative regulation.[49] Tort law and administrative regulation were modified throughout the 19th century to encourage industrialization in countries that were very different in themselves and with different judicial systems.

After much controversy throughout the 1970s and 1980s some economists and legal scholars in the United States were of the opinion that the civil legal system during the 19th century had clearly evolved in favour of the interests of industry. This transformation, however, was not achieved by means of a substantial modification of the laws that regulated industrial activity, but rather through a significant change in the legal interpretation of tort law.[50] The main idea is that American courts slowly stopped applying the strict liability rule,

---

[48] The regulation of labour relations is a good example of how both courts and legislation abandoned the principle of freedom of contract in common law and civil law countries; see Cabrillo (2007).

[49] Posner (1998), p. 401.

[50] See, especially, Horwitz (1977). An analysis of this can be found in G. Schwartz (1981) and Hovenkamp (1983).

which prevailed in the period prior to industrialization, and started to examine claims for damages caused by industrial installations following the negligence rule. It is not hard to understand why this change in the liability rules could have an important effect both on resource allocation and income distribution. According to the strict liability rule, the person or company that causes an accident should pay the cost of the damages produced, independently of whether or not they have taken the necessary measures to try to prevent such an accident taking place. Under this rule the manufacturer who, for example, causes a fire accidentally in the land adjacent to his factory, or who causes losses in agricultural production in the farms bordering his property because of badly controlled smoke emissions, should indemnify the injured parties. However, the legal decision would be quite different in a claim for damages in which the negligence rule was applied, since in this case the factory owner would only have to indemnify the injured parties if he had not taken reasonable precautions.

For those who defend the theory of the change in the liability rules in the US legal tradition, the judges were not neutral in the application of tort law but rather applied a utilitarian perspective which, in the language of welfare economics, allowed the external costs generated by a process of industrialization to be transferred partially to third parties. In other words, the American judges assumed a pro-industrial economic ideology in their interpretation of civil liability.

Apparently the story was quite different in continental Europe, since economic policy in the civil law countries followed a stricter regulation; there was a more interventionist tradition than that existing in Great Britain and the United States. It is not surprising, therefore, that the encouragement of industrialization by the legal community would take a different form from that followed in the Anglo-Saxon world. The goals, however, were similar. We could talk of a 'continental model' where industry would also be favoured by laws but administrative regulations would play the dominant role.

Though the legal system in continental Europe was dominated by administrative regulation regarding the creation of new industrial establishments, however, one should not exaggerate the differences between the two models, since they coincided on two important points.[51] First, administrative regulation would also appear in Anglo-Saxon countries. Secondly, the change in legal interpretation of tort law from strict liability to negligence was not necessary in civil law countries, such as France and Spain, as the civil codes upheld the negligence rule as a general principle from the beginning.

---

[51] The criticism by Dicey (1885 [1915]) that any administrative regulation is contrary to the rule of law greatly exaggerated the differences between the common law and civil law systems and helped sustain the idea of two incompatible legal models.

Legislators in civil law countries made use of administrative procedures to encourage industrialization, while a similar objective was pursued in the United States by applying the negligence rule. Both administrative and civil laws took into account the advantages that the new industries and technology offered to social welfare and sought formulas through which affected third parties would pay a part of the external cost. If we take again Spain as representative of civil law countries, we can find interesting similarities between Spanish decisions and those reached in the British and North American courts, which are often quoted to support the theory of the industrialist tendency of common law in the 19th century.

For instance, the Spanish courts maintained the thesis that the railways inevitably gave rise to accidents and risks, and that it was the obligation of the railway workers to take necessary measures to avoid these dangers. But if accidents occurred even when such measures had been taken, the companies could not be held responsible for what had happened. In this respect, we could mention the Spanish Supreme Court's decision of 30 May 1865. It denied the appeal presented by a landowner in Burgos against the decision of the Court of Appeals of that city. The Court acquitted the Isabel II Railway Company of the damages caused by a fire in a gorse thicket on the property of the appellant. Since the railroads crossed the appellant's land, the engines had started a fire on more than one occasion, causing considerable damage. The landowner claimed compensation before the Court of Appeals of Burgos, but the railway company fought the case. They argued that they recognized that the engines caused the fires, but claimed the engines were only working in keeping with their nature and that the fires had been completely unpreventable and beyond the control of the engine drivers. The Supreme Court accepted this reasoning and pointed out that since no carelessness or blame on the part of the engine drivers had been shown there were no grounds for imposing the payment of compensation to the aggrieved party.[52] The Spanish Supreme Court ruled similarly on many occasions.

To cite another example, let us look at a case resolved by the Supreme Court in its decision taken on 3 June 1901. On this occasion, the matter concerned an engine which caused a fire in a nearby haystack while manoeuvering in a station. In this case, the court applied the law mentioned above and ruled that there was no blame or negligence on the part of the engine driver. It pointed out, moreover, that the haystack had been placed near the railway line without any agreement that would limit the right of the company to use the line, and in full knowledge of the constant use that was made of the railway line and of the consequent risk to the merchandise.[53]

---

52 Jurisprudencia civil (1901), 921–3.

53 For a general overview of the role of administrative and tort law in 19th century Spain, see Cabrillo (1994).

The opinions of British and American courts in that period were not very different. Economists familiar with the arguments used by Pigou and the subsequent criticism by Coase will find themselves on well-known ground. As an example, let us look at two interesting North American cases in which the judges' arguments coincided with the enthusiasm for industrialization which we have seen reflected both in the text of the Spanish law referred to above and in the Spanish Supreme Court decision mentioned earlier. The first of these court decisions was in reference to an explosion in a factory which caused damage to a neighbouring farm. In 1873 a judge in New York State ruled in the case of Losee *v.* Buchanan that 'society has to have factories, machines, dams, canals and railways. These installations are called for to satisfy the multiple needs of the people and form the basis of our civilization.' He went on to add that, if any damage was caused to a third party's property because of an accident, the factory owner could not be held responsible for it.[54] Some years later, we find a similar opinion in the case of the Georgia Railroad and Banking Co. *v*. Maddox (1902), where the judge ruled that if a railway station had been authorized and was suitably run, the people who lived in the vicinity could not sue the company for damages since these were the inevitable results of the very existence of the railway system itself.[55]

This short study of tort law and the administrative regulation of dangerous industries endorses the position that the Spanish legal system concurred with the Anglo-Saxon systems in their desire to encourage industrialization and technical progress. It is possible to interpret the changes that took place both in civil law and common law countries as the expression of a new system of values that gained strength during the course of the 19th century. These new values – primarily, a belief in technical progress and industrialization as the driving force for prosperity and happiness – had spread throughout the Western world, and legal systems supplied similar answers to a common cause.

It is not a coincidence that new consumer preferences at the end of the 20th century were causing major modifications in the regulation of dangerous activities and liability rules. When the main objective is industrialization, the negligence rule and tolerant administrative regulation are applied. But when the value afforded to such assets as clean air and a healthy environment increases – even at the cost of more expensive production techniques and reduced industrial growth – we should not be surprised by the increase in restrictive administrative regulation and a recovery of the strict liability rule. No real differences can be found between developed civil law and common law countries.

---

54 Hovenkamp (1983), p. 687.
55 Coase (1960), p. 129.

5. OVERVIEW OF COURT STRUCTURES

To understand the form court structures have taken in any jurisdiction, it would be necessary to immerse oneself in the historical make-up and local realities that have shaped and continue to condition them. This is not our objective here. Rather, we aim to highlight basic features of civil law and common law court structures, providing an overview of their operations and statistics to allow for comparison.

There are two overriding features that greatly influence the role courts play in the allocation of resources in society.[56] The first factor is the jurisdiction they enjoy, that is, what types of disputes they may be called upon to hear. Such forms the basis for assessing the scope of courts.[57] Essentially, jurisdiction may be allocated within a unitary system of courts or fragmented into a multiplicity of different courts, each with their own separate hierarchical structures. *Ceteris paribus*, a court that enjoys greater jurisdiction and scope in its decision making enjoys greater authority in the assignation of resources in society. The establishment of separate autonomous courts truncates the scope of 'ordinary courts' and has been a preference of authoritarian regimes.[58] These courts are often staffed by a separate group of judges commonly with closer connections to the political system – particularly the executive – without the same guarantees of independence as ordinary judges, thus allowing for greater control over the administration of justice.

The second major factor of importance is the relation between the different layers of the court structure. One may highlight two basic models.[59] Within the coordinate model, lower and intermediate courts make the bulk of decisions and complaints that reach the top of the judicial pyramid are few and far between. This is usually associated with professional judiciaries – more prevalent in common law countries – as opposed to bureaucratic judiciaries – traditionally identified with systems adhering to the civil law tradition.[60] In an archetypal coordinate structure, legal proceedings are less integrated, testimony has traditionally been oral as opposed to written, and authorities have traditionally assigned considerable procedural responsibility to actors outside the organization (lawyers principally), with only limited review from above.[61]

---

[56] This framework is developed in Guarnieri and Pederzoli (2002). Though the authors focused on the political significance of courts, this division is propitious from the economic perspective of the allocation of resources in society.

[57] Ibid., p. 78.

[58] Ibid., p 79.

[59] Damaska (1986).

[60] See below, Chapter 3.

[61] As we shall see later, in common law jurisdictions, which adhere to *stare deci-*

The second basic structure refers to the hierarchical system, whereby cases move more easily up the judicial pyramid with a far greater number being subjected to re-examination by the highest court, a factor which enables it to control the courts beneath it. This is often associated with bureaucratic judiciaries, more prevalent in civil law countries. In an archetypal hierarchical structure, the legal system is organized according to specialized stages with information being collected gradually and expansive files developed as cases advance procedurally. Authorities administer proceedings steadfastly, curtailing the discretion of attorneys or their clients. Appellate review is commonplace before a decision is final.

No legal jurisdiction strictly adheres to either of the above, and recent cross-pollination, particularly in civil procedure, has led to the emergence of a debate on best practices that has transcended legal traditions. Court structures have taken multifarious forms and judicial pyramids exist, constituting a number of distinct autonomous subsystems.[62] Common to continental countries generally are clear divisions between ordinary courts which hear civil and criminal matters, administrative courts that adjudicate complaints involving public agencies, and specialized courts that hear cases related to constitutional law. Changes in the role of government have led to a greater number of issues being heard by administrative courts, outside the jurisdiction of ordinary courts. For the purposes of illustration, in the following we take a look at court structures found in three civil law countries (France, Germany and Spain) and two jurisdictions adhering to the common law tradition (the United States and England and Wales).

The French judicial structure is largely regional and fragmented, giving way to different courts hierarchies, as well as distinct management and career structures (see Figure 2.1).[63] It draws important distinctions between public and private law, civil and criminal law, and ordinary courts and the *Conseil Constitutionnel*. No court enjoys residual jurisdiction over all branches of the law.[64]

Ordinary cases, both criminal and civil, are adjudicated within a three-tier structure. Various *tribunaux* and specialized courts hear all criminal and civil cases. There are two general first instance civil courts, the 475 *tribunaux d'instance* and 181 *tribunaux de grande instance*, which are assigned cases according to their gravity.[65] Though traditionally the *tribunal de grande*

sis, the need for greater control by the higher courts is reduced, thus favouring the use of more coordinate structures.

62 Guarnieri and Pederzoli (2002), pp. 79–97.

63 For an authoritative discussion of the French judicial structures, see Bell (2001, 2006).

64 Bell (2006), p. 45.

65 Ministère de la Justice (2006), October.

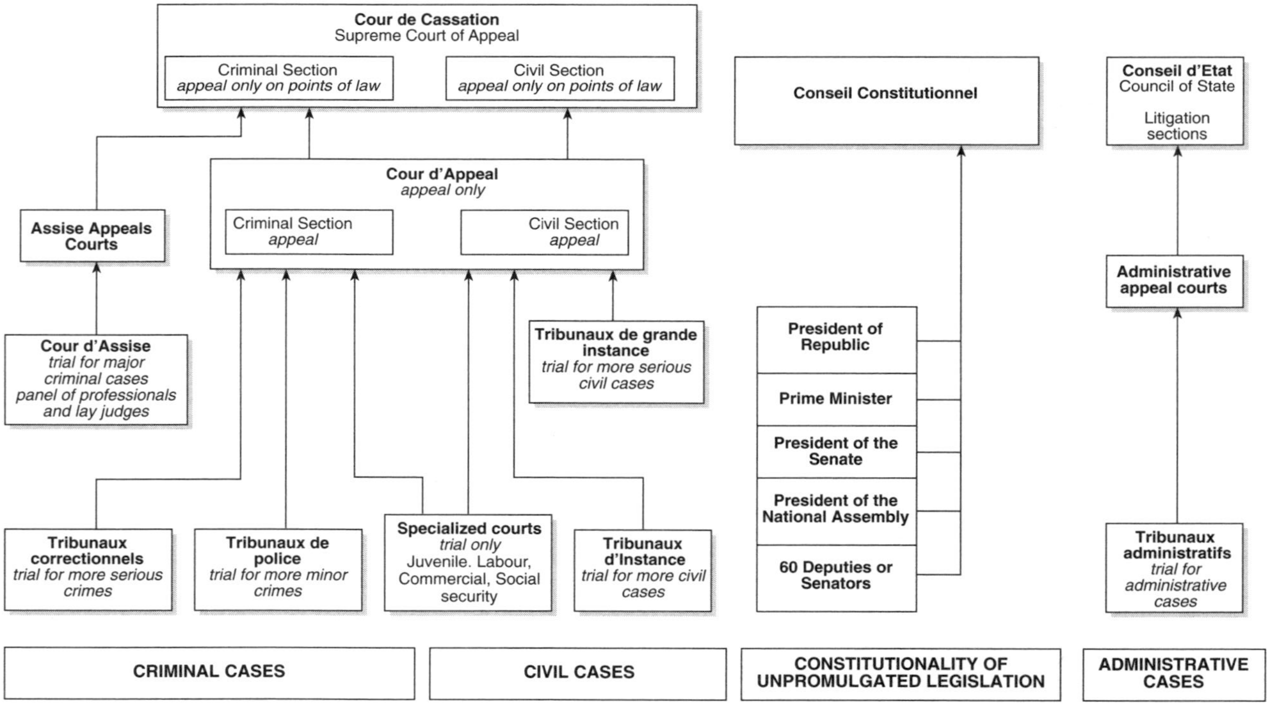

Source: Adapted from Guarnieri and Pederzoli (2002), p. 20

Figure 2.1 The French court system

instance has been a collegial court, in recent years much important civil work has been carried on by single judges.[66]

Various types of specialist civil courts exist. First formed in 1563, the *tribunaux de commerce* – of which there are 185 – deal with disputes among merchants. Judges at these commercial courts are lay persons elected indirectly by members of the local chamber of commerce. They have jurisdiction over contract and company cases, including insolvency. In 2005, 237 770 cases were handled by these courts, of which 28 903 were appealed.[67] Labour courts, known as *Conseils de prud'hommes*, of which there are now 271,[68] are also staffed primarily by lay persons, composed of equal numbers of employers and employees. They are a court of final resort for claims of under 4000 euros. These courts are composed of a conciliation panel of one employer and one employee, and a judgment panel composed of two from each group. Where there is no majority in support of a single position, a professional judge is called in to chair a session.[69] These courts handled 201 604 cases in 2005 of which 42 387 were appealed.[70] Other specialist courts include juvenile and social security courts.

The *tribunal de police* is the lowest-level criminal court, which handles minor offences, the *contraventions*. Cases are heard by a single judge, and some 98 per cent reportedly lead to convictions.[71] More serious cases (*délits*) are tried at one of the 181 *tribunaux correctionnels*. The judges are the same as those for the *tribunaux de grande instance*. Occasionally a *juge d'instruction* (an examining magistrate) will prepare a case for trial. Trial is commonly before a panel of three professional judges, and the conviction rate is very high (95 per cent).[72] The *cours d'assises*, located at the *Cour d'Appel*, hear a reduced number of very serious crimes. Trial is heard by three judges who sit with nine jurors. The *cours d'assises* decided 3245 cases in 2001, with 95.7 per cent resulting in convictions.[73]

Appeals may be heard by the *assises*, the criminal and civil sections of the *Cour d'Appel*, and the *Cour de Cassation*, serving as the final court of appeal. Whilst appeals to the *Cour de Cassation* are on points of law only, appeals to the *Cour d'Appel* may be on fact as well as law. Allowing for appeal on fact as well as law clearly increases the burden on the court of appeals. In 2005,

---

66 Bell (2006), p. 45.
67 Ministère de la Justice (2006).
68 Ibid.
69 Bell (2006), p. 92.
70 Ministère de la Justice (2006).
71 Bell (2006), p. 46.
72 Ibid.
73 Ibid.

the *Cour d'Appel* decided 219 494 non-criminal cases, of which 5607 were appealed. It also rendered a decision in 91 070 criminal cases.[74] The burden placed on the administration of justice by allowing appeal on fact and law is reduced, however, because of the documented nature of proceedings. A file on the case containing evidence produced by the lower civil and criminal courts is kept, but the court may order additional investigations as it deems fit. Litigants may make a *pourvoi en cassation* to the *Cour de Cassation* against a decision of the *Cour d'Appel*. The *Cour de Cassation* is the highest court in the French judiciary. There is only one for the whole Republic. Appeals are based on error of law only. Upon reaching a verdict it normally sends the case to a different appeals court for a decision on merits founded on its ruling. Its purpose is therefore to unify case law and ensure that the interpretation of texts is the same throughout the territory.[75]

Cases between citizens and public agencies are decided by a separate group of administrative courts divided into three levels, the administrative courts (*tribunaux administratifs*), administrative courts of appeal (*cours administratives d'appel*), and the judicial division of the *Conseil d'Etat*. The administrative courts and the administrative courts of appeal are staffed by a separate corps of judges from the *Conseil d'Etat*.[76] There are 36 first instance administrative courts spread across France. In 2005, they decided 155 562 cases.[77] The seven administrative courts of appeal, which hear appeals on points of law as well as fact, decided 23 553 cases. The presidents of these courts are members of the *Conseil d'Etat*. It should be noted that Council is not only a judicial body but also a major adviser to the government. In 2005, it decided 11 222 cases.[78]

The final branch of cases is related to the constitutionality of unpromulgated legislation. Unlike in the United States, judicial review of legislation in continental Europe is assigned to separate constitutional courts. The *Conseil Constitutionnel* is technically not a court but a council. Its role has changed significantly over time. Whilst formerly it was a body for adjudicating disputes associated with the legislative competence of the executive and Parliament, as well as contentious parliamentary elections, it today reviews the constitutionality of laws before they are signed by the President.[79] Unlike for instance in Germany, it does not hear applications from individual citizens

74 Ministère de la Justice (2006), October, p. 15.

75 For an overview of the role of the Cour de Cassation, see http://www.courdecassation.fr.

76 See Bell (2006), pp. 52–3; Guarnieri and Pederzoli (2002), p. 89.

77 Ministère de la Justice (2006), p. 31.

78 Ibid.

79 Ibid.

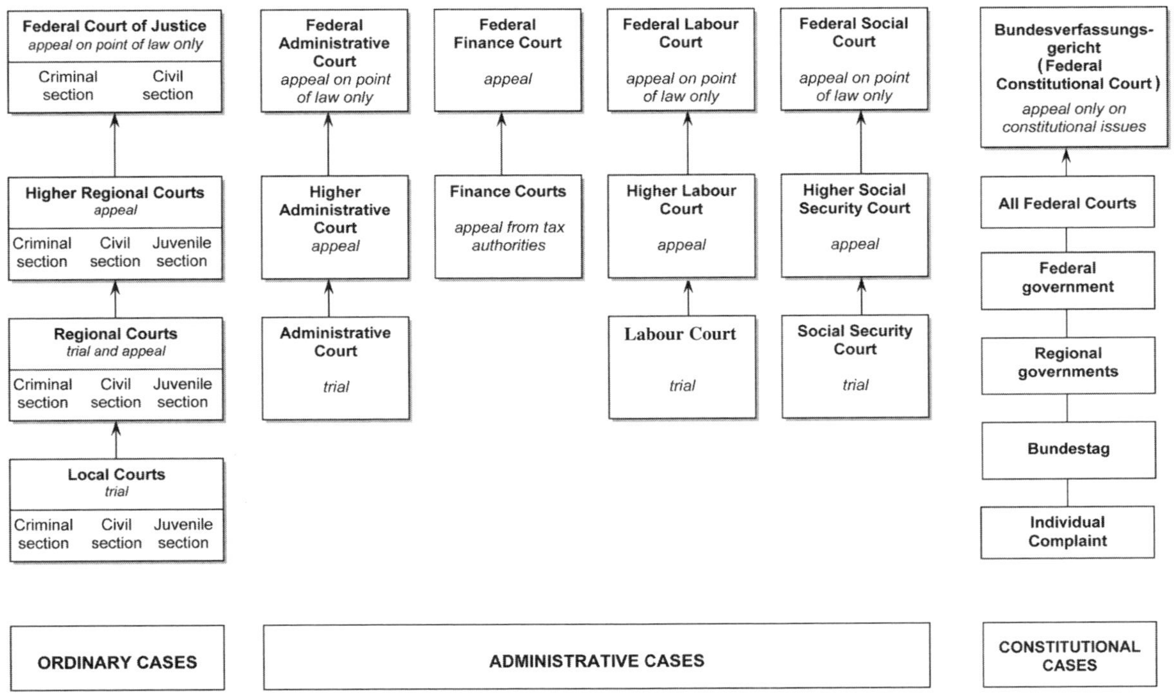

Source: Adapted from Guarnieri and Pederzili (2002), p. 94

Figure 2.2 The German court system

concerning the constitutionality of laws passed by Parliament relating to concrete situations, nor can it attend to applications from the administrative or civil and criminal courts. Applications are made by the President of the Republic, the Prime Minister, the President of the Senate, the President of the National Assembly, and 60 deputies or senators (commonly belonging to the opposition parties).

The German court structure represents an example of a continental law system within a federal structure (see Figure 2.2). It is characterized by being specialist and regional, though ultimately hierarchically integrated at a federal level. The courts are organized into five different groups, namely: (1) courts of general jurisdiction (*ordentliche Gerichte*) for both civil and criminal cases; (2) administrative courts (*Verwaltungsgerichte*);[80] (3) labour courts (*Arbeitsgerichte*);[81] (4) social welfare courts (*Sozialgerichte*); [82] and (5) fiscal courts (*Finanzgerichte*).[83] In addition, there is the Federal Constitutional Court (*Bundesverfassungsgerichtshof*), which is not part of the regular court system but forms its own judicial branch.

Courts of general jurisdiction (*ordentliche Gerichte*) have authority over all civil or criminal disputes which are not confided to the competence of one of the specialized courts.[84] A total of 1 949 031 first instance civil cases were decided by courts of general jurisdiction in 2004, of which 1 523 527 were heard at local courts (*Amtsgerichte*) and 425 504 were heard at regional courts (*Landesgerichte*). Moreover, 583 121 family-related cases were heard at special family courts. In total, 904 709 criminal cases were decided at first instance courts in 2004, of which 890 627 were heard at local courts, 14 066 at regional courts, and 16 directly at higher regional courts (*Oberlandesgerichte*).[85] All groups of courts are divided into trial and intermediate appeals courts based in the *Länder* and there is a final appeals court that is a federal court.

A striking feature of the German judicial system is the number of judges that man the courts. It is often contended that Germany has the largest number

---

80 See VwGO (*Verwaltungsgerichtsordnung*), available online: http://bundesrecht. juris.de/bundesrecht/vwgo/gesamt.pdf.

81 See ArbGG (*Arbeitsgerichtsgesetzt*), available online: http:// bundesrecht.juris.de/bundesrecht/arbgg/gesamt.pdf.

82 See SGG (*Sozialgerichtsgesetz*), available online: http:// bundesrecht.juris.de/bundesrecht/sgg/gesamt.pdf.

83 See FGO (*Finanzgerichtsordnung*), available online: http:// bundesrecht.juris.de/bundesrecht/fgo/gesamt.pdf.

84 See GVG, para. 13 (*Gerichtsverfassungsgesetz*), available online: http:// bundesrecht.juris.de/bundesrecht/gvg/gesamt.pdf.

85 Federal Statistics Agency, Germany. See http://www.destatis.de/e_home.htm. Moreover public proceedings were initiated in 4 994 776 cases at *Landesgerichte* and nine cases directly at the *Oberlandesgerichte*.

of professional judges in both absolute and per capita terms in the world.[86] This is reflective of the central and active role judges play in the justice system (see Figure 2.3). Though Germany, by European standards, does not have a small number of lawyers by any means – 125 015 in 2004 – it will surprise many readers to learn that there is one judge for every six lawyers. Of the 20 395 judges, 464 were active at the federal level and 19 931 at the state (*Land*). The courts themselves differ greatly in size. There were 15 146 judges (74 per cent) working at the ordinary courts in 2004, 2216 in the administrative courts, 1262 at the social courts, 1104 at the labour courts and 637 at the fiscal courts (see Figure 2.4).

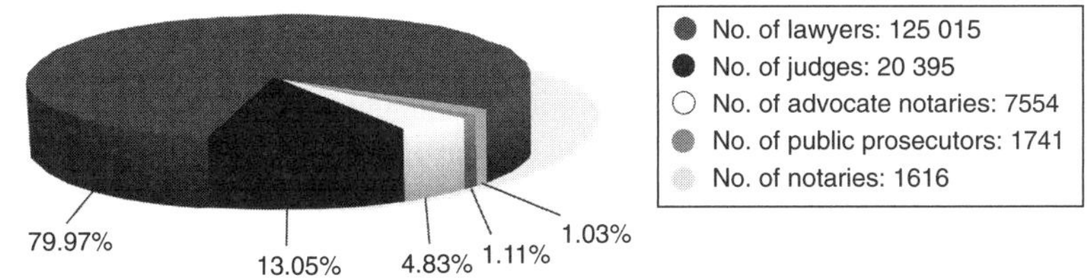

Source: Federal Statistics Office, Germany

Figure 2.3 Court actors in the German judiciary

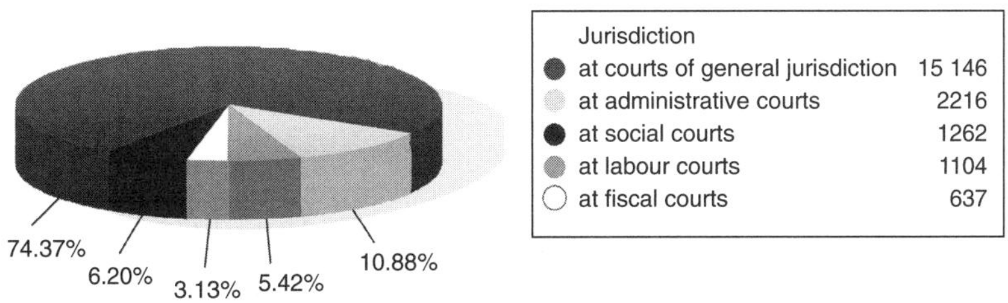

Source: Federal Statistics Office, Germany

Figure 2.4 Jurisdiction of judges in the German judiciary

86 Murray and Stürner (2004), pp. 38–9.

Regarding appeals, in principle litigants in German courts can appeal first instance decisions in a *de novo* proceeding. There are a number of explicit exceptions, however. Verdicts in criminal matters decided by the large chamber (*grosse Strafkammer*) [87] in regional courts cannot be appealed on fact but only on law. Thus, curious as it may sound, while for minor misdemeanors a *de novo* trial may be admissible, verdicts on serious crimes and felonies are – bar errors of law – final.[88] In civil cases appeal is generally available, except if the stakes are very small.

Appeals to the Federal Court of Justice (*Bundesgerichtshof*), the highest court in the field of ordinary jurisdiction (civil and criminal), are on points of law only. The facts decided by lower courts are binding on the *Bundesgerichtshof*, bar in exceptional cases such as where procedural error at the lower courts is clearly demonstrated.[89] It has twelve civil panels and five criminal panels with a total of 127 judges. It may also set up auxiliary panels, and has eight special panels primarily for disciplinary proceedings against lawyers, notaries, patent agents, chartered accountants and tax consultants, as well as for questions of agriculture law and cartels. It completed 3821 appeals on questions of law and refusal of permission to leave in civil cases in 2004. It dismissed 2154 criminal appeals as being meritless and gave a judgment on 174 cases.[90]

Decisions by the Federal Constitutional Court (*Bundesverfassungsgericht*) bind all constitutionally defined organs at both state and federal level as well as courts and agencies.[91] The Federal Constitutional Court exercises competency over a great number of issues, which may for the greater part be broken down into three broad areas.[92] First, it exercises 'abstract norm control' – that is, without any connection to a particular case before the courts – at the urging of the Federal Government, Länder or members of the Bundestag. This allows the court to examine the constitutionality of laws passed by Parliament as well as advise on the ratification of treaties. Second, it rules on issues referred to it by courts in the course of litigation on individual cases, thus exercising

---

87 Within the regional courts, criminal cases may be decided by small chambers (*kleine Strafkammern*) or large chambers (*grosse Strafkammern*), which refer to the make-up of the court that hears a case. In the case of the small chamber, there are three sitting judges, one professional and two lay. In the case of the large chamber, there are initially three professional judges and two lay.

88 Blankenburg (1996), p. 259.

89 One important exception is made in the case of patent cases, where the Tenth Civil Panel of the *Bundesgerichtshof* serves as a trial court.

90 Official statistics from *Bundesgerichtshof*; see www.bundesgerichtshof.de.

91 BverfGG §31.

92 Bell (2006), p. 166. For a precise look at the areas of competence of the *Bundesverfassungsgericht*, see BVerfGG §13.

'concrete norm control', with cases suspended until such a ruling is given. Third, it operates at the behest of individuals petitions known as constitutional complaints (*Verfassungsbeschwerden*), whereby individuals allege the breaching of their constitutional rights. Moreover, it rules on conflicts between Länder and the Federation or between different Länder or organs.

The lion's share of the cases decided by the Federal Constitutional Court has been constitutional complaints. From 1951 to December 2005 it decided 148 799 constitutional complaints, comprising 96.30 per cent of its total caseload. Of this number only 2.5 per cent were successful. Abstract and concrete control of norms accounted for only 2.18 per cent of its activity.[93] Conflicts between Länder and Federation or between Länder or organs accounted for 1.49 per cent.[94] It is interesting to observe that most of the constitutional complaints brought before the Federal Constitutional Court are against court decisions; in 2005, they composed 91.5 per cent of all constitutional complaints, effectively conferring upon the Federal Constitution Court the role of an additional court of appeals.

The Spanish court system is quite singular on the continent (Figure 2.5).[95] Though there are a number of specialized courts, such as juvenile or commercial courts, it is more cohesive. For instance, no distinction is made between judges who adjudicate administrative cases and those who adjudicate ordinary (civil and criminal) or specialized cases.[96] Although it is a national system, it is highly regionalized and local in nature. It has come under substantial strain in recent years, as Spanish society is becoming increasingly litigious.[97]

In Spain, many territorial areas will have courts presided over by non-professional judges (*jueces de paz*). These courts are maintained by the local municipality. The role of these judges is limited to very minor criminal and civil cases. The basic civil and criminal unit is a single-judge court, known as the First Instance and Instructing Courts (*Juzgado de Primera Instancia e Instrucción*), located in municipalities. These courts may be split into civil and criminal courts depending on the municipality. They handle lesser crimes for which no investigation before trial is needed (*instrucción*). In addition they conduct fact finding in cases related to more serious offences. In one or more centres in a province there will be specialist courts, staffed by ordinary judges who have passed a test in their specialism. More specifically, these include: administrative courts (*Juzgados de lo Contensioso-Administrativo*), which

---

93 See http://www.bundesverfassungsgericht.de/organisation/gb2005/A-I-1.html.

94 Ibid.

95 Guarnieri and Pederzoli (2002), p. 95.

96 Ibid.

97 See *Consejo General del Poder Judicial* (2006), p. 83.

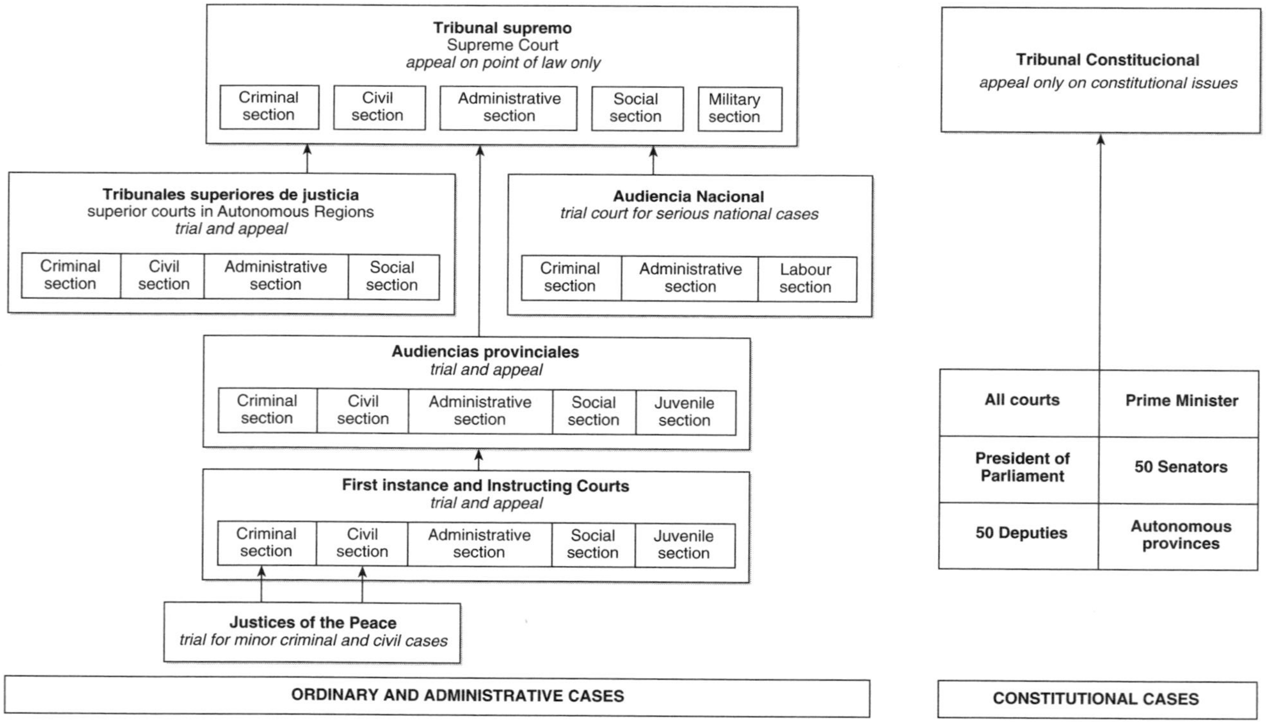

Source: Adapted from Guarnieri and Pederzoli (2002), p. 96

Figure 2.5 The Spanish court system

decided 99 655 cases in 2005;[98] labour courts (*Juzgados de lo Social*), which decided 259 492 cases in 2005;[99] post-conviction criminal courts (*Juzgados de la Vigilancia Penitenciaria*), which decided 178 259 cases in 2005;[100] and juvenile courts (*Juzgados de Menors*), which decided 28 859 civil and 34 785 criminal cases in 2005.[101] More recently, commercial courts have been established. More serious criminal and civil matters go directly to the *Audiencias Provinciales*. These are collegiate courts maintained by the local provinces.[102] Acting as a second instance court, they also hear appeals from decisions pronounced by the Court of First Instance and Instruction. In 2005, they decided a total of 101 426 cases.

At the level of the Autonomous Regions (*Comunidades Autónomas*), the Supreme Court dealing with appeals on points of law (*recursos de casación*) is the *Tribunal Superior de Justicia*. It is divided into three salas: civil and criminal, administrative, and labour. It has jurisdiction over questions of general civil law, local (foral) law and special law of the relevant Autonomous Regions. Moreover, it is authorized to hear civil and criminal cases against the presidents and members of autonomous regional governments, as well as the assembly, high members of the public administration, judges and magistrates in inferior courts. The court sits in three divisions: civil and criminal, administrative, and labour.

Cases that are considered of national or international importance are no longer decided within the court structure of the Autonomous Regions. The regionally located first instance criminal courts, known as *Juzgados Centrales de lo Penal*, deal with preliminary matters but the *Audiencia Nacional*, a national trial court, conducts trials. It is divided into three sections deciding – at first instance – criminal, administrative and social matters. It is responsible for, *inter alia*, hearing cases related to organized crime, terrorism and genocide. Pursuant to the reforms of 2004, there is always an appeal in criminal matters.

Located above the *Audiencia Nacional* and the superior courts in the Autonomous Regions (*tribunales superiores de justicia*) is the Supreme Court (*Tribunal Supremo*), which hears appeals on points of law from the two aforementioned. It may be seen as a Spanish equivalent of the French and Italian

98 Ibid., p. 111.

99 Ibid., p. 115.

100 Ibid., p. 101.

101 Ibid., pp. 90, 111.

102 Provinces (*Provincias*) are not to be confused with Autonomous Regions (*Comunidades Autónomas*). There are 50 provinces in Spain (Ceuta and Melilla are not integrated in the Spanish provinces). Autonomous Regions are a recent development, set out in the Spanish Constitution of 1978. There are 19 in total (including Ceuta and Melilla).

Courts of Cassation, whose function is to guarantee the uniform interpretation of law, including administrative law.[103] It enjoys jurisdiction in civil, criminal, administrative, social and military matters. Consequently, there are five different chambers which are in charge of cases in each of these areas.

The Constitutional Court (*Tribunal Constitutional*) is the court responsible for constitutional questions.[104] It has competency for, *inter alia*, controlling the constitutionality of laws (*leyes*) and legal/legislative decrees be they at a national or regional level; conflicts related to competencies between Autonomous Regions and the State or between the autonomous regions themselves; conflicts between constitutional state bodies; conflicts related to local autonomy (for example, of municipalities and provinces); questions regarding the constitutionality of international treaties; and amparo appeals for the violation of fundamental human rights and public liberty. Amparo appeals may be initiated by any person, national or international, physical or juristic, in defence of rights guaranteed by Articles 14 to 30 of the Constitution. They make up the greater part of the workload of the Constitutional Court (see Table 2.1). Amparo appeals in 2005 constituted 97.6 per cent of cases filed at the

Table 2.1 Cases filed at the Spanish Constitutional Court[105]

Type of case	Number
Appeals regarding unconstitutionality	16
Questions of unconstitutionality	206
Amparo appeals	9476
Positive conflicts regarding competencies	8
Negative conflicts regarding competencies	–
Conflicts between constitutional bodies	–
Conflicts in defence of local autonomy	2
Challenges regarding declarations without force of law and resolutions made by the Autonomous Regions	–
Requirements regarding the constitutionality of international treaties	–
Total	9708

Source: Spanish Constitutional Court (year 2005)

103 Guarnieri and Pederzoli (2002), p. 95.

104 See http://www.tribunalconstitucional.es.

105 http://www.tribunalconstitucional.es/memorias/2005/memo05_anexo03.html#Cuadro2.

Constitutional Court, followed a long way back by questions related to constitutionality, which made up 2.1 per cent of filings. Appeals regarding unconstitutionality and conflicts between competencies composed together only slightly over 0.2 per cent of all case filings.

Moving on to common law systems, the feature that is most surprising to European civil law scholars is the unitary nature of jurisdiction.[106] A single court frequently enjoys jurisdiction over civil and criminal matters, public law litigation and sometimes judicial review of legislation.[107] In the United States, legal structures are particularly fragmented, which is reflective of the federal and decentralized character of American political institutions. Unsurprisingly, this has led to a rather differentiated body of substantive law reflective of the nation's diversity. The law also reflects the common law tradition and the adversarial process which dictates many formal proceedings.

Article III of the United States Constitution and the first Judiciary Act were responsible for the development of three distinct types of federal courts, namely the district courts, circuit courts, and the Supreme Court. The 94 federal district courts are the trial courts of the federal system, with jurisdiction over civil and criminal disputes as well as many cases that would commonly be tended to in administrative courts in European legal systems (see Figure 2.6). Moreover, each district has a bankruptcy court as a unit of that district.[108] Certain trial courts enjoy nationwide jurisdiction over specific types of cases. The Court of International Trade deals with cases involving international trade and customs disputes. The Court of Federal Claims enjoys jurisdiction over most claims for money damages against the United States, in addition to disputes over federal contracts and unlawful 'takings' of private property by the federal government, as well as a host of other claims against the United States.

On average only 20 per cent of first instance decisions are appealed and only 5 per cent of these are subsequently reversed on appeal.[109] The United

---

106 Guarnieri and Pederzoli (2002), p. 81.

107 Courts of specific subject-matter jurisdiction are, however, also common in common law systems. In the United States, for example, these include: the United States Bankruptcy Courts, United States Tax Courts, United States Court of International Trade, United States Court of Federal Claims, United States Court of Appeals for the Armed Forces, and the United States Court of Appeals for the Federal Circuit. Whereas federal courts are generally created by the US Congress under the constitutional power set out in Article III, many specialized courts are created under the authority granted in Article I. See Posner (1996) for a discussion.

108 Three United States territories – the Virgin Islands, Guam, and the Northern Mariana Islands – have district courts that adjudicate federal cases, including bankruptcy cases.

109 Rowland (1991), p. 65.

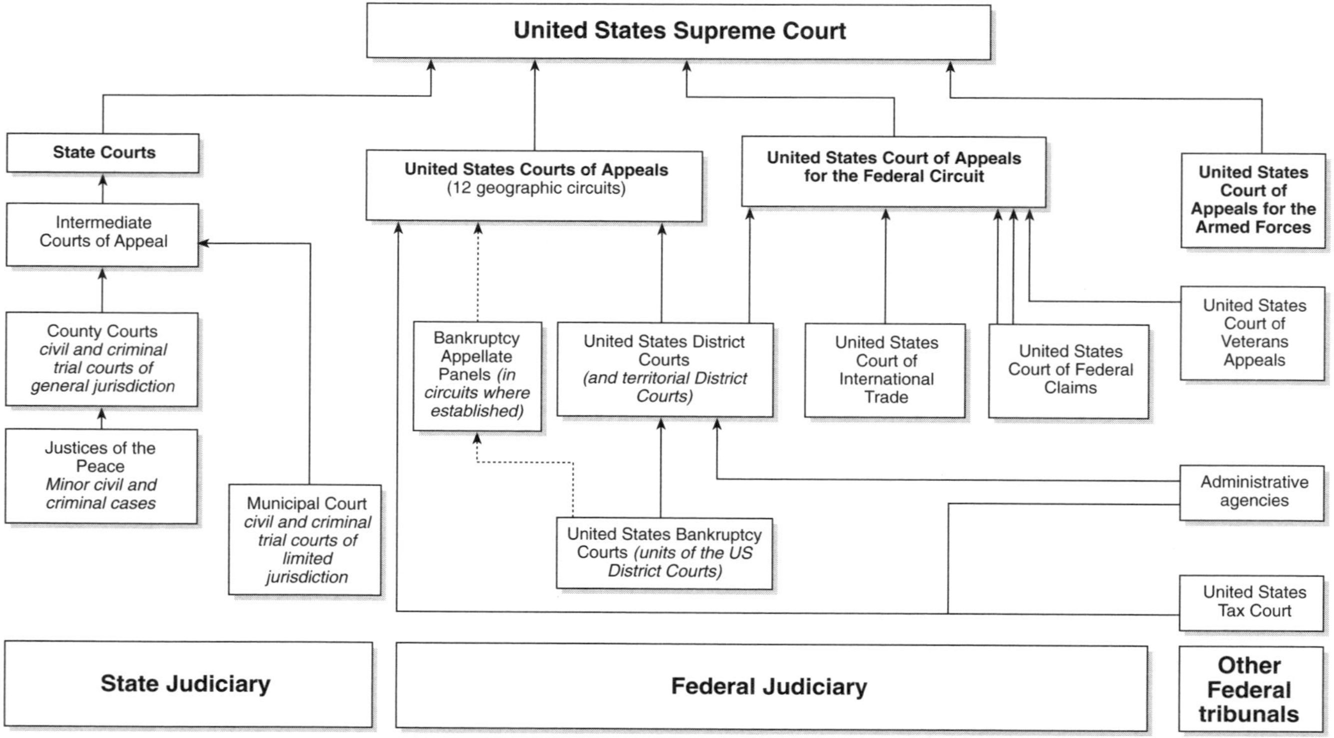

Figure 2.6 The United States court system

States has 13 federal circuit courts of appeal, 12 of which have jurisdiction over several states, and the Federal Circuit, which has nationwide jurisdiction to hear appeals in specialized cases, including disputes involving patent law and those decided by the Court of International Trade and the Court of Federal Claims. Federal circuit courts hear appeals from the district courts situated within their circuits, in addition to appeals from decisions of federal administrative agencies. Under the principle of *stare decisis*, its decisions are formally binding on lower courts.

There are two very notable characteristics of appellate courts in the United States. First of all, they are effectively courts of last resort, because it is extremely rare that cases make it up to the Supreme Court. They, therefore, are entrusted generally with the fundamental role of reversing error in trial court decisions and ensuring coherence of judicial decisions. Secondly, they are noted for their size. It is rare that the number of appellate court judges exceeds 15, tending to be far lower. These factors make them – from a European perspective – appear relatively small. Appellate court judges, therefore, know each other much better than trial court judges – particularly those in large metropolitan areas. Subsets of judges hear most cases, which can lead to different decisions emerging from a single court.[110]

The United States Supreme Court stands at the top of the federal judicial system. It consists of the Chief Justice of the United States and eight associate justices. From a civil law perspective, it is surprising to see the jurisdiction it enjoys, which includes many cases that in most European countries would be heard not by a single court but by a combination of a court of cassation (civil and criminal cases), a council of state (administrative cases), and a constitutional court (constitutional issues).[111] Within guidelines established by Congress, the Supreme Court, at its own discretion, hears only a very limited number of the cases it is asked to decide. Access to the court is by either writs of appeal or *certiorari*. It normally only accepts cases that raise 'substantial' federal or constitutional questions. These cases may begin at either federal or state law level. Four of the nine justices must vote to grant a writ of *certiorari*. The court receives approximately 7500 petitions a year, but *certiorari* is granted normally in no more than 100 cases. One cannot infer from the denial of *certiorari* any reflection on the merits of a case, but rather that a case is not sufficiently important to warrant the use of the court's scarce resources. Whereas the court enjoys widespread jurisdiction as well as ample discretion in the selection of cases it wishes to hear, the parsimonious number of cases that actually ever reach this instance confer great authority on trial and appeal courts.

---

110 See Atkins (1990) for a discussion.

111 Guarnieri and Pederzoli (2002), p. 84.

The federal system operates alongside 50 different state judicial systems. Most cases in the United States, of course, go to state courts, which are more numerous and are often located closer to litigants than federal courts. National government has effectively no control over the 50 state courts, providing neither the staff for the courts (state judges normally follow a distinct career path) nor the funds for their operation. State courts are required to adhere to interpretations of the United States Constitution by federal courts, but, should they fail to do so, the federal courts have not means to discipline them. In addition, state courts almost always have the final say on the interpretation of state laws.[112]

There are naturally differences between individual state court structures. As is the case regarding the federal judiciary, they are essentially organized around the principle of unitary jurisdiction, almost always divided into trial, appellate and supreme courts.[113] As in the federal judicial system, cases that actually make it all the way up to the supreme courts are extremely rare, as state supreme courts are similarly afforded the discretion to select the cases that they wish to hear. Cases that are considered important in establishing legal principles and for the resolution of differences in interpretation of the law are generally only heard by the supreme courts. Appeals in civil cases generally require the consent of either the appellate court or the judge that decided the original case and appeals are based on issues of law and not of fact. As in the federal system, the combination of widespread jurisdiction and ample discretion in the selection of the cases leaves the Supreme Court potentially open to criticisms of bias and ideology, and the small number of cases that reach this instance confers great authority on trial and appeal courts. Consistent with the strict separation between federal and state courts, federal courts may only overrule state courts where there is a federal question, that is to say a specific issue (such as consistency with the Federal Constitution) giving cause for federal jurisdiction. Appeals from losing litigants to the United States Supreme Court are therefore very rare and no more than 2 per cent of requests are granted annually.[114]

While the structure of the English court system is less complex than the American, it has some similar features (see Figure 2.7).[115] It is a unitary system that encompasses civil and criminal matters as well as public law litigation. In addition, despite the existence of two levels of appellate courts (the Appellate Committee of the House of Lords and the Court of Appeal), it is

---

112 Jacob (1996), p. 21.

113 Guarnieri and Pederzoli (2002), pp. 81–2.

114 Ibid.

115 As is conventional in much of the literature, when we refer to the English court system, we are in fact referring to England and Wales.

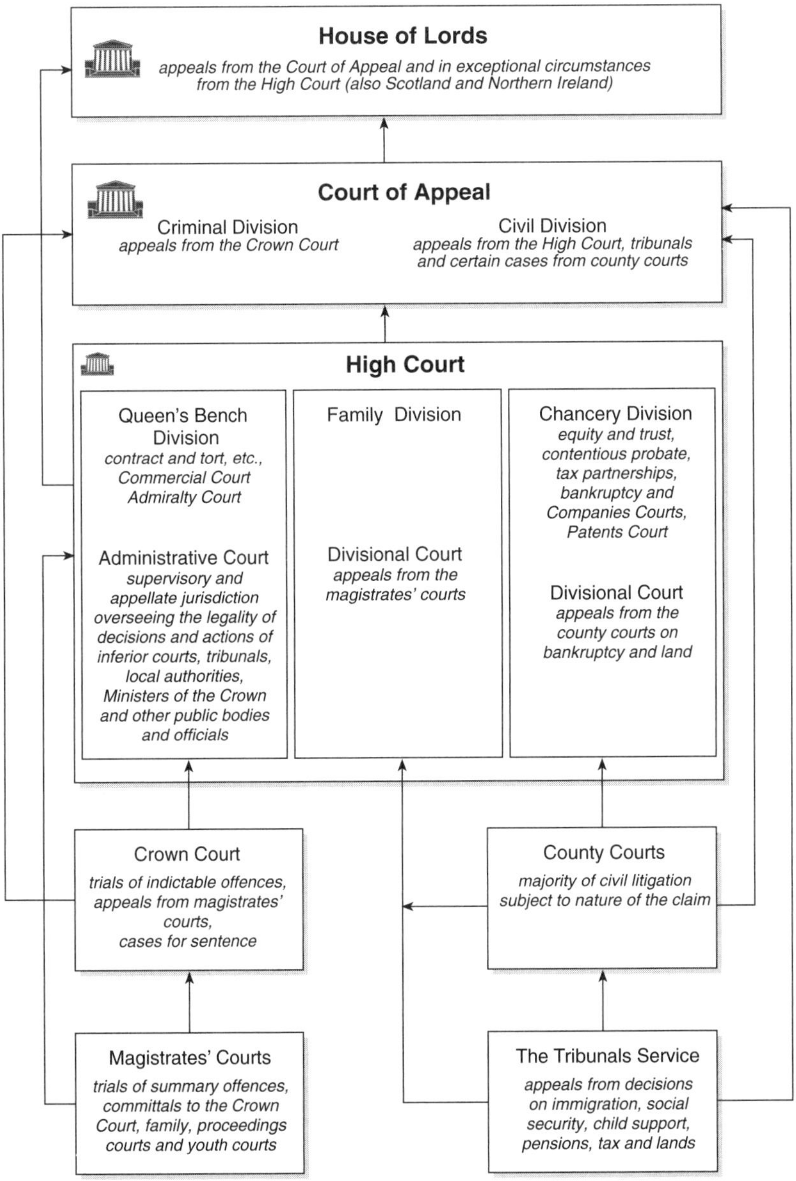

Source: The Court Structure of Her Majesty's Court Service (HMCS), available at http://www.hmcourts-service.gov.uk/aboutus/structure/index.htm

Figure 2.7 The English Court System

essentially a three-tier system with the Court of Appeal acting as the final appeal court in the vast majority of cases.

The county court is the factotum of the civil justice system. There are currently around 220 such courts in England and Wales. In 2004, 1 597 000 claims were brought for the recovery of debts or the recovery of property.[116] These courts also handle cases related to divorce, domestic violence and children. Cases usually involve financial claims of £50 000 or under. More complex issues are normally directly handled by the High Court. With over 30 000 bankruptcy petitions and 166 042 divorce petitions, there is a large proportion of routine uncontested cases. Circuit judges preside over most cases in county courts, though the more junior district judges handle cases with claims of up to £5000, which are automatically allocated to the small claims track.[117] Appeals can be made to the High Court or to the Court of Appeal.

More complex civil suits or those involving large sums of money may be brought to the High Court. The High Court has three divisions, the Chancery Division, the Queen's Bench Division and the Family Division. The Chancery deals with issues such as property and finance, including contentious probate, tax partnerships, bankruptcy, company law and patents. The Queen's Bench is the largest division, with 69 judges. It hears actions related to many types of contracts, if they are not assigned to the Chancery and tort. Typical claims include claims for debt, breach of contract, personal injury actions, defamation and professional negligence. The Family Division hears cases involving divorce, children, probate and medical treatment. It also serves as an appeal court for family issues first heard at the county court. First instance civil decisions normally can be appealed at the Court of Appeal (Civil Division), but the high cost of litigation in England generally discourages such appeals. Moreover, legal challenges to administrative decisions made by organs such as government departments or local councils (what is known in England as 'judicial review') are presented at the High Court.[118]

The lowest court for criminal matters is the magistrates' court.[119] It hears less serious criminal cases, which constitute up 95 per cent of those completed. They are generally presided over by three lay magistrates (justices of the peace), who are not paid but may claim expenses and receive an allowance for loss of earnings. Some cases may be presided over by a district judge. They normally cannot order sentences of imprisonment that exceed six

---

116 Department for Constitutional Affairs (2004a), pp. 50–51.

117 Guarnieri and Pederzoli (2002), p. 85.

118 Ibid., pp. 85–6.

119 Magistrates' courts also hear certain civil matters, such as family matters, liquor licensing and betting and gaming.

months (or twelve months for consecutive cases), nor can they impose fines exceeding £5000.

More serious criminal cases are tried in the Crown Courts, usually by jury. They are situated in approximately 90 locations, divided into eight regions in England and Wales. They heard 81 750 committals for trial in 2004.[120] The judges of the Crown Court are also judges of the High Court (who also sit in the High Court to take civil business), circuit judges (who also sit in the county courts to try less important civil business) and part-time recorders. The Crown Court has two other basic activities. It hears appeals against convictions and sentences passed by magistrates. Appeals against conviction entail a rehearing of the case in the Crown Court. Appeals involving only points of law go directly to Queen's Bench Division of the High Court. In 2004, it disposed of 30 979 committals for sentence and 12 578 appeals.[121] Appeals against a jury conviction are brought before the Court of Appeal (Criminal Division), but only on matters of law or the sentence handed down by a Crown Court judge.

The Court of Appeal is the second most senior court in England and Wales. It is divided into a civil and a criminal division. The Master of the Rolls is the head of the Civil Division, whilst the Lord Chief Justice is the head of the Criminal Division. In addition there are 37 Lords Justices. The Civil Division hears appeals from the High Court, county courts and tribunals. The Criminal Division hears appeals in criminal matters from the Crown Court. During 2004, a total of 7591 applications for leave for appeal were received, of which 1782 were against conviction in the Crown Court and 5809 against the sentence imposed. During 2004, the Civil Division disposed of a total of 3116 applications.

In comparison with American appeal courts, the English Court of Appeal shows a stronger propensity to reverse lower court decisions (Atkins 1990). Whilst aggregate reversal rates for federal courts in the United States for cases that come before them are commonly around 16 per cent, this number would appear to be substantially higher in England. During 2004, of the appeals heard by the Court of Appeal Criminal Division, over 38 per cent against conviction and over 69 per cent against sentence were allowed. Of the appeals disposed of at the Civil Division of the Court of Appeal, nearly 28 per cent were allowed.[122]

At the top of the judicial system is the Appellate Committee of the House of Lords, composed of 12 Lords of Appeal in Ordinary ('law lords'), as well as other Lords of Appeal, as required. On average, in the region of between sixty and eighty cases are considered annually by the Appellate Committee.

---

120 Department for Constitutional Affairs (2004a), p. 85.
121 Ibid., p. 21.
122 Ibid., p. 5.

For the year 2004, this number was 77.[123] Though it can hear cases from practically any field of law, it commonly hears cases related to human rights, public law, tort, intellectual property, taxation and commercial contracts.[124] The Appellate Committee of the House of Lords is authorized to hear cases from Great Britain and Northern Ireland, though not criminal cases from Scotland.[125]

As with the low number of cases selected to be heard in the US Federal Supreme Court, the parsimonious number of cases – though influenced by the high cost of proceedings – is largely a result of the Committee's desire to select cases it considers important. As seen above, this has the effect of shifting importance to lower courts that become the final instance in all but the rarest cases. It is interesting to note that over 41 per cent of appeals disposed of by the House of Lords were allowed.[126] In over 48 per cent of the appeals that came before it via the Court of Appeal, it actually reversed the latter's decision.[127] Though these numbers appear particularly high, the Supreme Court by comparison has an even higher reversal rate, averaging 66.6 per cent in the 27-year period between 1953 and 1979.[128]

These high numbers are indicative of the discretion awarded to these courts in the cases they wish to hear. As Atkins notes of the United States Supreme Court, it enjoys 'all but complete discretionary power over which cases it will hear'.[129] It is clear that the highest courts in common law systems generally enjoy a much lighter workload than, for instance, their European civil law counterparts.

In accordance with the Constitutional Reform Act 2005, the new Supreme Court will retain most of the judicial functions of the House of Lords and no longer be part of the legislative chamber, thus being separated from any non-judicial role. This includes the appellate jurisdiction of the House of Lords as well as the devolution jurisdiction of the Judicial Committee of the Privy Council. The Constitutional Reform Act 2005, in essence, creates for the first time in British constitutional history a separation of powers between the executive, the legislature and the judiciary.[130]

---

123 Ibid., p. 14.

124 Judges of the House of Lords are a completely different group of judges, with very different recruitment procedures. This is not surprising given that the Appellate Committee has jurisdiction over a far broader area, and that the Privy Council serves as a supreme court for a number of members of the Commonwealth.

125 Dymond (2006), p. 10.

126 Department for Constitutional Affairs (2004a), p. 5 and p. 14.

127 Calculations based on Department for Constitutional Affairs (2004a), p. 14.

128 Atkins (1990), p. 77.

129 Ibid., p. 78.

130 Dymond (2006), p. 29.

Comparing the US with the English judicial system, it would be prudent to highlight a few similarities and differences. The principle of *stare decisis* clearly acts as a factor of internal coherence in both systems. Moreover, difficulties in the appeals structure place greater importance on the role of first instance judges in both systems vis-à-vis their civil law counterparts. Whilst both systems are largely unitary in nature, the rising number of specialized courts in England has arguably led to greater fragmentation in the English courts. Administrative tribunals frequently handle numerous issues related to welfare policies and the rights and obligations of the welfare state. Though these administrative tribunals generally do not form autonomous, district entities outside the ordinary courts as in the civil law countries addressed above, they do represent a shift in direction and a divergence from US judicial development. Another important difference between the English and US courts is related to the lack of judicial review of legislation found in the former. The US judiciary is far more active in policymaking, whilst English courts observe the doctrine of parliamentary supremacy. As mentioned above, the English political system has traditionally lacked a well-defined separation of powers, the key principle that has encouraged courts in the US to grow in independence as well as stature.[131]

6. OPTIMAL TERRITORIAL JURISDICTION

In determining jurisdiction one of the fundamental questions is the determination of the geographical area over which authority extends.[132] From an economic perspective, a broad jurisdiction has the effect of avoiding the problem of different jurisprudential interpretations of a norm or identical legal problem, which otherwise would create greater legal uncertainty, therefore reducing the efficiency of the system of administration of justice. These benefits are particularly accruable where there is a high level of homogeneity in social or business norms and practices. As social and business norms become more heterogeneous among territories, more centralized decision making may not be capable of coping with this diversity, and differences in social and business preferences may not be properly accounted for. A degree of excessive centralization, furthermore, increases the costs for the parties that intervene in

131 See Atkins (1990); Shapiro (1981).

132 In the next section, we discuss specialization, which refers to the origin of a court's authority. Courts may be designed as either courts of general jurisdiction or courts of special jurisdiction, where courts of general jurisdiction are those empowered to hear a broad range of cases not reserved for special jurisdiction. Courts of special jurisdiction, on the other hand, are empowered only to hear specific kinds of cases.

the process. These transaction costs are reduced as a consequence of technical progress. For instance, a society in which travelling a distance of 20 or 30 kilometres entails numerous hours of travel can reasonably expect the territorial size of a specific court to be smaller than one in which travel only takes a few minutes. Similarly, the possibility of presenting documents to a court via technology naturally increases the size of the optimal jurisdiction of a court.

The solution to these problems – in practice – has generally consisted in giving precedence to reducing transaction costs at the first instance, establishing a high number of courts which allows for greater proximity to the parties involved in a trial. This is reduced as one ascends the court hierarchy, leading to a total centralization in the decision making in the case of supreme courts. The relevance of the principle of unification of jurisprudence has been such that it has led in some instances to extremely high transaction costs. One example of this has been the restrictions placed by the House of Lords as the highest court in the case of territories in the old British Empire, or the role of the Spanish Supreme court, which in the 19th century reviewed decisions by the Court of Appeals in Havana, Cuba.

The reduction in transaction costs, due to technical progress, together with the development of international relations and the success of some supranational processes of economic integration have resulted in the creation of new courts with jurisdiction extended over many countries. Whilst in theory there is potential for domestic courts to attract international disputes, structural limitations make these efforts difficult.[133] Nevertheless, the potential for competition between domestic courts is limited, due in large part to: (1) the transaction costs that would be incurred by foreign litigants in using these courts, (2) institutional factors that shape judicial activity, and (3) the fact that domestic courts have little incentive to attract this litigation.

International courts have undergone substantial development in recent decades, in terms of their numbers, competencies and caseloads. One may even refer to an increasing judicialization in the resolution of international disputes.[134] Judicialization refers to the increasing tendency today to substitute traditional procedures of diplomatic negotiation for the acceptance of a higher international court in the resolution of conflicts. This tendency can be found in multiple areas of the law and different courts. In relation to the former, there are different international courts which enjoy jurisdiction in areas such as human rights, crime, border disputes, territorial waters and various economic questions. With respect to the special scope in which they exercise their jurisdiction, there are courts, such as the International Court of

133 Gessner (1996).
134 Schneider (2006).

Justice, whose jurisdiction extends practically across the entire world; others, such as the International Criminal Court or the Dispute Settlement Body of the World Trade Organization, include a great number of countries; others are responsible for cases that affect countries that have formed a regional organization, such as the European Union or NAFTA.

Why do we witness the current tendency of courts to act at an international level in the resolution of disputes? The reason is clearly the greater efficiency of these models compared with the former ones grounded in diplomatic negotiations, frequently relying on a poorly defined legal framework. The creation of courts in this manner reduces costs in a double sense. First, they create a standard procedure, with clear rules and deadlines that facilitate the participation of parties and reduce delaying tactics, which are far more likely in traditional diplomatic negotiations. Secondly, the creation of these judicial organs is usually accompanied by the development of legal rules or standards, and – in time – a series of cases of reference has a similar effect to national law, not just in facilitating the resolution of specific cases but also in reducing uncertainty regarding law and litigation outcome, thus creating incentives for agreements between parties.

A good example of this evolution can be found in the development of the dispute resolution system in the World Trade Organization. In 1994 the Dispute Settlement Body (DSB) was created; its role is the application of new procedures in the resolution of conflicts between member states of the organization, which is an amplified, revised version of the old system used in GATT. This new body and its set of rules have permitted the resolution of a large number of cases. Of fundamental importance has been the fact that they can sanction the parties that are not complying with a ruling. In the first procedural phase, the WTO recommends an agreement prior to launching a formal claim against the organization. If agreement is not reached, the case is analysed by a panel of three experts, who write up a report and present it to the parties. Parties can appeal, and finally the DSB adopts its decision and gives the losing parties a deadline for compliance. If the losing party does not comply, a sanction is decided upon, which may include economic compensation to the winning party. In summary, the WTO Dispute Settlement Body may be seen as an application of basic principles of national law to a multi-national organization, and the advantages that are obtained by this procedure, as well as the costs (delays, excess number of cases, resistance to compliance with judgements), are becoming increasingly similar to those incurred by national courts.

The most interesting jurisdictional issue today is probably that of universal jurisdiction for the persecution of specific crimes. A case subject to universal jurisdiction may be dealt with by courts in any country without the existence of any specific link between the crime and the country hearing the case. The concept is not new. In the 18th century, for instance, piracy was considered a crime of universal jurisdiction, which meant that any country had the possibility of going after persons involved in this practice. In the 19th century Great Britain decided to oppose the trading of slaves effectuated by ships bearing any flag. In our times crimes against humanity are considered by some countries as subject to universal jurisdiction. Are there efficiency arguments behind this jurisdiction? Or put differently, is it efficient – for example – that a judge attempt to prosecute an ex-leader of a state for possible crimes against human rights which the latter committed when in power?

In these types of cases, the motivations of the judge and the state that hypothetically supports the case may be different. In other words, there may be a principal–agent problem, in which the judge has different objectives from those of the state. A judge may wish to put a dictator on trial for numerous reasons, in accordance with his own utility function.[135] A judge may derive satisfaction from the knowledge that he had a person on trial whose form of government he considered reproachable and punishable. He may also be motivated by the fact that being the judge responsible for a case against a despised international figure would raise his prestige in his own country, as well as afford him international recognition.

The state's interests may be compatible with those of the judge if majority public opinion and the government share the idea that it is fair to put the person on trial. There may, however, be a discrepancy between the principal and the agent if the state considers the costs of such a case to be greater than the benefits attained, in terms of – for example – a deterioration in international relations, or a loss of business opportunities for business-persons because of the decision of the judge, and so on.

In the assessment of the desirability of having a case, the social costs and benefits of having the case may be of little importance to the judge. Social costs, such as the loss of business by national firms in the country of origin of the former leader, may not be of any importance to a judge. In reality, the optimal behaviour for a country – though not for the judge – would be to act as a 'free-rider', leaving it to other states to support these costs. Suppose the case of a dictator whose actions are broadly considered within two countries (for example, France and Spain) to be violations of human rights. If a French judge is responsible for taking up the case in France, the principal beneficiaries of his actions include some who reside in Spain. Residents in Spain opposed to the regime generally receive the same personal benefits as if the case were held in Spain.[136] The costs mentioned above, however, must be covered by the

[135] See below, Chapter 3.

[136] Given that utility functions must be seen as complex, it is possible that some persons would receive greater benefit if the case were heard in their own country because of the international prestige related to the case.

French government and French firms. The conclusion is, therefore, that for a country exercising universal jurisdiction the net effects could be negative, though for individual actors, such as the local judge described above, the benefits of trying the case outweigh the benefits of not trying the case.

7. SPECIALIZATION

The logic behind the specialization of functions is the attempt to obtain advantages associated with the division of labour. The potential benefits of specialization and the division of labour have been well expounded in economics and the classic reference is, of course, Adam Smith. Smith suggested, 'The greatest improvement in the productive powers of labour, and the greatest part of the skill, dexterity and judgement with which it is anywhere directed or applied, seem to have been the effects of the division of labour.'[137] Increased division of labour increases productivity because the returns to the time spent on tasks are generally greater for workers who concentrate on a narrower range of skills.

Economic theory provides numerous explanations why the benefits accrued from specialization may be not realized. The first factor is the size of the market. Smith noted,

> When the market is very small, no person can have any encouragement to dedicate himself entirely to one employment, for want of the power to exchange all that surplus part of the produce of his own labour, which is over and above his own consumption, for such parts of the produce of other men's labour as he has occasion for. There are some sorts of industry, even of the lowest kind, which can be carried on no where but in a great town.[138]

The first major lesson we can draw from economic analysis is thus that the size of a market influences the gains to be had from specialization. Previous discussion on the political economy of the adjudication process and the impact of the expansion of markets and political processes would then *a priori* seem to be powerful arguments in favour of shifting the balance towards greater specialization.

---

137 Smith (1776 [1981]), p. 3.

138 'A porter', Smith suggests, 'can find employment and subsistence in no other place. A village is by much too narrow a sphere for him; even an ordinary market town is scarce large enough to afford him constant occupation. In the lone houses and very small villages which are scattered about in so desert a country as the Highlands of Scotland, every farmer must be butcher, baker and brewer for his own family. In such situations we can scarce expect to find even a smith, a carpenter, or a mason, within less than twenty miles of another of the same trade' (ibid., p. 31).

A second factor that limits the benefits to be had from specialization is coordination problems.[139] The greater the amount of specialization of function, the more difficult it becomes to coordinate activities. This can lead to principal–agent problems, increased monitoring costs, hold-up problems and so on. The second lesson of economics is, therefore, that increased specialization can bring about governance problems, which affect the returns to be had from a division of labour. We will argue below that these costs in civil law countries may be substantially lower than in common law countries, given the structure of the judicial system.

A third factor that limits the benefits to be had from specialization is the level of skills available in an economy. Where there is a higher level of skills, the gains from specialization are – all other things being equal – higher. Coordination among highly specialized workers enables economies to utilize vast quantities of knowledge. Where the level of human capital is low – as is the case in many developing countries – economic theory, therefore, suggests that the returns to specialization may not be as high as first hoped.[140]

In the debate surrounding specialized or general adjudicative procedures, judicial systems must decide between two alternatives: first, whether a court should have jurisdiction over any dispute that arises within a geographical area, that is, general jurisdiction; second, whether a court (or other adjudicative body) might have jurisdiction over disputes related to a specific subject matter over a geographical area, that is, specialized jurisdiction.[141] These organizational patterns could be applied to adjudicative bodies of first instance only, to appeals only, or to both first instance and appeals.[142]

Civil law countries enjoy a comparative advantage over common law countries in expanding the role of specialization of many judicial functions. There are numerous reasons for this, the most important being related to the role of the judge. First, the judges in civil law countries are already specialized in certain legal fields; administrative, criminal, and so on. Second, there is a higher ratio of judges to lawyers in civil law countries than in common law countries. This is clearly related to the more active role they take in proceedings and the nature of the tasks they assume. Third, the greater tendency in civil law traditions towards codification is more conducive to expanding the role of specialization. Fourth, having a career path, judiciary judges can be more easily introduced to – and readily accept – specialization, which makes

[139] Becker and Murphy (1992).

[140] There may still be substantial gains to specialization in developing countries, where the demand for litigation in a specific area is high and the human capital resources required to deal with the cases are available.

[141] Kornhauser (2000b).

[142] Ibid.

it easier to both expand and direct the size of the courts than in common law systems.

This is not to suggest that there are not common trends towards specialization in both common law and civil law countries, but that they have taken on a different form and pace. Courts in continental Europe have generally been prevented from entering into new areas of litigation, in favour of using new special courts or tribunals, such as administrative courts and commercial courts. In common law countries, to accommodate the increase in number and type and complexity of cases, there has been increasing use of quasi-judicial entities to perform these tasks.[143] Though there may be a tendency to think of this as a new trend, this would be inaccurate. One should also keep in mind that much of the administrative law structure in common law countries such as the United States has seen administrative agencies established as specialized courts, to determine the facts of a dispute and make initial legal rulings that are then appealed to courts of general jurisdictions.[144]

One of the most important advantages of specialization is that it allows procedures to be adapted to the dispute matter, hence promoting the goal of designing procedures proportional to the importance of a dispute. Another clear advantage of specialization is that as courts deal with the same issues repeatedly procedures become more routinized, which should speed up the adjudication process.[145] Specialization may also lead to more accurate decisions, given that judges have increased expertise in an area.[146] Likewise, it can lead to greater harmony in the law, as numerous courts are no longer dealing with the same subject matter. Specialization, as we have seen above, lends itself to situations where there is a steady demand for adjudication in a particular area. Hence, as frequency increases, so should – other things being equal – the gains to specialization. (This, of course, makes specialized courts more vulnerable to fluctuations in caseload in their area of activity.) This factor is furthered where issues are increasingly complex; here there is clearly a learning curve in deciding cases, that is, there are economies of learning. Moreover, judges have to make very specific investments in acquiring knowledge of technical issues. They will be more willing to do so, if they will be facing numerous cases of the same type in the future.

---

143 Cappelletti (1989), p. 22.

144 We do not mean to give the impression that both common law countries and civil law countries have been handling the issue of specialization within the core judicial body. Clearly, the make-up of the judicial branch has become far more complex and fragmented than used to be the case. See Cappelletti (1989).

145 Specialized courts also reduce the likelihood of venue disputes.

146 As we shall see below, however, specialization may also promote partisanship and bias, leading to sub-optimal decisions. What is considered accurate in a biased court may be sub-optimal from a societal point of view.

Having outlined multiple benefits associated with specialization, we now turn to some of the potential risks. One of the major costs associated with specialization was early identified by Adam Smith in the *Wealth of Nations*. Smith professed that 'The man whose life is spent performing a few simple operations has no occasion to exert his understanding or to exercise his invention . . . and generally becomes as stupid and ignorant as it is possible for a human creature to become.'[147] This line of argumentation was taken up by Richard Posner, who suggested that

> One does not have to be a Marxist, steeped in notions of anomie and alienation, to realize that monotonous jobs are unfulfilling for many people, especially educated and intelligent people, and that the growth of specialization has given to many white-collar jobs a degree of monotony formerly found only on assembly lines.[148]

This in turn may affect job satisfaction and the quality of people willing to become judges.[149]

Another risk of specialization is the danger of partiality. The problem is not merely confined to judges, given that the same dilemma is occurring with the creation of generic and specialized regulatory organisms, where impartiality is tested on many occasions. To denounce independence in favour of specialization would be an error that could debilitate an entire mechanism. In this vein, specialization may lend itself to greater partisanship and ideology. Judges, given that they are focused in a specific area, may become sensitive to ideology or more responsive to controversy.[150]

Given the aforementioned, it is clear that courts become more attractive for special interest groups when their jurisdiction is narrowed. This places even more emphasis on the importance of the appointments process, making it particularly attractive for interference by the political body. A distinction may, however, be made between different courts. For instance, one would expect

---

147 Smith (1776 [1981]), p. 782.

148 Posner (1996), p. 249.

149 Ibid., p. 251.

150 Posner's example of antitrust theory in the United States is instructive. Posner (1996), p. 251 suggests: 'Antitrust theorists notoriously are divided over the goals of antitrust law – over whether that law is designed and should be interpreted to promote social or political values having to do with decentralizing economic power and equalizing the distribution of wealth or whether the law should merely foster the efficient allocation of resources. They are also divided over whether specific practices are efficient or anticompetitive. These cleavages, reflecting deep and at the moment unbridgeable divisions in ethical, political, and economic thought, most basically over the justice and robustness of free markets, would not be eliminated by committing the decision of antitrust appeals to a specialized court; on the contrary, they would be exacerbated.'

greater problems in labour courts than in commercial courts. Labour courts are heterogeneous in make-up, with clear demarcations between employer and employee interests. Commercial courts, on the other hand, are largely homogeneous, with generally less appreciable demarcations among interests.

Moreover, whilst specialization can free up courts to hear disputes of a less specific matter, it can be very difficult to categorize many of the legal and policy issues that portend to adjudication.[151] It is not uncommon for categories of a dispute to overlap. As Komesar notes,

> Contracts, commercial law, constitutional law, and tort law litigation can each cover such a wide range of substantive subject matter that little would be gained in expertise by setting up courts for each category. These categories also overlap so often that specialized jurisdiction would produce a great deal of disputation about the coverage of each tribunal. As a general matter, broadening the categories would dilute the gains of specialization and narrowing the categories would lead to overlap in jurisdiction.[152]

This may reduce what Posner terms 'the cross-pollination of judicial ideas.'[153]

We have outlined the economic rationale behind specialization as well as its costs and benefits. Countries of the civil law tradition favour specialization, but those adhering to the common law tradition are increasingly experimenting with various models. Shifts toward specialization would appear to be the obvious consequence of the times we live in, but the path should be taken with caution, and each decision be subject to local and historical conditions. Moreover, one must emphasize the manner in which specialization influences judicial independence and good governance.

8. APPEALS

In our overview of court structures, we have seen that there are basic differences in the appeal structure between the common law and civil law traditions. In the civil law jurisdictions we examined, cases move more easily up the judicial pyramid and a far greater number are subjected to re-examination by the highest court. Appellate review is more commonplace before a decision is

---

151 Komesar (1994), p. 145.

152 Ibid.

153 Posner (1996), pp. 258–9. Posner maintains: 'Those who think that the basic concepts of securities law are totally different from those of tort law will not be troubled by this result. But those who agree with Holmes that there is a general legal culture that enables those broadly immersed in it to enrich one field with insights from another will see this as still another drawback of specialization.'

final. Within the common law countries lower and intermediate courts continue to make the bulk of decisions and complaints that reach the top of the judicial pyramid are particularly rare.

But, why should appellate structures exist and what importance should be assigned to the appellate structure? Economics has put forward some useful replies in response to these and other fundamental questions. One key strand in the literature refers to the error correcting role of appeals.[154] It is inevitable that courts will err some of the time in their decision making. A society worried about accuracy in court decisions can make two fundamental choices to reduce the level of error. First, it can allocate increased resources to trials, that is, longer proceedings, a larger number of judges, more skilled judges, and so on. Second, it may allow for appeals. The economic argument behind allowing appeals is that litigants who have been wronged form a subset of all cases and, instead of having to increase the allocation of resources to all cases, gains can be forthcoming by doing so over a subset of cases. Individuals possess private information on when they have been wronged and appeals can allow courts to access this information. This works when courts can differentiate between those that have been wronged and those that have not been wronged.

A litigant who has been wronged has incentive to pursue an appeal where his expected benefits from doing so exceed his expected costs; that is, where the probability of success (p) multiplied by the gains (G) is greater than the costs of pursuing the appeal (C) ($p.G > C$). Where the probability of success from appealing is 0.7 and the gains from appealing are €100 000, a wronged litigant will appeal if the costs of doing so are less than €70 000. Note, a litigant who has not been wronged, however, will similarly pursue an appeal where his expected gains exceed his expected costs. If the probability of success from appealing is 0.2 and the gains from appealing are €100 000, a litigant who has not been wronged will still appeal as long as the costs associated with doing so are less than €20 000.

It is evident that societies should encourage litigants who have been wronged to come forward and dissuade those that have not been wronged from doing so. One means for doing so is by increasing the accuracy of appellate decisions, that is, the probability that incorrect decisions are reversed and that correct decisions are deemed accurate. In the above example, if the probability of success in appealing is raised to 0.8, the wronged litigant will pursue litigation as long as the costs of doing so do not exceed €80 000. If the probability of success from appealing is reduced to 0.1 for a litigant who has not been wronged, then he will only pursue appeal if his costs of doing so are less than €10 000.

---

154 See Shavell (1995a, 2004) and Kornhauser (2000a).

A second mechanism for increasing the separation between aggrieved litigants and those who have not been wronged is related to fees (and fee structures). Given that litigants who have been wronged have greater expected payoffs from appealing vis-à-vis those that have not been wronged (€70 000 versus €20 000 in the aforementioned example), making it more costly to use the appeal process will ensure that a higher *proportion* of cases appealed are by those litigants who have been wronged in the former instance. The difficulty associated with this measure is naturally its potential in some cases to dissuade aggrieved litigants from coming forward, should fees be set too high. It is interesting to note, however, that no court system that we are aware of makes use of high court fees for separating litigants. In fact, court fees for appeals are generally quite low.

This brings us to our third mechanism, namely the potential use of subsidies. Subsidies can be used to encourage persons with legitimate claims to come forward, if the costs of accessing the appeals structure are otherwise too high. There are many forms that subsidies can take. The court could decide to waive all costs of appeal, or the costs of certain actions. It may also consider different costs structures, such as allowing for costs to be reimbursed after an appellate decision has been made.

There are naturally instances where it is in societies' interests that wronged litigants do not appeal. From a social welfare maximizing perspective, appeals can only be justified where the associated social harm of an egregious court decision is greater than the costs of appeal and the expected social harm after appeal. The expected social harm after appeal refers to the probability of error in appeal multiplied by the social harm. From a societal perspective, therefore, the social cost of error must be greater than a certain threshold, which is in turn influenced by the social costs of appeal and the probability of error in appellate decisions.

The error correcting role of appeals has a substantial impact on the optimal level of investment in accuracy at first instance courts (see Figure 2.8). Consider for instance an adjudicatory system with no possibility for appeal. It makes investments to ensure quality at trial (such as lengthening proceedings and increasing the number of judges). Let investments in the quality of trial be denoted by X. As it makes these investments, the probability of an erroneous decision occurring (denoted by p) decreases. The harm caused by erroneous decisions is denoted by H. Note, we have assumed diminishing returns to increases in investment (X). The total costs curve is the sum of X and p(X)H. The optimal level of investment in the quality of trial is denoted by Q*, the point where the sum of the costs of trial and the expected costs of error are minimized.

Now let us consider the case with appeals (see Figure 2.9). Where appeal is permitted the harm incurred by error (H in trial) is no longer the same. The

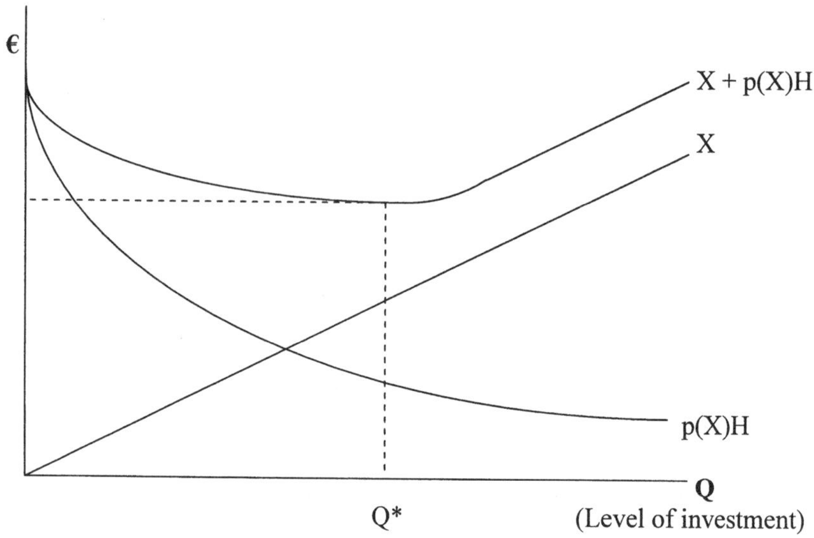

Figure 2.8 Optimal investment at trial courts with no appeal

harm from an error in trial is in fact the costs of investment at appeal plus the expected harm from failing to reverse an error. Let this be denoted by H'. Given the potential of the appeals process to rectify errors at trial, the optimal investment in quality at trial is reduced. This is denoted by Q**.

More recently, economic analysis has started to look not just at the role appeals play via reducing error after it has occurred but also at the importance of appeals as a mechanism for preventing error in the first place.[155] Appeals function as a type of threat to judges, given that if they make wrong decisions these may be reversed upon appeal. Judges, therefore, have strong incentives to make correct decisions and appeal structures can be a cost-effective mechanism to ensure accuracy, without – in many cases – ever having to be used. As is the case in error correction, the error prevention role of appeals is superior to the case of random monitoring of appeals generally, given that appeals allow for a subset of individuals to come forward with private information regarding errors in adjudication. There may, however, be some use to (limited) random monitoring, given that judges, to prevent litigants from appealing, only need to exert enough effort to make appeals not worthwhile. In other words judges do not necessarily make the socially desired (legally defined) optimal decision, but make decisions that do not deviate too much from the

155 Shavell (2006).

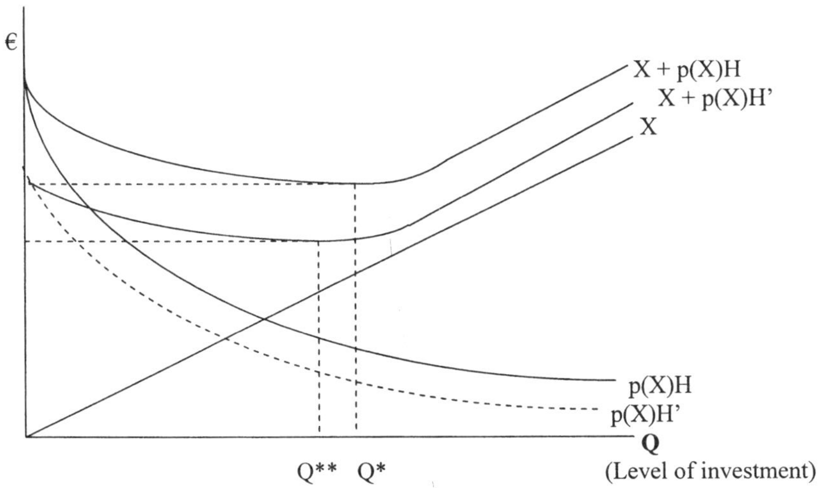

Figure 2.9 Optimal investment at trial courts with appeal

socially optimal. Nevertheless, where judges consistently do enough to prevent appeal by making it not worthwhile for parties to appeal, the accumulated costs of doing so over time may be substantial. There may, therefore, be some use for random monitoring to pull up judges who engage in these practices.

Note, there will clearly always be some amount of uncertainty in judicial decisions that will lead to a certain number of appeals. This can err on the side of wrongful or rightful claims; one cannot say on average whether litigants with legitimate claims will be more likely or less likely than those who have not been wronged to come forward on the basis of uncertainty.

The interpretation of appeals as error prevention and error correction works very well if we view judges as sharing a common objective function, principally the overall reduction of errors in the system. Appeal structures emerge in these 'team models' to reflect this common goal. Once, however, we accept the fact that judges may differ in their objective functions things are no longer as clear-cut. Potentially higher-level judges (let us denote the highest level by T) may wish to impose their preferences on those below them (at T-1). Judges, in order to prevent reversal of their decisions, will have strong incentives to conform with those above them. It is easy to see in this vein how the preferences of judges at T may be incorporated into the decisions of judges at T-1, and how judges at T-2 incorporate the preferences of judges at T-1 and so on). Efforts may be made to reduce the severity of this problem. For instance, where judges at first instance do not know who may potentially hear appeals of their decisions and if they suspect that these persons are interested in reducing error, they have strong incentives to still make substantial efforts to arrive at correct decisions. Randomness may reduce the risk of conformity. Similarly, allowing judges to voice disaccord in majority opinions may reduce the risk of conformity, a factor generally not allowed for in civil law countries.[156]

Like conformity, ideology may be a problem. As discussed below, use of collegiate courts makes it more difficult for ideology to dominate a judicial decision. As with conformity, introducing randomness into the equation, where judges do not know who will potentially hear their decisions upon appeal, may mitigate the problem, thus leading to more accurate decisions. Similarly, paying particular attention to the selection of higher court judges may mitigate this problem. We will devote greater attention to judicial preferences in the next chapter.

The functioning of appeals as a mechanism for error prevention, as for error correction, rests on the incentives for wronged individuals to come forward and appeal. But as with litigation in general, private incentives to appeal are not necessarily aligned with societal interests. Poorly designed, appeals may have a dilatory effect. The knowledge that an appeal can be lodged against first instance decisions may result in a situation where parties do not invest much time and effort in first-level proceedings. This is highly likely where a rehearing is or *de novo* proceedings are virtually guaranteed. Where a complete rehearing is practically guaranteed, the optimal societal level of investment in the quality of trial court proceedings approaches 0. Cases are not fully developed until they actually reach the appellate courts, the obvious result of which must be court delay. Appeal proceedings, therefore, should be subjected to some selection criteria.

It is not uncommon to find the right to appeal guaranteed by statute or some underlying constitutional principle. This can be inefficient in many cases and result in delay, as the appellate court cannot refuse to listen to appeal. This contrasts with appeals by leave or permission, which require the appellant to move for leave to appeal. The decision to allow appeal may rest with the lower court, the appellate court, or both. In civil law countries, it is commonly allowed to appeal first instance decisions on fact as well as law, a factor which clearly increases the caseload of appellate courts. Moreover, this shifts the optimal level of investment in proceedings in first instance courts regarding fact finding, a factor which *should* be reflected in the number of work hours spent on a case.

---

[156] There may also be costs to dissenting opinions, which are discussed in the next chapter.

The error prevention and error correction function of appeals is clearly related to the role of higher courts in the harmonization and development of law. It is common to find this role explicitly stated in the designated functions of higher courts. The Federal Court of Justice in Germany (*Bundesgerichtshof*) states in its homepage, for example, that it is 'With few exceptions . . . a court of appeal dealing with questions of law. Above all, its tasks are the safeguarding of legal uniformity through the clarification of fundamental questions of law and the development of law.' Similar provisions can be found in high courts in most countries. As we have seen above, higher courts in civil law countries frequently have to deal with a substantially larger number of cases than their common law counterparts. There are several structural reasons for this, an important one being the reluctance in many civil law jurisdictions to give their highest courts more ample discretion in the selection of the cases they are to decide.[157] Similarly, differences in precedential practice and the writing of judicial opinions may be a cause of and caused by the number of cases that are heard. Civil law jurisdications do not adhere to the principle of *stare decisis* in adjudication, and precedents are confined to a more 'persuasive' role. Whilst in civil law countries judicial opinions are rather terse and jurisdictions do not generally allow dissenting judges to attach a dissent to a majority opinion, in common law countries individual appellate court judges do far more than vote in favour of reversing or upholding on appeal, frequently offering a detailed rationale for their decisions. One cannot per se argue which appeal structure is more or less efficient, in part because this in turn depends on the structure of the lower courts and the quality and accuracy of their decisions. However, it is clear that the highest courts in many continental countries must decide several thousand cases every year, many of which are largely irrelevant for the clarification or development of the law.

A characteristic of appeal courts throughout the world is that they are collegiate in nature. This inverted pyramidal structure, with the size of a panel deciding a case increasing as a case rises up the judicial hierarchy, would appear to be a common feature of almost all court systems.[158] Judges are normally selected from a broader panel to hear cases. This is of importance from both the perspective of error correction and prevention and that of harmonization and development of the law. For example, randomness in appellate structures can reduce both the likelihood of conformity and ideology. The size of panels from which judges are often selected are, however, too small to really mitigate these tendencies, and judges generally know each other very well. A cost of randomness is clearly uncertainty, as different

[157] In the United States, for example, four out of nine judges must vote to grant a writ of *certiorari*.

[158] Kornhauser (2000b) p. 53.

decisions may emerge from the same court. Richard Posner, himself a federal appellate judge, advanced numerous reasons why appellate courts tend to be collegiate in nature.[159] Collegiality may (1) reduce the importance of individual judges (and, importantly, the costs of erroneous decisions by a single judge); (2) reduce the costs of error by poor appointments; (3) enable better deliberation, and (4) allow for a division of labour among tasks. The principal disadvantages of collegiate courts may be the cost of collective decision making and the fact that a number of judges are tied up, preventing them from hearing other cases. To wit, numerous jurisdictions are experimenting with the idea of reducing the number of judges in panels and having only one professional judge hear certain types of cases.

An interesting difference between the Supreme Court in the United States and the highest courts in civil law generally is that cases are not heard by a panel in the former but rather by the entire bench. A justification for this measure lies in the fact that the Supreme Court in the United States enjoys enormous jurisdiction and an exceptional ability to choose its cases. The costs of error in cases of such importance are therefore enormous, as are the costs of poor appointments. Moreover, having all judges decide cases reduces the chances of capture and any one ideology dominating a particular decision.

9. STREAMLINING PROCEDURES

Standard procedure is frequently seen as inadequate in certain cases, given that it leads to excessive delay and costs that are not proportional to the importance of the issue in dispute. One reaction has been the use of summary procedures and summary courts. Though summary procedures in recent years have received renewed attention, they have been in use for a long time. Van Rhee notes, for instance, that already in the early stages of the development of the Romano-canonical procedure, a summary procedure was designed for the handling of a select group of cases more speedily than ordinary procedure permitted. Accordingly, elements of ordinary procedure could be omitted in the search for a balance between quick administration of justice and an acceptable outcome for the parties. It was well established that ordinary procedure would be too slow for certain categories of cases.[160] Today, practically every country has and is experimenting with different forms of summary procedure as a tool to reduce delay, with varying degrees of success.

159 Posner (1996).
160 van Rhee (2004), p.1.

The *kort geding* in the Netherlands is frequently exalted as a success.[161] Formerly used as a form of preliminary injunction, it has developed into a form of summary proceeding whereby parties present their cases at the hearing and the judge indicates their probabilities of success. Frequently it results in almost immediate settlement. Germany has also had ample success with what is commonly known as the Stuttgart model. An aim of the model was to have cases prepared at a preliminary state with sufficient detail for issues to be decided in one sitting. England and Wales have also had some success with the aforementioned, and summary judgments based on documentary evidence relative to the strength and weakness of claims have succeeded in removing bad claims that would have otherwise remained in the system.[162] Moreover, different tracks are now in use in most continental European countries catering for the different needs of cases. One area currently on the European agenda that has been quite successful has been debt collection. Most issues regarding debt collection are such clear-cut cases for standardization that this should hardly come as a surprise.

Experiences – even when seen just from the perspective of delay reduction – have not always been positive. It is reported that Spain and Greece have had their difficulties with streamlining procedures, in large part because too many exceptions to standard procedure were developed, which actually led to increased delay.

Whereas legal scholars have consistently lamented the fact that undue delay is hindering the work of the courts and denying parties their legal rights, recent shifts in thinking have been towards recognizing the importance of the allocation of judicial resources proportionate to 'the nature of the issues involved'.[163] As mentioned in Chapter 1, a major reason for these delays has been the fact that legal scholarship – and lawyers – have over-emphasized accuracy above costs, where accuracy refers to the paucity of error in the legal process. Increased accuracy has consistently been assumed desirable and courts thus designed procedural rules (as well as substantive law) on the basis of the inherent value increased accuracy.[164] However, where costs – or time – are not given consideration, there is little means to quantify the benefits of accuracy or understand when accuracy is desirable.[165] Applying the law to the facts of a case without paying attention to costs and time is a blatant abuse of judicial resources. Increases in accuracy are accompanied by social costs, because they demand a lengthier and higher-value legal process.[166]

161 See Zuckerman (1999).
162 Andrews (2005), p. 175.
163 Woolf (1995).
164 Kaplow (1994).
165 Ibid.
166 Shavell (2004), p. 454.

It follows from the above discussion that there is an optimal level of accuracy in legal proceedings. There is a trade-off between two costs: the costs of error, and the costs of the procedure in question.[167] The logic behind this position is easy to understand. As procedures become more summary, the probability of an error being committed – all other things equal – increases. Alternatively, as proceedures become lengthier and of higher value (through training for judges, newest technology, and so on), the probability of error is reduced – all other things being equal. Miller points out two extremes:

> we could imagine a judge simply tossing a coin; this would be an extraordinarily efficient means of dispute resolution, but it would be unlikely to achieve accurate results. On the other hand, we can imagine a system that erred in the other direction: all evidence would be admitted; all witnesses would be subject to examination, cross-examination, and impeachment; evidence would not be excluded as repetitive, and so on.[168]

It is clear that in the latter system the chances of arriving at a more accurate decision are higher than in the former, though there is no reference to costs.

The basic trade-off between error costs and procedural costs are captured in Figure 2.10. According to the graph, it is assumed that there are diminishing

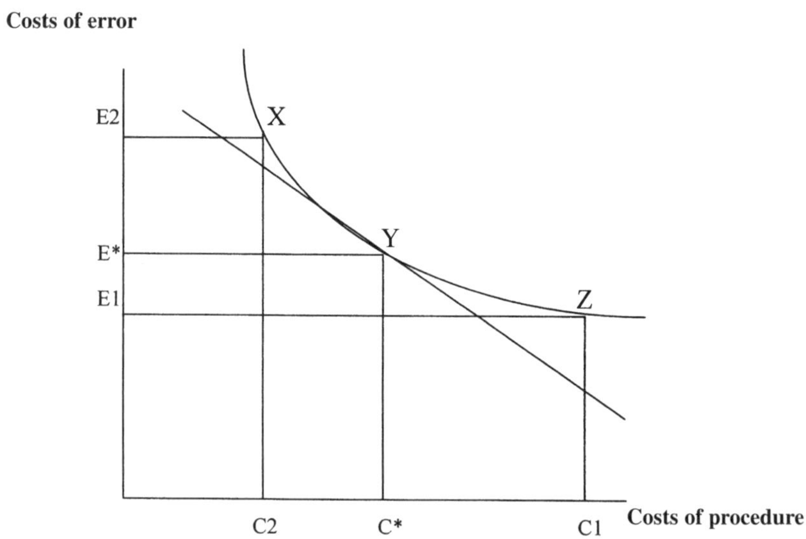

Figure 2.10 Procedural costs and the costs of error

---

[167] See Miller (1997).
[168] Ibid., p. 906.

returns to procedural expenditure. As procedures become more elaborate, the savings from error reduction diminish. The efficient point in the graph is Y, which minimizes the sum of both the costs of error and the costs of procedure. This occurs at a cost of procedure C* and at error costs of E*. A judicial system that finds itself at point X, for instance, is spending too little on procedure as the sum of the error costs and the costs of procedure are greater than at point Y. A judicial system, on the other hand, that finds itself at point Z on the graph may have more 'accurate decisions' (given that error is reduced to E1) but has substantially higher costs of procedure (C1), which do not offset the benefits to be had from greater accuracy.

The economic analysis of the trade-off between error costs and procedural costs holds other factors constant. Streamlining procedures and the introduction of summary courts is generally done in the belief that a legal system for a specific issue finds itself at point Y in the graph. (Recall that at point Z procedural costs do not compensate the level of error correction.) Let us now assume that estimates are right – that too many resources are being spent on procedures that do not compensate – and a society introduces reforms that move a jurisdiction from point Z in the graph to point Y. What would be the effect on the overall level of case filings? This is captured in Figure 2.11.

It is a fair assumption that the demand for litigation is downward sloping; that is, as the costs of litigation decrease, the demand for litigation increases. A reduction in the procedural costs borne by litigants means that it becomes cheaper for people to sue. Given that the costs of procedure are partly borne by litigants (largely in the form of lawyers' fees), one can expect to see more lawsuits. A society which previously had litigation costs of C1 would now

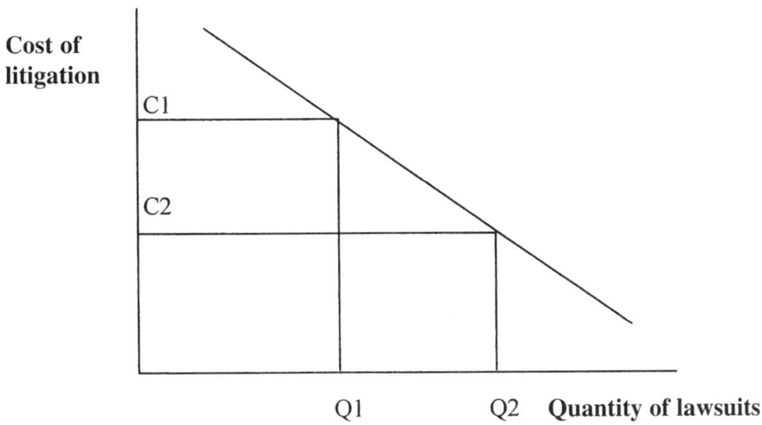

Figure 2.11 The demand for litigation

have litigation costs of C2, and the number of lawsuits would shift from Q1 to Q2.

The above suggests that by streamlining procedures one cannot necessarily be assured of reducing delay in courts. Whether or not streamlining procedures actually leads to an increase in court delay depends on the shape of the demand curve for adjudication; that is, if the demand for litigation is highly elastic – given present levels – slight reductions in price may lead to large increases in litigation.

Though streamlining procedures may lead to greater access to justice, it will not necessarily lead to greater substantive justice. Where procedures are streamlined, decisions are less accurate. The gains to be had by those who were previously excluded from going to court must be weighed against the necessary costs incurred by those who already had access to justice, which come in the form of less accurate decisions.

There are other costs of simplifying procedures that at first may not appear obvious. For instance, a standard of liability may be set in order to achieve optimal deterrence given a specific level of enforcement. Increases in litigation (a shift from Q1 to Q2 above) may actually lead to over-deterrence. The costs of over-deterrence may again be superior to the societal gains of a reduction in procedural simplicity (the benefactors of which are largely those persons who would have otherwise been locked out of the adjudicative system). The latter costs of over-deterrence may be temporary, as (future) defendants and law enforcement begin to modify their behaviour.

Whilst it is clearly incorrect to use elaborate delays as a means of reducing litigation, economic analysis shows us that there are numerous considerations, from a welfare maximizing perspective, that should be borne in mind by administrations interested in streamlining their procedures. We emphasize, however, that the overall tendency to allocate judicial resources proportional to the value of a case is to be applauded, particularly given that judicial procedure has traditionally emphasized accuracy over cost and delay. Moreover, as will be discussed later, the issue of whether or not societies are actually too litigious is not at all clear-cut, particularly given the fact that private incentives to litigate commonly diverge from that which is socially optimal.[169] A 'tolerable' amount of delay is necessary. It should further be noted that a high demand for court services may actually be an indicator that courts are working quite efficiently.

---

169 Shavell (1997).

3. Judges

1. INTRODUCTION

This chapter is dedicated to the analysis of judges, the central figures in the administration of justice. From an economic perspective, the reasons behind judges' behaviour are more enigmatic than for either political actors or those engaged in the private sector. Conditions of judicial appointment are frequently designed to curb motivational factors common to practically all types of employment found in the market. Traditional tools of public administration, such as the carrot and the stick, are less available to influence judges' behaviour, the obvious reason for which being judicial independence.[1] It would be foolhardy to assume that judges are purely motivated by social welfare maximization considerations.

Several factors influence the way in which judges' work is performed, but the factors that sway judicial behaviour are less straightforward than for other economic agents. Judges still respond to incentives, though, by design, the number and nature of these incentives may be limited. We shall see that the effects of changes in remuneration are ambiguous. Increasing judicial salaries does not generally lead to an increase in effort, given that productivity is not tied to effort. A judge who values leisure time highly may even have greater incentives following a pay rise to reduce his effort level. On the other hand, it may lead to better candidates entering the judiciary. Moreover, where there is a substantial difference between rewards for first instance, second instance and third instance judges, the more monetary-minded judge may also have incentives to increase his efforts in order to move to a higher income bracket.

Reputation and shaming are two issues that may factor highly in judges' considerations and can encourage them to make a better effort, but their utility depends on the social value of establishing a reputation and the costs of being shamed. For example, establishing a reputation for being cooperative in a group that has an established ideological slant can hardly be considered desirable, nor can using the power of shame in order to ensure conformity with an inefficient norm.

---

1 Posner (1993).

Socialization can be particularly important in influencing judges' preferences, as well as effort levels. The differences in recruitment between civil law and common law countries suggest socialization is a more powerful variable in influencing judicial behaviour in the latter. Moreover, identifying with a particular group can influence judicial decisions, particularly if the cases involve the special interests of these groups. Political interference in the adjudication process is always undesirable, but politicians can more subtly influence the direction of the courts through political appointments, furthering the selection of candidates with similar preferences to their own. Similarly, the level and nature of accountability vis-à-vis court users and other stakeholders can substantially influence judicial behaviour.

2. WHAT MOTIVATES ECONOMIC AGENTS?

To understand the behaviour of individuals, economists often think in terms of utility maximization. In looking at judges' utility functions, it is interesting to start by reflecting on the functions of agents who participate in the other two mechanisms for allocating resources – the market and the political system.

In the private sector, economic agents try to pursue their private benefit as far as possible within certain given restrictions. The management of a private sector enterprise is facilitated by giving 'employees' incentives to work hard and output is easier to value, given that it is based on revenue maximization.[2]

Understanding the behaviour of actors in the political system is more complex. The system contains two types of economic agent. Firstly, it includes politicians, who have been the subject of intensive study by public choice theory. According to this approach, the main objective of a politician is to retain or to acquire power, within a specific framework of restrictions, the most important of which in democratic systems is the need to win elections.

The second type of economic agent is civil servants. Most activities in the public sector are carried out not by politicians but by the latter. According to economic theory, civil servants aim to maximize their own interests but in a different manner from politicians. They are not interested in being re-elected, as they do not need to be. Civil servants generally remain in their positions despite political change and their careers will only be affected if they become identified in some way with the group in power. Their objective is to increase their influence and power by making their department as large as possible, by being responsible for the largest possible number of staff and by having the

2 There is generally a single objective, namely revenue maximization. This is not the case in the public sector, which commonly has multiple objectives.

largest possible budget. They, therefore, adopt a strategy of persuading the decision-makers that their proposals are reasonable, where the decision-makers are the politicians who draw up state budgets and the members of parliament who accept them.[3] Civil servants will oppose any rationing measures which may mitigate the importance of their functions or allow them to be taken over by a different department at a lower cost. And they will often succumb to pressure by politicians in favour of certain interest groups, if this ties in with their own objectives. If the civil servant has a low-level position whereby he cannot aspire to this type of influence or hope to increase his earnings by stepping up his effort, then he will try to maximize his leisure and convenience at work, working the shortest possible hours and doing his best to adapt working hours, holidays and other working conditions to his personal interests.

3. RECRUITMENT

A useful distinction can be drawn between two types of judiciary, namely bureaucratic, to which civil law jurisdictions generally belong, and professional, characteristic of common law judiciaries (see Table 3.1).[4] Whilst this is obviously a simplification and actual circumstances are more complex, judiciaries in democratic countries can, nevertheless, generally be located on a continuum between these two archetypes. Within Europe, the French judiciary has traditionally represented the bureaucratic model, whilst the English judiciary has most closely been associated with the professional model. Obvious limitations to this distinction include the fact that lateral entry for judgeship by qualified professionals has become a common feature of almost all legal systems, including civil law countries.[5] Moreover, some jurisdictions, such as England and Wales, make great use of lay judges, which is not captured by the aforementioned. Part-time working has also started to grow in importance, which not just facilitates the role of judges with families, particularly women, but permits practitioners in other legal professions to be employed as part-time judges whilst keeping their commitments in private practice.[6] In addition, common law jurisdictions, such as England and Wales, have recently begun to explore the use of judicial career paths.[7]

3 Niskanen (1971).
4 Guarnieri and Pederzoli (2002).
5 See Bell (2006).
6 Ibid., p. 15.
7 See, for instance, Department for Constitutional Affairs (2005), available at http://www.dca.gov.uk/publications/reports_reviews/judicial_career05.pdf.

Table 3.1 Types of judiciary

Bureaucratic judiciary	Professional judiciary
Selection by exam at young age normally after university	Appointment after acquiring professional experience
Training takes place primarily within the judiciary	Experience normally as legal advocates, but sometimes as legal academics
Hierarchy of ranks determines organizational roles and promotion	No formal provisions for advancement
Generalist approach to work performance and role assignment. Judges are recruited for a wide set of roles, not a specific position, and change jobs often	Judges recruited for specific tasks and promotion not widespread. There are weak controls by higher-ranking colleagues
Low degree of internal independence vis-à-vis other judges	Strong guarantees of internal and external independence

Source: Guarnieri and Pederzoli (2002), pp. 67–8

Similarities between the recruitment of judges and that of traditional bureaucrats are self-evident in continental judicial systems. Let us consider Spain (see Figure 3.1). Judicial trainees are recruited by public competition among law graduates – though a limited number of positions in each rank is by special competition among experienced lawyers. Recruitment is thus – generally – at a young age, not long after leaving university, and new judges are trained at a special school, a measure to compensate for the recruit's lack of practical legal experience. Career judges are civil servants and, like other civil servants, hold their posts for life. The fact that candidates enter the judiciary at a much younger age than in countries of the common law tradition, in which it is necessary to have proven experience as a lawyer before becoming a judge, stresses this similarity with other civil service professionals. Whereas in the UK or the United States the position of judge is generally attained as the culmination of a professional career in law, in Spain graduates in law become judges when they pass the relevant competitive examinations. Moreover, in many cases candidates reflect on the option of entering other professions in the public administration.

In England and Wales judges have traditionally been selected on quite an informal basis, in a fashion often considered to be lacking in transparency. Whereas until the 1970s the number of barristers and judges was still quite low

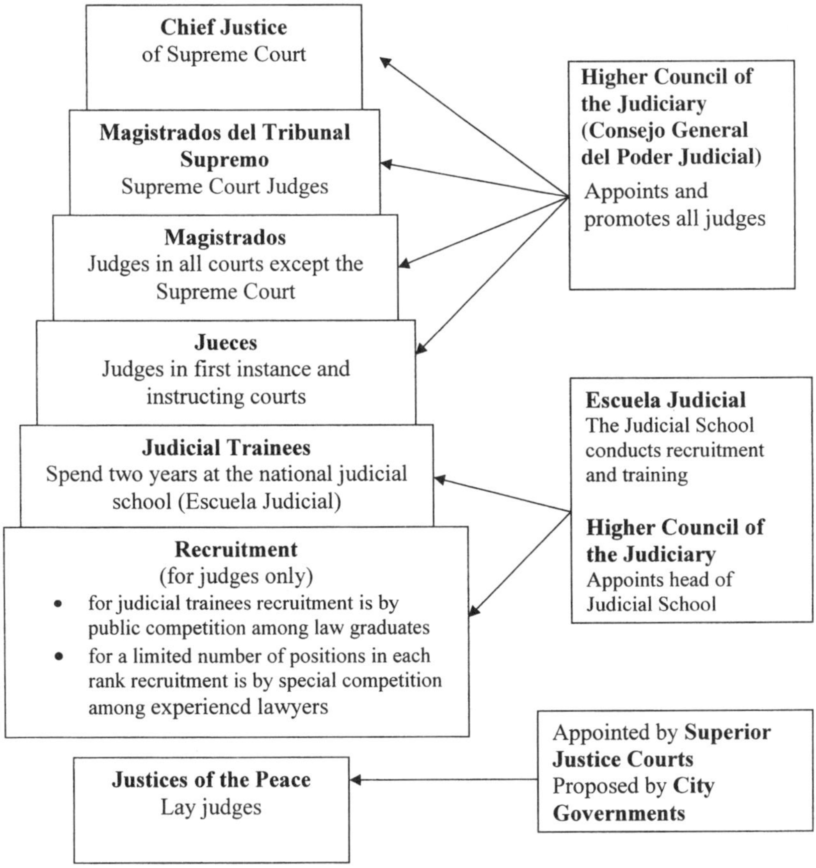

Source: Adapted from Guarnieri and Pederzoli (2002), p. 44

Figure 3.1 Appointment and career structure of Spanish judges

and the Lord Chancellor could get directly involved in appointments, the increase in numbers and complexity has made this impossible to sustain. Until the 1990s the procedure for appointing judges resembled more joining a club than an appointment to a job.[8] It was only in the 1990s that formal interviews by selection panels were introduced for the lower court posts, a practice that was eventually extended to the High Court. With the Constitutional Reform

8 Bell (2006), p. 312.

Act 2005, the position of a Judicial Appointments Commission is now guaranteed, comprised of lay and judicial members, with a lay chair. The system of judicial appointments has become more transparent and professional, with emphasis on the possibility of a judicial career. This process – it is hoped – will also lead to the selection of judges outside a narrow elite, who more adequately represent all groups that make up society.[9]

Currently, only 18 per cent of judges are female, with most of these being drawn from the lower ranks. There are only eleven female High Court judges from a total of 108 (10.2 per cent) and three female justices from a total of 42 (including heads of division) at the court of appeal (7.1 per cent). There is only one High Court judge (0.9 per cent) of ethnic minority origin and there is no such law lord (see Table 3.2). Efforts are currently being made to find a better balance, but some factors have been highlighted that hinder this endeavour.[10] First, the low number of positions that have to be filled within the judiciary at higher ranks means that there are few places actually available. Second, the available pool from which to draw qualified candidates does not seem to be representative of society. Women, in particular, have traditionally left the bar after a shorter period of time, leaving fewer to choose from.[11] Despite the fact that entry rates for men and women in both the barrister and solicitor professions are similar, there is no indication that attrition rates (that is, the rates at which individuals leave the profession) are becoming more equal. Third, even among the women that remain in the profession and are eligible candidates, fewer apply for the position of judge.[12] This does not seem to be the case for minorities.[13] According to one recent study, the main reason given from white, female barristers for not applying for judicial office were the demands from practice, followed by a personal assessment that their chances of receiving the position were low. Non-compatibility with family responsibilities was also considered a factor, especially for some High Court positions where judges have to work on circuit.[14] Parity of appointments between the sexes is, therefore, unlikely in the foreseeable future.

---

[9] See Department for Constitutional Affairs (2005).

[10] See Department for Constitutional Affairs (2004).

[11] Moreover, fewer women make it to partner in elite law firms, thus reducing the likelihood of them distinguishing themselves among peers, a factor of importance for higher positions in the judiciary in common law countries.

[12] Ibid., p. 18.

[13] Between 1998–99 and 2002–3 the percentage of applicants from minority ethnic backgrounds rose to 10 per cent and the percentage of appointments to 8.9 per cent. Ibid., p. 17. In total values this is reflective of the percentage of those of minority ethnic backgrounds in the population.

[14] Ibid.

Table 3.2 Annual diversity statistics (1 April 2006)

Post	Total	Female number	%	Of ethnic minority origin	%
Lords of Appeal in Ordinary	12	1	8.3	0	0.0
Heads of Division	5	0	0.0	0	0.0
Lord Justices of Appeal	37	3	8.1	0	0.0
High Court Judges	108	11	10.2	1	0.9
Circuit Judges *	631	71	11.3	10	1.6
Recorders	1401	199	14.2	67	4.8
District Judges **	449	99	22.0	14	3.2
Deputy District Judges **	840	229	27.3	36	4.3
District Judges (MC)	134	31	23.1	5	3.7
Deputy District Judges (MC)	158	34	21.5	142	3.8
TOTAL	3775	678	18.0	142	3.8

Notes:

* including Judges of the Court of Technology & Construction
** including Family Division

Source: Judiciary of England and Wales (available at: http://www.judiciary.gov.uk/keyfacts/statistics/diversity_stats_annual/2006.htm).

This trend contrasts sharply with those found in some civil law countries, such as France and Spain. This process does not affect all legal professions equally, as it is the profession of judge that has experienced the largest growth in the number of women. Although the term 'feminization' is used increasingly in the literature on labour economics, its meaning is not univocal. Those sectors or markets where women compose a majority are considered 'feminized'. Feminization refers to the process by which an activity that was formerly predominantly undertaken by men is increasingly being undertaken by women. The profession of judge has until very recently been dominated by men. The entrance rate of women to the profession in continental civil law countries, however, has been spectacular in recent years. Whilst the highest positions in the judiciary remain dominated by men, the vast majority of new judges in many jurisdictions are now women. The most striking example has been France, where 80 per cent of those entering the magistrate profession were women in 2006. The number of new female judges was only slightly less in Spain; and the evolution is similar in other countries belonging to the civil law tradition.

Why is this tendency taking place and why has it taken hold in some legal systems more than others? The first explanation would be to attribute this phenomenon to the increasing participation of women in the workplace and their increasing access to higher levels in professions. It is interesting to note, however, that, in those countries referred to above, the growth in the number of women becoming judges is greater than the growth in the number of women entering other legal professions. If we analyse, for example, the composition of lawyers working in the most prestigious law firms by gender – and, especially, if we look at the number of women who acquire the status of partner – we see that the level of participation by women is still clearly minoritarian. The question is, then, why does this occur in the judiciary and not in large law firms? The answer lies with the differences pointed out above in the training and selection of judges, and especially, in the fact that in civil law countries in these regions, the judge is a civil servant from the beginning of his professional activity, without having generally worked as a lawyer in the private sector.

The cost–benefit analysis carried out by those who consider becoming civil servants in these countries is relatively straightforward. For high-level professionals – such as lawyers and judges – to work in the public administration means renouncing a higher income that could be earned in the private sector. There are considerable advantages, however, in terms of greater job security, comfort in performing one's duties, and reduced work hours. In the case of women this makes it easier to combine professional life with motherhood and family life. It is true that this is also applicable to men. Empirical evidence shows conclusively, however, that men value these factors significantly less than women.

The shortage of women and minorities active in the judiciary has traditionally been considered regrettable and substantial literature exists affirming that it is of importance for a judiciary to adequately represent all groups that compose a society, given the special characteristics of the profession. By the same logic, one may lament the fact that men entering the profession today are now clearly under-representative.

4. SALARY

As is generally the case for civil servants, judges' remuneration is not directly linked to productivity. An increase in earnings is, therefore, not usually the main objective of judges when practising their profession. However, though not linked to productivity, earnings do depend on the position occupied by a judge and a higher position will result in higher remuneration. The salary structure and the system for entering the profession – by competitive examination in France, Spain and other civil law countries – seem to exclude lawyers whose objective is to have high earnings. This is not to suggest that there is no place for the more monetary minded, given that it is not unusual for a judge whose knowledge is appreciated by the market to ask for leave of absence in order to become a practising lawyer. This possibility does not differentiate the judge from all other civil servants, as it is also found in other high levels of the state administration (tax revenue inspectors, state attorneys, and so on).

Like other civil servants, judges can also maximize their leisure and convenience at work. A judge who is keen to work a limited number of hours will be aware that he is unlikely to be promoted but this behaviour is unlikely to have much effect on his remuneration in comparison with colleagues at the same level. This has important implications for the policy of judges' remuneration. If, in a judge's utility function, leisure represents a significant, non-monetary payment, a rise in earnings will not necessarily be an incentive for making a greater effort. Unless the salary rise is linked to productivity, it is unlikely to have any positive effect at all on the judge's activity. It could even be argued that certain leisure activities require a certain level of economic resources and an increase in the latter would serve as an incentive to increase these activities, which might lead to more time devoted to leisure than to work.

The positive effect of increasing judges' remuneration without effort being tied to performance would therefore not be greater productivity but attracting more valuable people in the first place, who consider monetary earnings as one of the most important criteria in choosing their profession. The aforementioned analysis suggests that a negative effect on productivity might be caused by reducing judges' incompatibility working outside of the profession, allowing them to carry out more productive activities in addition to their main function. This possibility would create incentives to reduce to a minimum the activity which provides them with a fixed remuneration, irrespective of productivity, and to devote more time to activities in which remuneration depends on performance. The comparison of judges with university professors in certain subjects, for whom it may be easier to obtain additional earnings, seems to confirm this idea. Hence, incompatibility constraints for judges may serve not just to protect judicial independence and integrity but also to increase productivity.

Singapore serves as an example of a country that has placed great emphasis on remuneration for public service in general and judges in particular. It is reported that, in order to attract the best jurists to the bench, salaries are determined by taking 90 per cent of the average salary paid by the six best law firms of Singapore to their lawyers with comparable professional experience.[15] Similarly, judges in other judicial systems frequently receive compensation

15 Langseth (2004).

higher than other members of the public administration with similar qualifications, which serves as a type of honesty premium, as well as a reward for the recognized responsibilities that accompany the job.

The issue of remuneration among federal court judges has come in for some heated discussion recently in the United States. In his 2006 'Year-End Report on the Federal Judiciary', Chief Justice Roberts considers the issue of raising federal salaries so important that he dedicates the entire report to it. He suggests that 'it had been ignored for too long and has now reached the level of a constitutional crisis.'[16] Chief Justice Roberts argues that judicial salaries are so low that 'it changes the nature of the federal judiciary when judges are no longer drawn primarily from among the best lawyers in the practicing bar.'[17] Posner posits, however, that federal judges have traditionally not been hired from the very top rank, adding:

> But that has always been true, so the question is whether the enormous political costs of stratospheric increases in judicial salaries are worth bearing in order to bring the ablest private lawyers into the federal judiciary. I think not . . . .It would mean overpaying the vast majority of judges in order to get the handful whose reservation price is high.[18]

Posner further highlights the fact that, although increasing salaries would result in more interested parties for the job, merit is not the sole or even most important criterion in the selection of candidates. Moreover success in practice, according to Posner, which may be used as a principle factor in addressing the merit of candidates, has not been a very good indicator of success as a judge.

Posner's analysis indicates that fears expressed by individuals who see federal judgeship in Chief Justice Robert's words as 'a stepping stone to a lucrative position in private practice' that 'threatens the viability of life tenure' and 'the Framers' goal of a truly independent judiciary' do not seem to be vindicated by the statistics.[19]

Useful insights can be gathered by looking at the following two tables. Table 3.3 indicates the average pre-tax salary for a 45-year-old judge in seven countries, as reported in a 2001 study by the European Association of Judges. We have included two common law countries in the table, England and Ireland; the rest follow the civil law tradition. The first observation one can make is related to the difference in salary between common law and civil law

16 Roberts (2007), p. 1.
17 Ibid., pp. 3–4.
18 Posner (1996), p. 30.
19 Ibid., pp. 30–32

Table 3.3 Average salary of 45-year-old judge (in euros)

	First instance (1)	Second instance (2)	Third instance (3)	3/1	3/2	2/1
France	63 883	65 313	82 528	1.29	1.26	1.02
Germany	52 584	57 672	80 724	1.54	1.40	1.10
Italy	59 160	78 146	91 552	1.55	1.17	1.32
Portugal	66 794	68 803	73 906	1.11	1.07	1.03
England	127 000	241 000	254 000	2.00	1.05	1.90
Ireland	80 071	122 478	133 005	1.66	1.09	1.53

Source: European Association of Judges (2002)[20]

judges in Europe (even accounting for differences in PPP), where salary in the former would appear to be significantly higher. This can clearly have a significant impact on status. Note, the fact that judges in common law countries tend to have more experience upon entering the profession would seem to be negated as an explanation for the salary differential, given that we are looking at the average salary of a 45-year-old judge. The second factor of interest is how countries greatly differ in salaries between judges in the different instances. In Portugal, for example, the difference in salary between a first instance and a second instance judge is merely 3 per cent, between a third instance and first instance 11 per cent. Remuneration clearly is not seen – or used – as a factor in motivating judges.

This figure contrasts significantly with England, where the difference in salary between first and second instance judges is 90 per cent. Interestingly, judicial salary does not increase significantly between second and third instance judges (5 per cent). Significant differences in payscale will clearly offer some reflection of the status of judges in their respective courts.

Let us now turn our attention to Table 3.4, which shows the minimum salary of a 35-year-old entry-level judge and offers a comparison with the minimum salary of a 35-year-old entry-level civil servant with a university degree. In the civil law countries listed, the salaries of entry-level judges and entry-level civil servants are very similar. A money-oriented individual would, therefore, have little incentive (initially at least) to choose one profession over the other. This reflects the point we made above that many individuals might as easily go into the traditional civil bureaucracy as pursue a judicial career in

20 Available in German under the title 'Richtereinkommen im Europäischen Vergleich' at http://www.drb.de/.

Table 3.4 Comparison of salaries of 35-year-old judge and civil servant (in euros)

	Judge	Entry salary Civil Servant	Comparison
France	37 758	36 588	1.03
Germany	35 316	34 932	1.01
Italy	37 185	28 930	1.29
Portugal	40 985	40 000	1.02
England	127 000	50 000	2.54

Source: European Association of Judges

civil law countries. Again, where salary is a reflection of status, entry-level judges are not held in the same esteem vis-à-vis civil servants in civil law countries as in common law countries.[21]

5. IDENTITY AND SOCIALIZATION

When judges identify with certain social groups, there is potential for this to influence their decisions in court.[22] Legal scholars and reformers alike are conscious of these dangers, and to mitigate this problem propose having the judiciary composed of a broad range of groups that make up society. The fear is that a judge may try to pass a sentence in favour of the group to which he considers he belongs and with whose welfare he identifies.

Tendencies of judges to identify with groups may be based on less than obvious factors. It has been stated, for example, that the clear attitude in favour of tenants in Spain amongst judges is largely due to the fact that they have to move frequently during their careers and so have often been in the position of tenants. Judgments passed in favour of the latter would, therefore, imply support of this group and their interests. This notion is not new in the economics literature. Nearly 250 years ago, Adam Smith stated that it was preferable

21 Figures for Irish civil servants were not available, but, given the high entry-level salary of judges, one can expect a similar position to that found in England

22 In his study, Judge Posner states that trying to change the world has no part to play in judges' utility functions. Here we argue, however, that preferences and ideology among other factors influence the behaviour of judges. This does not mean that judges consider they must try to change society but that their preferences may affect their decisions. Such preferences are – we contend – largely determined by the social group they belong to.

for courts having to decide on matters related to divorce or adultery to comprise clerics who were not married, because married men would identify too easily with the interests of husbands and their decisions would favour the latter. This was based on the idea that they might one day find themselves in a court of justice in a similar situation.[23] In recent times this argument has frequently been raised against male judges, who have been perceived as being excessively benevolent towards wife-battering husbands.

Although such interests may be relevant in some cases, they may not be very important in the everyday activity of judges. This is mainly because there are not many subjects in which a specific decision is likely to lead to a significant improvement in the 'personal' situation of judges. It is a different matter, however, when judges, in their capacity as citizens or consumers, feel that a specific interpretation of a law will favour the society in which they live.

5.1 A Basic Model

As the above analysis will have made clear, we argue that judges' personal preferences may be a relevant factor in their way of administering justice. Economic theory has made important efforts in recent decades to include the creation and maintenance of preferences in analysis. Since the pioneering work by Stigler and Becker (1977), economics has considered the possibility of no longer considering people's tastes and preferences when trying to explain them from the point of view of economic analysis. In Becker's work, preferences enter the model by including in the utility function two specific types of capital – what are known as personal capital (P) and social capital (S).

$$U = U(x_1, \ldots x_n, P, S)$$

where x_i represents the various goods a person consumes.

From the point of view of economics, the most important conclusion that can be drawn from this model is that, since our actions today affect our personal and social capital, and these affect our future preferences, this 'extended' utility function will be stable while the traditional utility functions (or sub-utility functions)

$$U = U(x_1, \ldots x_n)$$

will not. But, for our purposes, what is most relevant is that the extended utility functions can often help us understand the behaviour of people and of

---

23 Smith (1762–66 [1978]), p. 147.

social groups. The decisions taken by each individual and the social context of these decisions help individuals establish their preferences, which, in turn, determine their patterns of behaviour (Becker 1996; Becker and Murphy 2000).

Personal capital is determined by a whole range of activities and experiences throughout a lifetime. It is a stock variable, which is determined by the accumulation of investments made during all the periods before the one under consideration (I_{Pi}), minus depreciation in this capital during each of these periods (D_{Pi}). Personal capital, therefore, at a specific time, t, will be:

$$Pt = \sum_{i=1}^{t-1} Ipi - \sum_{i=1}^{t-1} Dpi.$$

In view of the nature of a person's life cycle, investments in each period may have different values, which, moreover, will vary for each person. It is, however, reasonable to asume that, although personal capital changes over a lifetime, it becomes more or less stable at a relatively early age – specifically, at the end of the educational period, once the basic experience for a specific professional activity has been acquired.

Social capital theory was developed in the sociological literature by J. Coleman (1990), based on a concept laid down by G. Loury. The idea is that, in many types of social organization, a set of practices are undertaken which are very useful for the social and economic progress of a specific person belonging to one of them, building up values, interpersonal relationships and principles of authority and confidence which are accepted by the members of the group. Coleman states that social capital is defined by its function, which is basically to facilitate action by those forming part of the group. Social capital, therefore, is productive in that it allows the members of the group to achieve certain objectives which would be much more difficult to achieve without it. In view of its special characteristics, it also acts as a public good which belongs to no one in particular and can be used by all the members of the group. And a relevant aspect of social capital is that one of the important factors for creating it is the development of a set of shared ideas or a way of interpreting reality which is shared by the group members.[24]

A specific person's social capital is therefore based on both the strategies used to enter a specific group and the group's activities and preferences, which will be internalized by each of its members, not only because they can be adopted without external incitement but also because the fact that they are

24 Coleman, 1990, pp. 300–321.

adopted will improve their position within the group and will therefore raise their well-being. Like personal capital, the social capital of a specific group h is a stock variable, which is formed by the accumulation of investments by all the people belonging to the group (Z_i^h), minus any depreciation (D_i^h), which would reflect a weakening in the group structure or a reduction in its capacity for achieving the common goals. If we call the contributions made by each member of the group h to the group's social capital Z_j^h, then the social capital of this group comprising n members over time at time t would be:

$$S_t^h = \sum_{j=1}^{n} \sum_{i=1}^{t-1} Z_{ji}^h - \sum_{i=1}^{t-1} D_i^h.$$

Figure 3.2 presents the dual relationship which exists between each of the members and the group's social capital. On the one hand, each of them (j =1,2...n) contributes over time to the formation of the social capital S^h. On the other, this social capital becomes an argument for the utility function for each of them.

This model can be applied to the group of judges in a specific social structure as they are a clearly defined professional group in which all the members share the same specific activity, usually as a full-time occupation, and most of them have undergone a similar process in order to join the group. However, this process differs from country to country, so it may significantly affect their patterns of behaviour.

In order to become a judge in Spain, as in other continental European countries, it is first necessary to study law. During this period, students become immersed in what we could call the basic values of lawyers, which, in most European countries, do not tie in with criteria of economic efficiency.[25] Candidates then need to pass through the filter of competitive examinations, in which they are examined by members of the group they hope to enter, that is, judges. In their own interests, they therefore begin to adopt the values of those who determine their professional future. After passing the competitive examination, the new judge becomes a member of the group. Training is then completed with courses at the Judicial School and practical experience in courts, which not only provide some of the technical knowledge required but also help complete the socialization process. This process is important when joining any group, whether it is a company or a professional group, because it

---

[25] It is possible to distinguish between the main value systems in the different legal professions but we believe it cannot be denied that studying law gives a specific view of social life which is unlike that received by a student of, for example, economics or psychology.

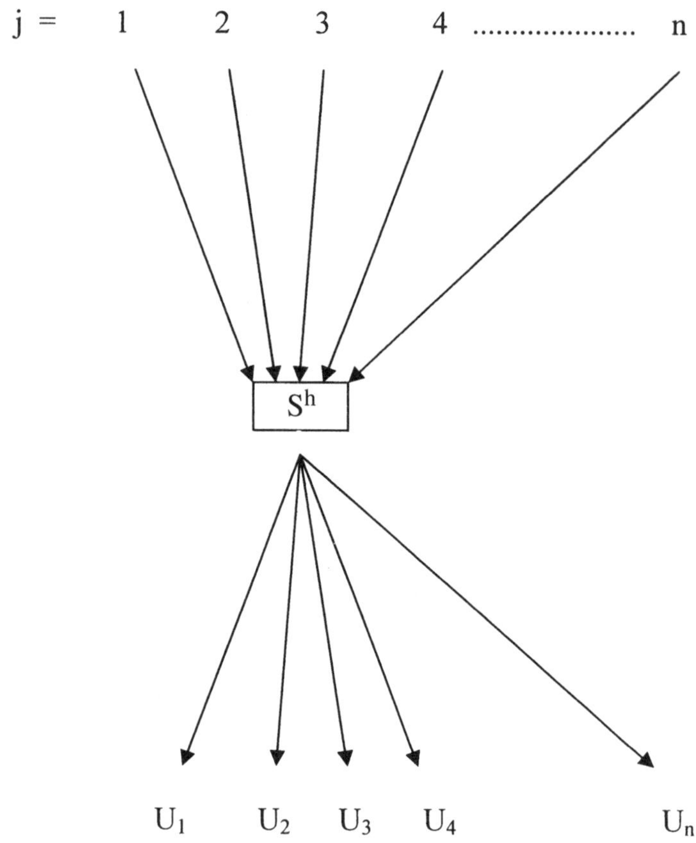

$$U_j = U_j\,(X_1, \ldots\ldots\ X_n, P_j, S_j^{\,h})$$

Figure 3.2 Social capital and utility functions

reduces transaction costs in everyday life and also reinforces any collective actions taken by the group. A person may reject a specific social system, especially when the expected benefit of non-compliance is greater than the expected cost, but the incentives to conform are always high. In the case of judges, the cost of non-compliance consists of sanctions by supervisory bodies or informal sanctions by other members of the group and, in either case, it may seriously affect a judge's career. And the group will function better if its members have adopted a set of basic principles creating confidence in the group and reducing the costs of inspection and maintaining discipline within the organization.

Since there are many judges and since their social capital has been formed throughout a long historical process, the role played by each individual in the process of creating this capital is fairly limited. It can reasonably be assumed that each judge acts as a person who accepts a value system rather than as someone who can play a relevant role in creating such values. However, some judges, as with members of other groups, may to some extent become 'opinion leaders' by going beyond the mere acceptance or transmission of values. This is unusual, however, at least in continental civil law systems. It is true that courts of justice function according to a hierarchy, so that not all judges are equally influential as interpreters of a specific legal text. But there have been few judges – at least in Spain – who have really had a decisive personal influence on the social capital of the group.

This may be different in common law systems, especially in the United States, where any lawyer is fully aware that certain judges have made important contributions in the past to the country's legal culture, and not only in the judicial area. It is still common, for example, for the Supreme Court at any specific period in history to be known by the name of the judge who presided it at the time. But there are two factors that must not be forgotten. First, the role played by judges, and especially by the Supreme Court, is much more relevant than that played by judges in Europe. Second, the US Supreme Court has a very small number of judges, who are appointed for life and so may hold their positions for very long periods.

As with any other group, judges do not act in a vacuum but within a specific social and economic framework which will greatly influence the formation of their ideas. Judges' preferences are therefore based on two important elements. First, there are the dominant ideas within their society at a specific time. This means not only the principles which govern society as a whole but also those prevailing in smaller social units, such as the family or a religious group. Second, there is the set of values which is transmitted to the judge by the professional group. With regard to the former, a country's social and cultural tradition as well as the specific time may affect judges because society is affected by these. It is therefore no surprise to find more judges who are against state intervention in private economic relations and in favour of the principle of freedom of contract in a country such as the United States of America than in a nation like Spain in which free market principles have always been less marked.[26]

Though in principle the importance of social groups is applicable to any organizational model of the administration of justice, it is clearly of greater

---

[26] For other examples of how judges have responded to dominant values in a society at different moments in time, see above, Chapter 2, Section 4 on common law and civil law.

importance in continental civil law structures than in traditional common law models, where receiving a judgeship is only possible after working for a certain length of time in legal practice.

6. POLITICS

Though a very relevant subject, our analysis has not yet made any explicit reference to the possible influence of political motivations in judicial decisions.[27] In many countries, it is not unusual for the appointment of judges to senior positions to be the subject of political debate. There are concerns that if decisions have to be taken regarding certain activities carried out by government or members of government, the political leanings of judges might incline them to favour or disfavour a specific group. When a political body is involved in this type of appointment, debate is frequent and sometimes inevitable. Consider the case of appointments to the US Federal Courts of Appeal and the Supreme Court (see Figure 3.3). Debates on the appointment of these judges are often heated, leading to criticism of the efficiency of the appointment's procedure, where, instead of emphasizing a prospective judge's technical competence, focus is often shifted to his position on sensitive matters in political debate, such as the issue of abortion or affirmative action.

Although there is extensive empirical literature on the role of political suasion on judicial independence and court decisions in the United States, it is still fairly recent, so conclusive results cannot yet be drawn. There are two reasons for discrepancies in results found in the literature. First, it is difficult to determine what is actually meant by the political independence of judges. Second, when empirical studies are carried out, the sample of cases and courts is limited and clear results have not been forthcoming. Ashenfelter et al. (1995) studied federal civil rights cases and reached the conclusion that it is not possible to find firm correlations between the party which supported the appointment of certain judges and the judgments passed by them in the courts. However, in a study of environmental protection cases, Revesz (1997) found a significant link between the ideas that are considered dominant in the political group which supported the appointment of a certain judge and the decisions passed by this judge in the Federal Court of Appeals of the DC Circuit. In a recent study of more than 4000 cases heard by Federal Courts of Appeal, Sunstein et al. (2003) concluded that whether a judge had been nominated by the Democratic or the Republican Party was in

[27] The problem of state judges elected by popular vote in the United States is perhaps the best example of a blurring between politics and the judiciary.

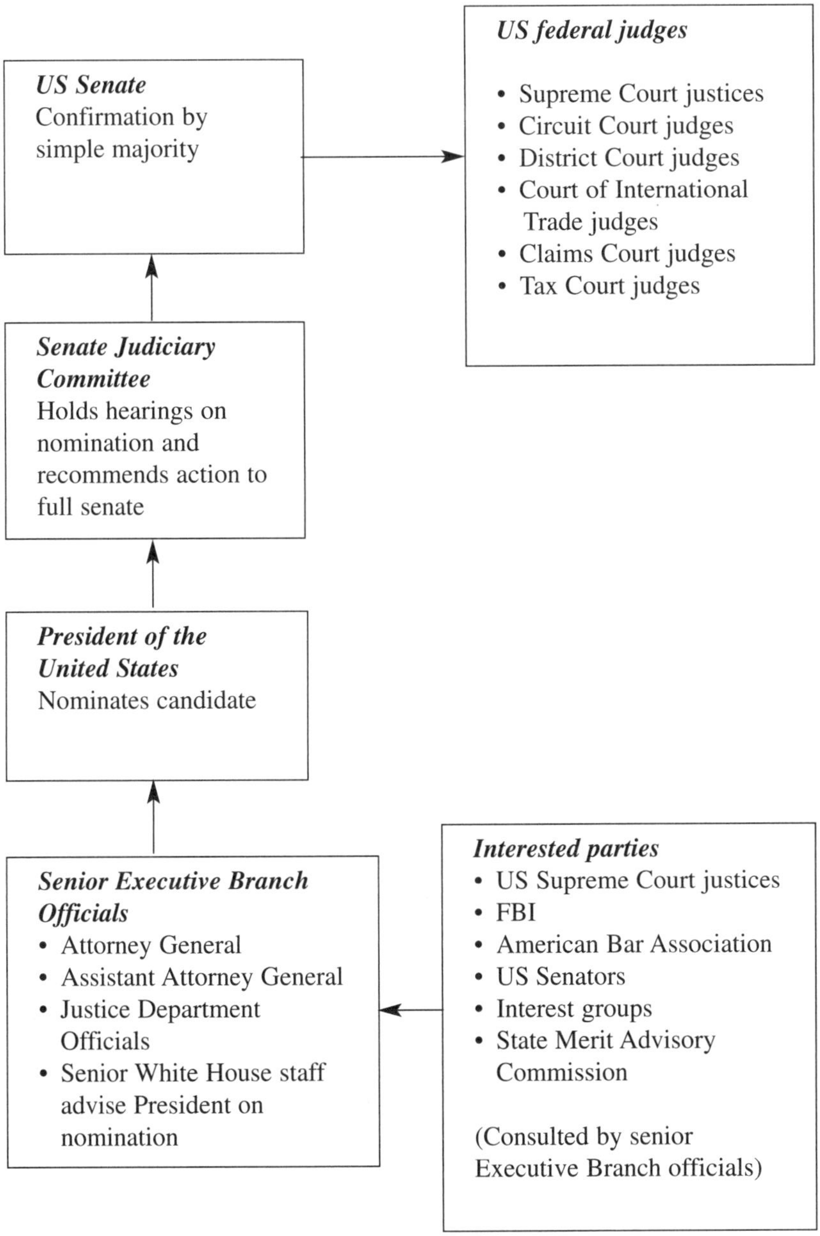

Figure 3.3 Appointment of Federal Court judges in the United States

a large number of cases a good indicator of how judges decided. This difference, which seems clear in subjects such as abortion, sexual harassment, positive discrimination, the death sentence, legislation on the disabled, or piercing the corporate veil, is much less relevant in other matters, such as opposition to expropriations.

Reference can be made to a 'political conditioning' of judicial decisions. What is being discussed in the debate in the United States is not that the judges nominated by a Democratic or Republican government will vote in the courts in line with the specific interests of certain individual politicians or parties, but that the parties support the appointment of people whose preferences are the same as those which dominate in the party. It is not, therefore, a question of 'buying favours' in advance but rather of orienting future decisions in line with certain ideas.

Whether or not the political nature of appointments leads judges to find in favour of or against the executive power is a different matter. This is what is being referred to in countries such as France, Italy and Spain when people talk about the politicization of justice. This is a much more serious problem because, whilst ideological preferences are inevitable, favouritism shown towards specific individuals is not. Any doubt that arises in public opinion regarding the objectivity of judicial decisions can be very damaging for the image of the judicature. Moreover, it can reduce legal certainty, pushing up the costs of economic activity and thus having a negative effect on the generation of wealth.

Ramseyer has put forward a most interesting study on the independence of courts from political interference, which is relevant to our discussion here.[28] According to Ramseyer independence is not found in constitutional text. Comparing the US judiciary with the Japanese, he found that both constitutions aim to insulate judges from political encroachment, but whilst Americans appoint individuals with preferences associated with their party, they do not further intervene thereafter, whereas the Japanese continue to do so. This occurs despite the fact that US politicians could restructure the courts in order to further intervene in the process. The variation in judicial independence is due to the state of the electoral market. Where one party expects to stay in power indefinitely (as was the case of the Liberal Democratic Party (LDP) in post-war Japan until 1993), the government has incentives to interfere in the courts. Similarly, where parties expect the electoral process to end soon, courts will also not be kept independent. Court independence may, however, emerge where neither one of these conditions arises: where parties do not see the end of an electoral process as a possibility or where no party expects to remain in

---

28 Ramseyer (1994).

power indefinitely (as is the case in the United States), judicial independence may emerge as a cooperative outcome. Judicial independence therefore resembles a cooperative outcome in an indefinitely repeated Prisoners' Dilemma. Where there are high political risks for any one group interfering with the judiciary, this equilibrium can be quite stable.

7. THE COSTS OF DEFENDING ONE'S POSITION

The degree to which specific preferences or ideology may affect the behaviour of judges depends on the costs of pursuing them. Consider a frequent situation in a court in which one of the judges does not agree with the judge who drafts the leading opinion or with the majority opinion of the bench. If the judge's objective is to maximize his preferences, he will have incentives to devote time to preparing arguments against those of the other judge, trying to convince his colleagues of his own opinion. If he is unsuccessful – and is duly authorized, as is the case in some countries – he may cast a dissenting vote. If convenience and leisure are more important to him, however, he will not hesitate to support the leading or majority opinion, as this will save him a lot of hassle. Defending preferences therefore involves an opportunity cost which each judge may or may not be prepared to accept, depending on the relevance of the case and the likelihood that his opinion will influence the decision of the judges in that court, or those in a higher court if there is an appeal.

The decision not to support one's own ideas and willingly accept the majority opinion may also be the result of utility maximization in the long term, in that a judge who does not present objections to the leading opinion may expect to receive similar treatment from his colleagues when the time comes. This attitude seems to reflect long-term cooperative conduct which could be interpreted in terms of a repeated game, with the well-known result that integration in a specific social group and frequency of dealings are incentives for cooperation. A judge may, therefore, consider the opportunity cost of defending his own ideas to be too high.

Recent literature has analysed these 'panel effects' on the opinions of a judge acting on the bench. Let us assume that there are only two possible ideologies which can influence an opinion, A and B, and that our judge has ideology A. The degree to which he is prepared to devote time and effort to obtaining a decision in line with his ideology will be determined by whether the other two judges[29] are of the same persuasion or are of the opposite ideology. Sunstein et

[29] Here we assume that a bench comprises three judges, but the results would be similar with a larger number.

al. (2003) call these effects ideological weakening and strengthening. The first case arises when a judge is in the minority because his ideology is different from that of the other two members of the bench; that is, the bench structure is BBA. The second case arises where our judge forms a bench with two others who share his view of the problem to be adjudicated; in this case the bench structure is AAA. Economic theory suggests that in the first case a judge is unlikely to fight to have his position prevail, unless current law and previous decisions indicate that the decision favoured by the judges with ideology B would be rejected by an appeal court.[30] In the second case our judge would see that his ideas had support and would therefore be strong in defending them. The judge's final vote is, therefore, determined not only by his own preferences but also by those of the other members of the bench. A judge might vote against his own ideas on a bench if he knew that at least two votes would be B. The internal relations strategy might therefore prevail over the judge's preferences.

If we accept that there is a set of ideas which is shared by most of the judges and which forms the group's social capital, we can infer that disagreements based on ideological preferences will not be relevant in most cases. And when there are ideological differences, these will be minimized by panel effects and the trend towards consensus decisions will be strengthened. When preferences are shared by the group of judges, they may therefore play a very important role in the orientation of court decisions.

8. PERFORMANCE INDICATORS

It is axiomatic that actors in all organizations are rewarded in return for services rendered. This extends to all types of organization and the judiciary is no exception. Some estimates of performance have to be developed. Public sector organizations and actors have traditionally resented the idea of their performance being monitored, and this is especially the case for the judiciary, which has often hidden behind arguments of judicial independence. Establishing performance-monitoring standards and indicators for judges, court staff and courts can be an effective way of enhancing both the efficiency and accountability of judicial systems.

Performance monitoring requires first and foremost the definition of what is to be measured.[31] Secondly, the means of measuring must be determined.

30 The appeals structure is clearly one of the most important accountability tools within the judiciary. This was discussed at length in Chapter 2, Section 7.

31 This may include factors such as judicial efficiency, integrity, quality of and access to justice, transparency and public confidence.

One must argue against an over-reliance on quantifiable criteria. Performance monitoring must be directly linked to training programmes, so that the system does not only demand improvements but also provides for the necessary tools to bring about behavioural change.[32]

Indicators must be developed by or in close consultation with the judiciary itself. Though judges should be at the forefront in developing performance standards, other stakeholders should be included in the process, including prosecutors, judicial clerks, lawyers and court users. From the perspective of the judiciary, performance indicators can shield it from arbitrary attack by outside parties, such as politicians, the media, and vested interests.[33] Not only do statistics and performance indicators assist in conceptualizing the true nature of the size of caseloads, delay or inefficiencies, but they also serve as a managerial device within the court that can help in the better allocation of scarce resources.[34]

Certain quantitative measures are called 'hard data', as they are more easily verifiable. Quantifiable data should be made available both for courts as a whole and, more importantly, for individual judges. Verifiable quantitative hard data include:

- the number of cases handled by a court and a breakdown of the nature of these cases, and comparison of these figures with total demand and previous years. This information should be sufficient to indicate both clearance rates and congestion rates and allow for comparison both over time and across courts;
- the number of cases handled by individual judges, both absolutely and in relation to the total demand, with a comparison with peers and prior years;
- the average time to resolution in a particular court and for individual judges, and the percentage of cases completed within reasonable or prescribed time;
- the types of cases handled by individual judges and courts;
- the proportion of cases that are appealed against, both for a court and for individual judges;
- the number of cases dealt with by a judge that are turned over on appeal.

It is clear that there should not be over-reliance on any specific factor or even on the sum of these 'hard data', but, if they are taken as a whole with

---

[32] Hammergren (2002), p. 22.

[33] Fix-Fierro (2003), pp. 6–7.

[34] Balanced scorecards have been introduced in some jurisdictions, such as Singapore, which we discuss below. See Langseth (2004), on file with authors.

other less quantifiable standards, a more informed picture of the performance of courts and individual judges may begin to emerge. Moreover, it is fundamental that indicators are not designed purely to assess the notion of delay, but to address the quality of the judiciary and the service it provides. For instance, we have seen above that there may be trade-offs between delay and accuracy.[35] Emphasizing delay solely may lead to an unsatisfactorily large increase in error. Similarly, indicators must look beyond sole reliance on caseload statistics. As Posner notes,

> A case is not a standard measurement like a quart or a constant (that is, inflation-free) dollar. If an increase in cases were associated with a decrease in composition of the docket toward a class of relatively easy cases, the figures on caseload growth would exaggerate the actual increase in the workload of the courts, and in the workload associated with a particular class of cases, for example criminal. To translate *caseload* statistics into *workload* statistics, cases must somehow be weighted by their difficulty.[36]

For instance, the Trial Court Performance Standards and Measurement System, developed by the National Center for State Courts in the US, has established 22 different standards that look at five different areas to assess court performance:[37]

- Access to Justice
- Expedition and Timeliness
- Equality, Fairness, and Integrity
- Independence and Accountability
- Public Trust and Confidence.

To assess each of these standards and give an indication of performance in the five aforementioned areas, it has developed 68 field-tested measures.

But it is notoriously difficult to develop a close to perfect checklist for several reasons. First, judicial performance depends on a host of criteria that relate not only to the judiciary itself, but also to external factors.[38] Second, checklists from other countries cannot be easily imported, given the inherent differences between countries and the vast number of variables involved. Third, it is very difficult to develop actual scores or a grading system, given that there is no science in determining the score of a particular court or individual judge, and the importance of individual factors may easily be over- or

---

35 See above, Figure 2.8.
36 Posner (1996), p. 64.
37 See http://www.ncsconline.org/D_Research/tcps/Introduction.htm.
38 See Hammergren (1999).

under-measured. Fourth, we do not know precisely what measures determine judicial performance, so we must invariably view results with caution. Quantifying results may lead to the impression of good science, but should not divert observers away from using common sense. Fifth, the process of developing indicators is a sensitive one and will probably involve compromises. These compromises may come from the fact that judges fear certain information impeaches judicial independence. In other instances, compromises may be more pragmatic and cost-based.

For performance indicators to have the desired impact, it is necessary to assess both what is to be measured (for example, access to justice, quality of justice, judicial efficiency), how it is to be measured (for example, public perception survey of the judiciary, access to information on citizens' rights), and who is going to measure and collate this information. If performance bonuses are to work properly, they must be well designed, well disseminated, transparent, and measured in a professional manner.

Whilst performance indicators may be used for the purposes of performance bonuses, this practice is not necessarily welcome in many judiciaries. In Spain, the Higher Judicial Council (*Consejo General del Poder Judicial*) publishes a workload model which serves as a benchmark to asssess the efficiency of a judge. It effectively assigns a number of work hours to different tasks and the judge is supposed to complete a certain number of hours per year. In truth, however, its main purpose is to monitor the need for extra judges and additional money from government, and any use in promotion assessment is unclear.[39] Its utility as a device to increase judicial performance is, therefore, limited.

Other jurisdictions will rely principally on informal means, particularly shaming, to pull those judges up whose performance is assessed as inadequate. Posner reports, for instance, that the Administrative Office of the US Courts compiles and makes available to the public numerous statistics related to the performance of individual federal district judges, including: the number of motions that a district judge has under submission for more than 30 days; the number of bench trials in which the judge has failed to render a decision within six months; and the number of his cases that are still pending after three years.[40] He observes that where a judge has fallen behind in any one of these categories, the chief or circuit chief 'comes down on him with greater or less vigor', with the result that 'there is usually although not always some improvement in the next reporting period.'[41] Judges, however, may enter into

---

39 Bell (2006), p. 184.
40 Posner (1996), p. 222.
41 Ibid.

a type of 'game playing' where judges, knowing the indicators that have been developed, wait the full 30 days before deciding a motion, or the full six months before rendering a decision. A plausible solution offered by Posner, which could be applied in most jurisdictions, would therefore be to report the number and *average* age of all motions and bench trials at the close of the reporting period, as well as the number that have been pending for more than the prescribed times.

9. A PUBLIC COMPLAINTS SYSTEM

Feedback from court users is a *sine qua non* for promoting better court management and better court performance. One innovative means of gathering feedback has been through the use of balanced scorecards. In Singapore, eJustice Scorecards have been deployed in several divisions, including the civil, criminal, family, small claims, information technology and corporate divisions. The scorecards software offers valuable feedback on the organization's performance by integrating financial measures with other key performance indicators, such as customer perspectives, internal business processes and organizational growth, learning and innovation. It provides important monthly information on different aspects of performance in a single management report.[42] Where the public can voice feedback on all actors in the justice sector, levels of efficiency and probity can be raised. Whilst increasing the efficacy of a public complaints system may actually in the short term increase the likelihood of scandal and reproach directed at judges and the courts, in the long term it serves as a fundamental democratic tool, both increasing citizen participation and deterring unwanted behaviour. The establishment of a credible and effective complaints system must be made well known to the public. The general public needs to be aware of these avenues and of the complaints procedures.

Many courts in less developed countries are beset by corruption. One of the features of corruption in the judiciary is that it frequently resembles extortion more than bribery. From the perspective of anti-corruption strategies this is actually encouraging because it means that there is often a clearly identifiable victim of corruption. Where corruption is a form of reciprocal behaviour and both sides (that is, the bribe giver and the bribe receiver) are happy with the outcome, there is no readily identifiable victim. When there is no readily identifiable victim, there is often no one to report what has happened. This is known as a consensual crime. Where corruption resembles extortion, however,

42 See Langseth (2004).

the victim is actually the 'bribe giver', which means that corruption no longer operates in secrecy. Victims of corruption are very useful partners to procure information and secure convictions and law enforcement needs to tap into this channel.

A challenge faced by any judicial complaints mechanism is how to deal with the number and nature of complaints. Experiences from several countries confirm that complaints are often filed by disgruntled litigants and may be largely unfounded and there is strategic use of accusations of corruption. This needs to be taken into account in the design of the complaints system. Steps should be taken to ensure that judges are protected from frivolous or unfair attacks by unhappy litigants who seek to use the disciplinary system as an alternative appellate process or simply for revenge.[43] This puts pressure on disciplinary boards in terms of capacity. Complaints should be handled in a speedy and effective manner to limit the negative professional and personal impact on the judge concerned, who turns out to be falsely accused. Citizen education about the role and responsibilities of judges should include information about how to file complaints when judges fail to fulfil their duties. Further, a strict separation of performance evaluation and the handling of complaints, as well as discipline, would appear to be vital.[44]

10. DISCIPLINING JUDGES

The issue of judicial accountability was near-taboo in most countries until the last decade, as judges were hailed as divine-like figures. Historically the divine model may have been necessary to separate the judge from partial roles in societies where blood relationship and rules of reciprocity governed.[45] As Noonan notes:

> Symbols of impartiality such as the blindfold and the scales became important factors in creating the standard of a judge above the litigants and the interests of the litigants. Important as these symbols have been, they risked creating an image of a judge that masked completely the play of human personality in judging.[46]

Accountability can no longer take a back seat in discussions on judicial independence. To wit, history teaches us that where the judiciary is perceived as being unaccountable it is a great threat to its own independence, as the executive enjoys

43 USAID (2002), p. 115.
44 Ibid., p. 117.
45 Noonan and Winston (1993), Introduction.
46 Ibid.

greater support and greater incentives to reorganize or indeed dissolve the judicial body in its entirety.

There is no single best option for the nature of judicial discipline, and countries commonly rely on a combination of the following factors: elections, criminal prosecutions, commissions, collegial supervision, the media, and civil society.[47] What is certain, however, is that the judiciary itself should be primarily in charge of disciplinary matters, a factor that is furthered by it having well-established internal supervisory structures. Though modern standards of judicial performance necessitate accountability, judicial independence is and should always be the primary factor to wield influence over measures, given that judicial independence is perhaps the single most fundamental institutional support for the furtherance of the rule of law.

The role of well-functioning disciplinary structures should be given more attention in order to improve judicial incentives and judicial performance. The role of other factors that are complementary to these structures must be duly recognized. One factor is transparency in court and judicial procedures, which affords citizens the possibility of supervising their courts. Open court proceedings, for instance, for interested citizens, the media and civil society are an important safeguard against malfeasance or the appearance of malfeasance.[48] Public commentary on matters such as the efficacy, integrity and fairness of proceedings and outcomes is important and should not be unduly restricted by legislation, judicial orders or the application of contempt-of-court offences.[49]

The first line of a disciplinary/monitoring structure is inevitably collegial. Collection and dissemination of performance indicators, such as case statistics, as we have seen above, can ensure judges pull their weight and improve court management and performance. But an interesting aspect of these statistics is that they allow for comparison of caseloads and other factors among judges. Where this information is disseminated among judges this affords them an opportunity to compare their efforts with other judges, thus granting them a monitoring role over their colleagues.

The second line of supervision in most democratic systems rests with a superior such as a senior judge or president of the court. The role of the superior is often to ensure that judges are pulling their weight and in some instances to make some recommendations concerning remedial action.

Thereafter, the authority for disciplining and removing judges varies. In some countries the chief justice or judicial council is responsible, whereas in

47 Dakolias and Thachuk (2000).
48 See Kelly (2000), p. 11.
49 See United Nations Office on Drugs and Crime (2004), p. 114.

others external institutions are responsible.[50] There may also be some mixture of both.[51] In several countries the disciplining and removal processes for higher court and lower court judges diverge.

It is common for judges to receive some protection against sanctions based upon the exercise of their core judicial functions. This covers both civil actions against the judge and disciplinary actions based on these core functions. In some cases, such as in France and Italy, the state can be sued for a judge's mistake. Personal liability for civil crimes is not common but it is often allowed for criminal actions.[52]

Some jurisdictions have started to use codes of conduct for judges, which serve as an ethical guide, but others prefer to use case law, which in the case of Spain is based on the Higher Judicial Council (*Consejo General del Poder Judicial*) and the Supreme Court, the two bodies that hear judicial disciplinary cases in Spain.[53] Though numerous countries have developed rather detailed structures regarding judicial discipline, only seldom do judges outside of the developing world receive a serious sanction and dismissal is a very rare occurrence. Several countries have constitutional protections that very narrowly define the grounds on which a permanent judge can be removed, particularly from the higher courts. Formally, impeachment type procedures are frequently the main option for removal. In England, for instance, judges of the High Court and Court of Appeal cannot be removed from office except by an Address from both Houses of Parliament.[54] Interestingly, this process has not been invoked against such a judge since 1830.[55] In Germany, a federal judge may be removed by a resolution passed by two-thirds of the Bundesrat and Bundestag, for breach of democratic duties of office. In the United States, the only means for removing federal judges is generally considered to be a cumbersome impeachment process.[56]

---

50 Judicial councils are commonly found in continental Europe, with substantial differences between their authority and composition. For a discussion of judicial councils generally, see Guarnieri and Pederzoli (2002). For a discussion on their role in discipline, see Bell (2006).

51 Whilst under external authorities we generally refer to the parliament or the executive, in a few countries powers of investigation and prosecution have even been awarded to an Ombudsman, most notably in Sweden and Finland (see Dakolias and Thachuk 2000).

52 Dakolias and Thachuk (2000), p. 381.

53 Bell (2006), p. 186.

54 Ibid., p. 323.

55 Dakolias and Thachuk (2000), p. 402.

56 This claim is now disputed by some. See Prakash and Smith (2006).

Nevertheless, there are numerous lessons from experiences with judicial discipline bodies that are relevant for our discussion here.

First, disciplinary hearings should generally be public, a proposition which is frequently resisted. In the case of France, resistance was so great that it had to be decided by the European Court in Strasbourg, which eventually obliged such hearings to take place.

Second, this process is best managed by the judiciary itself. History teaches us that judicial disciplinary bodies are one of the key areas in which the executive encroaches upon judicial independence. We also know, however, that investigations and disciplinary actions are rare, and removals very infrequent, when the judiciary is responsible for its own discipline. One of the reasons for this is clearly that the judiciary has great disincentives to highlight problems within its ranks, given the associated reputation costs. To wit, this is a common problem in all bodies of self-regulation. In order to get beyond this bias, a statutory obligation to investigate all complaints would appear to be important, as would transparency in the entire process. Moreover, to mitigate the problems associated with self-regulation, disciplinary bodies may also include members of the public and the bar.

Third, there is a need to have a system to address not just serious wrongdoings, such as bribery and corruption, but also less serious wrongs. These commonly include demeanour problems such as name-calling, abuse of contempt power, insulting attorneys, gender bias and other unprofessional conduct. This conduct would generally be seen as a non-removable offence, whereas more serious issues, such as corruption, and most criminal offences would be regarded as removable offences.

Fourth, the need for disciplinary bodies is dependent upon the working conditions within the judiciary. Where working conditions are extremely poor, it should come as little surprise that judges and their staff are more likely to engage in improper behaviour. The overall incentives to engage in improper conduct must therefore be addressed and too much weight should not be given to the notion of discipline. The goal is voluntary compliance with honest behaviour and not to discipline as many judges and their staff as possible.

Fifth, the actions of disciplinary and monitoring bodies should be transparent and accountable. Findings should be put on the internet. Results from more important disciplinary proceedings may be used as guidelines for judges and judicial staff in the future.

Sixth, judicial disciplinary bodies should explain their actions to both the media and citizenry in a systematic manner, and a policy of public outreach should be nurtured.

Seventh, though there are numerous investigative and disciplinary mechanisms that can be selected, all of these require a well-functioning public complaints system. Citizens need to have mechanisms to voice eventual complaints against judges and their staff in order to initiate disciplinary or even criminal action; this would reduce the levels of undesirable behaviour in the judicial domain (see Section 9 above).

11. APPENDIX: CONTRACTUAL SOLUTIONS TO THE INDEPENDENCE PROBLEM? THE EXAMPLE OF AN INTEGRITY BONUS

Economists are often interested in incentive alignment. They speak in terms of principals and agents. Agents in the case of the judiciary are the judges (and their staff), the principals are the citizenry. The central issue investigated by principal–agent theorists is how to get the agent to act in the best interests of the principal when the former has an informational advantage over the latter, as well as different interests. The above discussion will have made clear that guarantees of judicial independence greatly restrict the powers of alignment of judges' preferences with those of citizens.

In some instances, judiciaries are plagued by corruption, and corrupt actors hide behind judicial independence in order to shield themselves from investigation and prosecution. One possible solution may be the development of an integrity bonus. Like a performance bonus for good performance, an integrity bonus would be given to judges and judicial staff for honest behaviour. The design of this mechanism would be as follows.

Judges and judicial staff would voluntarily sign a contract indicating that they are not willing to participate in corruption or malfeasance. Among the clauses in the contract, judges and their staff would agree to abide by all the conditions of a modern code of conduct, including full and voluntary disclosure of their assets, and would agree to let themselves be monitored. Moreover, the contract would provide for a possible sanction or an avenue for dispute resolution when judges are found not to have abided by the terms of the agreement. Judges and judicial staff who voluntarily agree to let themselves be monitored and do not violate the terms of the agreement would be awarded an integrity bonus, perhaps quarterly. The size of this bonus, to have a real impact, should probably be between 15 and 20 per cent of basic salary.

There are a number of advantages to using such a mechanism:

1. Voluntary solution

This is a voluntary mechanism, not imposed by a third party. Judges and administrative staff should sign such an agreement not as a group but as individuals. It is a contractual solution to the problem and does not violate the principle of judicial independence.

2. Solving the first-mover problem

One of the problems with the judiciary in some countries is that many external to the judiciary do not consider it fair to improve the conditions and pay within the judiciary while it is perceived as being corrupt. The judiciary on the other hand argues that it is doing the best it can, given the poor conditions and salary it has available to it. This agreement solves the first-mover problem, since both sides would move at the same time. Incentives would be given to the judiciary to be honest and at the same time it would receive better financial remuneration.

3. Getting around loopholes in the law

Contractual solutions may get around loopholes in the law. On some occasions, laws may not be forthcoming or may be hopelessly incomplete. A contractual solution voluntarily obliges parties to adhere to terms which are not encompassed in the law.

4. Separating mechanism

Such a system may function as a means to separate the good from the bad. Parties who trust the system and feel that they have nothing to hide will agree to the terms of the binding agreement, and will also agree to let themselves be monitored. Those that are unwilling to sign the agreement will be widely known and may incur reputation losses and arouse suspicion. If it is properly designed and conducted, with time more and more parties should be willing to sign the agreement, given both the financial benefits involved and the impression that is made by not signing it.

5. Solving the enforcement problem

Where judiciaries were formerly reluctant to monitor for and sanction improbity among its actors; such a contractual agreement would solve the enforcement problem.

The question of who is going to monitor such agreements is crucial. It would be necessary that the monitor (and enforcer) of such agreements be selected in direct consultation with the judiciary. The monitor cannot be imposed, for instance, by the executive.

6. Exportation later to other sectors

This mechanism may be pilot tested in the judiciary, forming an action learning approach. Pursuant to successful implementation, it could then be exported to other sectors.

4. Litigants

1. INTRODUCTION

We all make an elevated number of contracts everyday. In the vast majority of cases, these contracts are realized in the manner envisaged by contracting parties, in the sense that one of the parties delivers the goods or services solicited according to the terms of the agreement and with the quality expected. In other cases, however, one party does not comply with that which was agreed, in terms of obligations, either partially or completely. These situations in the majority of cases are resolved by agreement between the parties. For instance, where a party supplies goods with a defect it may agree to substitute them for another without defect, or offer monetary or other compensation for the difference in quality. If a good was delivered late and a penalty clause was included in the contract for such cases, the issue may be resolved by reducing the sum the purchaser of these goods has to pay. If the buyer fails to pay the agreed sum by the agreed-upon date, he may return the merchandise to the seller.

Cases where one of the parties does not comply with an agreement and refuses to compensate the other party are relatively few. A disgruntled individual has various options. First, he may do nothing. Indeed, in many economic transactions that fail to live up to our expectations, this is the solution we adopt. A meal of mediocre quality in a restaurant or a session at a cinema with poor sound will rarely lead to anything but a modest complaint, at the most. There are two reasons that explain this behaviour. First, the costs we incur as a result of the actions of the offending party may be too small for the investment of our time and resources in acquiring the compensation we consider adequate. Second, the issue of whether contractual obligations have or have not been abided by may actually be debatable. There is no clear rule that establishes what constitutes a satisfactory meal or satisfactory sound at a cinema. Moreover, the restaurant and cinema proprietors will point out that the vast majority of clients did not complain. Within a few seconds we conduct a cost–benefit analysis, whereby we intuitively calculate the benefits that we may obtain by bringing forward a formal complaint, the costs we may incur in terms of time and resources, and the probability that our efforts will be successful. This analysis leads us into taking a decision. Note, although the probability of success may be very high and we know that we will receive compensation to the value of the good or service in question, efficient conduct on our part may be not to file a complaint, because the transaction costs of complaining may be greater than the compensation.

Let us suppose, however, that a law establishes that the injured party has the right, in addition to the return of the amount paid, to compensation for time and effort associated with the filing of a complaint (we would have to add that the administration is omniscient and can quantify with precision the costs incurred by each person). In this case, our behaviour would change, because complaining may now be the most convenient strategy. The existence of a law establishing compensation for time and effort is clearly not necessary in many cases for parties to decide to seek compensation. In the case of a cinema session, poor sound may not be sufficient reason to warrant a complaint. Let us suppose, however, that we are not discussing the quality of a cinema but damages to a house we have recently purchased from a construction company at a cost of several hundred thousand euros. The cost–benefit analysis is in reality similar to that discussed above, but the costs we incurred are far higher. Though the costs of filing a complaint are higher, the benefits we expect to obtain are much greater than in the case of the cinema; we are, therefore, far more willing to incur the transaction costs associated with demanding compensation. For this reason, we may decide to sue or threaten to sue the construction company for damages, demanding reparations, or the monetary value of such, which has been calculated by professionals that we have contracted.

The construction company itself may pursue various options. First, it may accept the claim, which indicates that the problem has been resolved. Second, it may refuse to pay up or conduct the necessary reparations. Third, it may partially refuse the claims or initiate negotiations in order to try to come to some agreement which would result in the payment of only a part of the amount claimed, discussing technical aspects of the work (a concrete defect does not exist or is less than that alleged by the buyer) and/or the manner in which one can interpret the law (even if the defect exists, it may not be the obligation of the constructor to repair it – for example, because a certain period of time has passed since the house was handed over). These negotiations may or may not result in agreement.

In the case of a company refusing to pay up or conduct the necessary reparations, or where the parties do not arrive at an agreement regarding the size of reparations in negotiations, the buyer has the possibility of taking the matter to the courts. Litigation before courts thus generally constitutes the last option for the resolution of a conflict and only in rare cases is it actually invoked.

Until now we have been looking at the case of non-compliance in contract, where a party considers the contractual terms of an agreement not to have been honoured. This is not, however, the only situation that can give rise to litigation. Frequently, the damage caused by a person or firm is produced without the existence of a prior relationship between the injurer and injured party. In some cases it may be the undesired result of a specific action. The case of a factory that contaminates the air and reduces agricultural production on a nearby farm, or a car that runs over a pedestrian, does not involve any type of contractual non-compliance, nor is it usually the result of any criminal behaviour. Producing a specific product or driving a car per se does not constitute illicit behaviour. The undesired effects of these types of actions are the reason for torts, in which the injured party finds himself in a similar situation to that of a party seeking compensation for non-compliance with contractual obligations. The strategies for acquiring compensation under tort law are similar, as is the cost–benefit analysis, though they are subject to the specific particularities of the law.

2. PRIVATE SUIT AND SOCIETAL INTERESTS

A private individual who has suffered a harm has incentives to sue when the expected costs of suit are less than his expected benefits. Accordingly, suit is more likely the greater the probability of winning, the higher the award and the lower the (expected) costs of trial. The individual's expected benefits may be either the gains from trial or possible settlement. In terms of costs, parties generally have to pay court fees, and a series of other expenses, such as lawyers' fees, fees for technical reports, and evidence related fees. The first, lawyers' fees, are beyond doubt the most important, and their size and payment structure are often determining factors for a private individual or firm in deciding whether to go to court to enforce a right. In some instances, parties may be able to recover most of these costs, a subject we shall return to at greater length below.

Private incentives to sue are misaligned with what is socially optimal.[1] Consider the situation where a defendant can totally avoid an accident if he makes a modest investment in his level of care. Where plaintiffs have incentives to sue, because the cost of doing so is less than the expected benefits, the rational defendant will foresee this possibility and increase his level of precautions. This will lead to the situation where litigation will not occur.[2] If the costs of suing, however, exceed the benefits of doing so, in the same example, the

1 Shavell (1982, 1999b).

2 We are excluding for the moment the possibility of errors, and strategic behaviour by plaintiffs.

rational defendant has no such incentives. The rational defendant will again foresee this possibility and has, therefore, no incentive to increase his level of precaution, that is, take the due level of care. Plaintiffs will not generally include in their calculations the social benefits from suit, which are principally in the form of deterrence.[3]

Consider, on the other hand, the case where a defendant increases his precaution but this has no effect on the level of accidents. As always, plaintiffs will sue where their expected benefit from doing so is higher than their costs. Where the expected benefits are higher than the expected costs, litigation is socially wasteful, because the defendant could have done nothing to influence the accident. Plaintiffs are interested in their own (potential) costs of litigation, as opposed to the total societal costs, which include those incurred by the defendant and total court costs. Recall that society is interested in minimizing the total social costs of accidents, which include the sum of precaution costs and the costs of accidents. In this case, increasing the level of precaution has no impact on the costs of accident, so it is socially wasteful.

Note, we have selected two very basic cases, at each extreme: one where the defendant can avoid an accident and its associated costs, with only a modest increase in expenditure, and the other where the defendant could do nothing to alter the level of accidents. These examples serve the purpose of highlighting the basic misalignment between private incentives to sue and that which is socially optimal. In many cases, however, the analysis becomes more difficult. Consider for example once again the case of automobile accidents. A society could reduce the level of automobile accidents to zero, if it were to ban their use and this measure were perfectly enforceable. Such a measure would, however, be completely imprudent, the reason being that drivers derive utility from using their cars. Though harm is a social cost, curtailing it is itself a costly endeavour. There are, therefore, trade-offs involved between curbing the nature of generally socially desirable activities and the level of harm caused by these activities. These trade-offs become difficult to measure.

A subject we shall return to at greater length in Chapter 7 is the practical implications of the aforementioned. Shavell identifies two cases, those of automobile accidents and product liability, which would appear to be good candidates for excessive litigation.[4] Automobile accidents comprise up to 50 per cent of all civil litigation in the US, and one suspects similar percentages in other societies. Individuals already have sound incentives to avoid accidents, based

---

[3] In rare cases it may lead to precedent or clarification of the law. Even in these cases, however, the final goal remains deterrence-based, given that precedence and clarification of the law have the effect of better allocating risk between parties and imposing a cost on those that do not adhere to the law.

[4] Shavell (2004), p. 395.

on injury to self, criminal sanctions for drunkenness and speeding, fines for traffic violation and so on. Tort liability which ties up the courts, therefore, would only seem to have a modest effect on changing the behaviour of motorists. Similarly, litigation costs associated with product liability are generally quite high, but companies already have strong incentives to retain their customer base, establish a reputation and avoid being identified with having low-quality or dangerous goods.

Consider, however, the case of environmental issues, such as low-level pollution damages, where the harm is likely to be spread out among many victims. In this case, the personal costs of litigation can easily be higher than the individual damage suffered by any one victim. Injured parties are therefore unlikely to bring a suit and tort feasors have little incentive to internalize these costs. Moreover, even if a suit is brought, tort feasors only compensate those victims that bring suit, and not the other injured parties, resulting in a sub-optimal level of precaution and deterrence. This is one of the strongest arguments in favour of class action lawsuits and joinder claims.

There is more reason to believe that social and private incentives to sue are better aligned in contractual disputes, given that the parties have better incentives to factor the costs of disputes into contracts and allocate risks between parties. Contracts, therefore, aim to reduce the chances of litigation and, should litigation be initiated, the mutual costs associated with resolution. Again, there are some limitations to this argument. It is subject to the nature of the contract as well as the degree of information parties have with respect to the details of the contract. Many agreements are standard form contracts, where parties do not always read the details. The extent to which the market removes inefficient clauses from these contracts and better allocates risk between the parties is still open to debate.[5] The argument in favour of market correction of inefficient clauses rests on the assumption that only a certain number of informed purchasers of a good or service need to read the contract and contest inefficient terms, and that these benefits are then spread out among the entire group of purchasers.

The problem of excessive suit may not be as severe under negligence as in strict liability.[6] A harmful outcome is less likely to produce a suit, because under the negligence rule, for a suit to prevail, negligence must be shown. Theoretically, negligence could prevent the problem of excessive suit; in the real world, however, victims will still bring (some) suits against non-negligent injurers, and injurers may still act negligently.[7] Moreover, judges may make

5 Gazal (1998).
6 Shavell (2004), pp. 393–4.
7 Ibid., p. 394.

errors, thus introducing uncertainty into the judicial system owing to the difficulties of asserting the 'due level of care'. This may also increase the level of suits. Interestingly, however, it would appear that under the rule of strict liability fewer cases would actually make it to trial, given that – unlike under a negligence rule – it is easy to establish who is going to win the case. There is greater room for disagreement between the parties under the negligence rule. Moreover, it is probable that the administrative costs associated with claims will also be higher.[8]

Civil litigation in effect offers a type of private enforcement against undesired behaviour (as opposed to public enforcement).[9] Reliance on private incentives for the deterrence of harmful behaviour has some limitations. In some cases, tort feasors may be judgment proof,[10] so victims have no incentive to bring a case forward, hence some injurers may not be deterred. In others, the costs of suit may be higher than its benefits and victims are disinclined to enforce their rights. Where this is the result of diffused harm among victims, the obvious solution would be to allow the bundling of claims. Another problem is that victims with positive value claims may be disinclined to sue where they do not have the immediate financial means to cover legal costs. This problem could be mitigated by parties being allowed to sell their claims to third parties.

Private individuals may seek to enforce their rights by subsidizing the costs of doing so for the sake of deterrence.[11] In other words, they can incur substantial costs in the present – beyond the benefits associated with the resolution of a particular dispute – in order to deter actions that harm them in the future. Imagine the case of a landowner who saw his land being used occasionally by a 'rogue farmer'. Though the damages incurred by the landowner may be modest, he can choose to take action against the rogue farmer as a means to deter other rogue farmers from doing the same in the future.

This becomes more difficult, however, where victims are anonymous, that is, in a society where it is not clear who the victims will be in the future. In

---

8 For a discussion of negligence versus strict liability, see Schäfer and Schönenberger (2000).

9 The classic article on public versus private enforcement is Landes and Posner (1975). See also Friedman (2000), Chapter 18, for a discussion on the uses and limits of private enforcement versus public enforcement.

10 According to *Black's Law Dictionary*, 'judgment proof' is a phrase that refers to: (i) All persons against whom judgments for money recoveries are of no effect; e.g., persons who are insolvent, who do not have sufficient property within the jurisdiction of the court to satisfy the judgment, or (ii) who are protected by statutes, which exempt wages and property from execution.

11 To wit, in criminal law, victims generally assume substantial costs and do not receive any monetary compensation for doing so.

this case, victims would not have incentives to take measures to ensure private enforcement and deterrence, as they may not identify themselves as potential victims in the future. Imagine now that the landowner considers it likely that the rogue farmer is an itinerant and will move on after a short spell on his land, and, moreover, he considers it very unlikely that the rogue or other rogues will return to his land in the future. The deterrent effect of litigation is blunted and he is unlikely to take any action. As future victims become more difficult to identify, it becomes increasingly likely that individuals are willing to take little or no action. In the case of the landowner, for example, he may enter into talks with other landowners in the locality to commit to take preventative measures and litigate in the face of other rogues entering the district. They may even develop a fund to cover potential legal costs. Now consider, however, that the rogue farmers do not travel merely within one district or county, but throughout the land. Collective agreements become more difficult to reach and sustain, and free-rider problems and other problems of collective action may raise their heads and the system breaks down – if it were even in place. As victims are not identifiable, individual victims may consider it rational not to take any measures towards private enforcement.

Moreover, several types of tortious acts are only ever prosecuted with a low probability. To deter harmful actions in these types of cases, an injurer should be forced to compensate more than the harm caused to the injured party who brought suit. Assume for instance that the chances of detection are only 0.1, that the damage caused is €100 000 and that the tort feasor expects to cover exactly the damages caused if detected. The expected costs of these actions for the injurer are thus only €10 000. For an injurer to internalize the true amount of harm caused, he would have to pay damages of €1 000 000. In this case, a multiplier may be used (damages × 10). One of the problems with this mechanism is that it can encourage fraudulent suits. Theoretically, this problem could be reduced if the injurer were still forced to pay €1 000 000 (thus internalizing the costs of his actions) but the victim only received a part of the compensation. The remainder could be paid, for instance, to the court. Nevertheless, there are still larger incentives to initiate suits, given the potentially high stakes for the tort feasor, especially suits that are filed simply to extract a claim (that is, predatory and negative value suits).

Given these incentive problems, numerous types of cases are dealt with in large part under criminal law, though in fact some of these harmful actions may both be tortious and criminal.[12] In this discussion here, we will be

---

[12] It is common to distinguish between civil and criminal torts. Where wrongful actions are not explicitly prohibited by criminal law, we speak of a civil tort. Where a party wrongfully intended the damage to follow an act, it is an intentional tort; otherwise it is considered an unintentional tort, a distinction commonly adhered to by insurance

concentrating on civil litigation, as opposed to criminal, unless otherwise indicated.

3. THE EUROPEAN VERSUS THE AMERICAN RULE

There are substantial variations in legal systems regarding the recovery of costs. In the literature, the 'American rule' refers to the characteristic that each party, both the winner and the loser, covers his own costs, independent of the outcome of a case. On the other hand, the 'European rule' – also known as the 'English rule' – refers to the practice whereby the winner can shift his expenses on to the loser. We shall use the term 'European rule' for our purposes here, given that use of the term 'English Rule' may be misleading, as this rule is commonly found in civil law countries. This fee shifting is not applied in all circumstances; in cases where the expenses of the winner are considered exorbitant, for instance, the American rule may be applied, or expenses may be capped.[13]

The difference between the American and European rules can be easily understood from the following simple equations.[14] According to the American rule,

$$EB_p = A.P_p - C_p$$
$$EC_d = A.P_d + C_d,$$

where EB_p represents the 'expected benefit for plaintiff of litigation', A the 'amount' in question, P_p the 'probability with which plaintiff expects to win the case', P_d the 'probability with which defendant expects plaintiff to win the case', C_p 'the cost borne by plaintiff in making his case' and C_d 'the cost borne by litigant in defending his case'. Neither the plaintiff nor the defendant takes their opponent's costs into consideration. Note, where $A.P_p$ (expected benefits for plaintiff) is greater than C_p (plaintiff's costs), the plaintiff will file a suit.

companies when indemnifying claims. A criminal tort refers to harm or damage stemming from a violation of criminal law, affecting a private individual, the public at large, or the state.

13 There are numerous types of cost-shifting rules. One type is offer-of-settlement rules, which are found in most – if not all – common law countries. A common element of these rules is that one party (often a defendant, but perhaps the plaintiff) makes an offer to the other to settle. If the final judgment is less than the proposal made by the offeror, then the offeree faces subtantial costs for refusing to settle, typically based upon the litigation costs of the other party. For a discussion of other possible rules, see Bebchuk and Chang (1999).

14 Throughout the text, unless otherwise indicated, we assume risk neutrality.

In the European rule (loser pays), we have:

$$EB_p = A.P_p - (1 - P_p)(C_d + C_p)$$
$$EC_d = P_d(C_d + C_p + A).$$

Unlike in the American rule, the loser pays the winner's legal fees, which obliges the parties to factor their opponent's legal costs into their calculations.

The first observation we can make about the European rule is that it discourages more suits from coming forward than the American rule where the plaintiff has a low probability of winning. Let us imagine a case where the amount in dispute, A, is equal to €100 000. The costs for the plaintiff of presenting the case, C^p, are equal to €20 000 and the costs for the defendant in presenting his case, C_d, are equal to €20 000. For $P_p = 0.25$ with the American rule: EB_p = (€100 000 × 0.25) – €20 000 = €5000. The plaintiff has incentive to sue. On the other hand, with the European rule: EB_p = (€100 000 × 0.25) – (0.75 × €40 000) = –€5000. The plaintiff would not bring suit.

The second observation we can make is that beyond a certain probability of winning the European rule increases the likelihood of suit. Interestingly, where the parties both bear equal legal costs, this threshold probability is 0.5. Substituting $P_p = 0.5$ into our example, then under the American rule: EB_p = (€100 000 × 0.5) – €20 000 = €30 000. Under the European rule: EB_p = (€100 000 × 0.5) – (0.5 × €40 000) = €30 000. We see that the payoff under both rules is the same. If we plug in the value $P_p = 0.7$ we can see that the European rule becomes even more attractive. Under the American rule: EB_p = (€100 000 × 0.7) – €20 000 = €50 000, with the European rule: EB_p = (€100 000 × 0.7) – (0.3 × €40 000) = €58 000.[15]

Figure 4.1 captures the aforementioned tendencies. It shows how, as the probability of winning a case increases for a plaintiff, the European rule becomes more attractive relative to the American. Given the legal costs that we assumed in the above examples, at the threshold value (EB_1, P_1) plaintiff will file suit under both rules. Note that the expected benefits of suing at the threshold may still be negative, depending on the the size of the amount in dispute, as well as the size of the legal costs borne by the

---

15 These tendencies can be shown algebraically. Consider a completely identical claim under the different cost rules, with all other things equal. The European rule is more valuable to a plaintiff than the American where: $A.P_p - (1 - P_p)(C_d + C_p) > A.P_p - C_p$. Rearranging, we have $P_p > C_d/(C_d + C_p)$. This indicates that those with a high probability of winning at trial will find the European rule more valuable. For those cases where $P_p < C_d/(C_d + C_p)$, an individual is less likely to bring suit under the European rule.

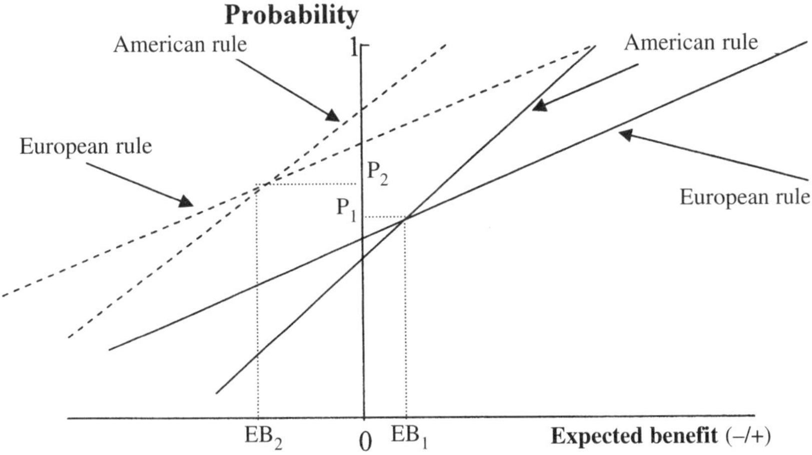

Figure 4.1 Threshold point between American and European rules

parties.[16] This is depicted by the intersection of the dotted lines (EB_2, P_2). Unlike at P_1, where the expected benefits of litigation (EB_1) are positive, at P2 the expected benefits of litigation (EB_2) are negative. It is worth noting, however, that in the latter case the point of positive returns to litigation occurs at a lower probability under the European rule than the American. A modest increase in the probability of success can therefore bring about litigation under the European rule.

The third observation we can make is that, whilst the European rule *may* result in fewer cases, the costs involved in litigating these cases may actually be higher. The reason is the following. Increases in legal expenditure may affect the expected probability of winning a case.[17] Under the European rule,

---

[16] One may consider a case where it is difficult for plaintiff to show that he has been wronged and plaintiff is willing to spend a lot fighting the case. Let the amount in dispute remain at €100 000, but the plaintiff's legal costs are now 70 000, and the defendant's legal costs are €90 000. Furthermore let the probability of plaintiff winning be equal to 0.6. Under the American rule: EB_p = (€100 000 × 0.6) – €70 000 = – €10 000. Under the European rule: EB_p = (€100 000 × 0.6) – (0.4 × €160 000) = – €4000. In neither case will suit be brought.

[17] Plaintiffs generally set their costs to maximize their expected returns to litigation. This is more complex than it may first appear, because a plaintiff's expected gains are not just dependent on his own increases in expenditure but also on how defendant reacts to plaintiff's increases in expenditure. The same can be said for a defendant who conditions his spending according to his expected costs of trial, and must invariably consider how to maximize spending taking plaintiff's reaction into account. The effects of greater legal expenditures, therefore, depend on the specific

parties who are litigating will be encouraged to increase spending as they do not internalize the costs that they produce, given the opportunity to shift costs to the losing party. For instance, a plaintiff who increases his spending by one euro will actually only have to pay this euro if he loses the case. If there is only a 0.3 chance that he will lose the case, he eventually only pays 30 cents on every euro he spends. Moreover, with the European rule, the stakes of the lawsuit are increased. As the stakes of the lawsuit increase, so too do the incentives to increase expenditure on legal fees. These two factors may lead to some relatively disproportionate spending. For instance, in a recent case involving the supermodel Naomi Campbell against a popular British tabloid, Ms Campbell came out victorious and was entitled to modest damages of £3500.[18] Ms Campbell was, however, also entitled to recover her legal costs which totalled more than £1 000 000.[19]

Let us now return to the fundamental problem we identified above, namely the misalignment of private incentives to sue with what is socially optimal. From this perspective, the general consensus among law and economics scholars is that there is no systematic advantage of one legal rule over the other, and hence the effects of fee shifting are ambiguous.[20] Where plaintiffs have strong cases, and thus enjoy a high probability of winning, the European rule will increase the level of litigation. Some of these cases may be socially excessive, as discussed above. This tendency is somewhat reduced where good cases do not win with certainty or there is error in the judicial system. Moreover, risk aversion can further reduce the likelihood of these cases coming forward, given that the difference between winning and losing a case is substantially amplified under the European rule. Where litigants have only a low probability of succeeding in litigation, it would decrease the volume of litigation. Fee shifting may serve as a type of subvention to parties with socially desirable cases whose legal expenses involved in bringing suit may exceed the harm suffered. It can also be used to discourage so-called 'predatory' or unmeritorious suits. Again, this does not suggest that there is a systematic advantage of one rule over the other.

Until now we have only looked at the effect of the European and American rules on litigated cases. Below, we shall make further reference to this distinction as part of our analysis on settlement and behaviour.

---

functional relationships between the two parties' expenditures, as well as each litigant's expectation of his opponent's reaction. See Cooter and Rubinfeld (1989) for a game-theoretical analysis of these tendencies based on the American rule.

18 See *The Economist* (2005b).

19 Clearly courts may reduce this spending by putting a cap on reimbursable legal spending or shifting to the American rule.

20 Shavell (2004), Katz (1987, 1990), Spier (forthcoming).

4. SETTLEMENT

Litigation is often seen as a battle or war, restricted only by the rules of the legal game. In this vein, Franz Klein, the father of the Austrian Code of Civil Procedure – a precursor to a new era in civil procedure in Western Europe – professed:

> Youth is thought the basic moral principle, one must also help the enemy in hardship, but in litigation this is something altogether different. Litigation is a war, in which the parties in a state of bitter hatred aim to mutually destroy through every available means their perceived enemy, and the law grants them this right.[21]

Roscoe Pound, in his now famous speech on 'The causes of popular dissatisfaction with the administration of justice', advanced the notion of a sporting theory of justice. He proposed that

> The sporting theory of justice . . . is so rooted in the profession in America that most of us take it for a fundamental legal tenet. But it is probably only a survival of the days when a lawsuit was a fight between two clans in which change of venue had been taken to the forum.[22]

Further, he lamented the fact that

> it is a matter of course that a judge should be a mere umpire, to pass upon objections and hold counsel to the rules of the game, and that the parties should fight out their own game in their own way without judicial interference.

Nearly one hundred years later, Lord Woolf would profess that in civil litigation in England and Wales 'the principle of "party-control" permitted litigation to become a battle-field where the parties waged war with little prospect of judicial intervention, unless the case proceeded to trial.'

Despite these observations, we know that the vast majority of cases settle before reaching trial.[23] From an economic perspective, settlement is feasible where parties expect mutual gains from reaching an agreement. More precisely, settlement is possible where the defendant's expected costs of trial are greater than the plaintiff's expected benefit from trial.[24]

Consider the case under the American rule where $EB_p = A.P_p - C_p$, and $EC_d = A.P_d + C_d$. Settlement can occur where $A.P_d + C_d > A.P_p - C_p$, or rewritten

---

[21] Free translation, original cited in van Rhee (2005), p. 12.

[22] Pound, American Bar Association Reporter (1906).

[23] For a good overview of settlement and up-to-date bibliography, see Daughety (2000) and Hay and Spier (1998).

[24] Again we assume risk neutrality unless otherwise indicated.

$C_p + C_d > A.P_d - A.P_p$. To illustrate, let A = €100 000, $P_d = 0.4$, $P_p = 0.5$, C_d = €20 000 and C_p = €20 000. The expected cost for the defendant from trial is equal to €40 000 + €20 000 = €60 000. The expected benefit for the plaintiff from trial is equal to €50 000 – €20 000 = €30 000. One can clearly see that there is room for settlement, given that €60 000 > €30 000.

Under the European rule, we have $EB_p = A.P_p - (1 - P_p)(C_d + C_p)$ and $EC_d = P_d (C_d + C_p + A)$. Settlement is possible where $P_d(C_d + C_p + A) > A.P_p - (1 - P_p)(C_d + C_p)$. Let us assume the same numerical values as above. The expected cost of trial for the defendant is equal to 0.4 (€20 000 + €20 000 + €100 000) = €56 000. The expected benefit for the plaintiff from trial is equal to €50 000 – 0.5(€20 000 + €20 000) = €30 000. Again, one can see that there is room for settlement, given that €56 000 > €30 000.

Preliminary observations

Differences in beliefs can prevent settlement from occurring, with the result that parties end up at trial. Economists often view these differences in beliefs as a form of over-optimism. Optimism can be related to the probability of winning, the size of the award and/or legal costs. Once a suit has been filed, differences in beliefs under the European rule tend to increase the chances of trial, given that a 'loser pays' system amplifies the differences of opinion regarding trial outcome. This factor may be limited somewhat by risk aversion, because the stakes at trial are now higher. The riskiness of trial is amplified where legal fees are mostly incurred at trial and not in settlement. Note also that as the value of the issue in dispute increases, so too do, *ceteris paribus*, the chances of going to trial, given the fact that the difference in beliefs on trial outcome is amplified. This holds for both rules.

4.1 The Bargaining Surplus

We have seen above that settlement may occur where the defendant's expected costs of trial are greater than the plaintiff's expected benefits, and that this difference may be considered a bargaining surplus. Simple bargaining models attempt to look at means of dividing this surplus. The simplest of all bargaining games is based on the notion of take-it-or-leave-it offers.[25] There are two players,[26] Player 1 and Player 2, who move sequentially. Accordingly, Player 1 moves first and proposes a division of the surplus, *S*. Let us denote the division of the surplus proposed by Player 1 for himself as *a*, and the division of

[25] These games are played under symmetric information, which means that the players all have the same information.

[26] In the following we are going to assume that the players behave rationally.

the surplus offered to Player 2 as b, hence ($a + b = S$, where $a \geq 0$ and $b \geq 0$). Player 2 then decides to accept or reject this offer. Where Player 2 accepts this offer, the proposal is agreed upon. There is a simple equilibrium in this game, and that is for Player 1 to offer Player 2 only slightly more than what he would get by not accepting the offer, let us denote this value by ε, that is ($a = S - \varepsilon$, $b = \varepsilon$). Player 1, therefore, acquires practically all of the bargaining surplus in take-it-or-leave-it games. For the sake of simplicity, let us assume that if Player 2 does not accept the offer he gets zero, as shown in Figure 4.2. In such a case it would be enough for Player 1 to offer a minute share (let us say 1 per cent) to Player 2 to win his acceptance. Thus the equilibrium would be a almost equal to S and b almost equal to zero.

Consider a simple numerical illustration. Let the EC_d of going to court be equal to €60 000 and the EB_p of going to court be equal to €40 000. The bargaining surplus is therefore €20 000. Let us assume that Plaintiff makes the first move, that is, an offer to Defendant, and Defendant moves second, deciding to either accept or reject this offer. The only equilibrium in this game is for Plaintiff to offer €60 000 – ε, thus acquiring the entire bargaining surplus of €20 000, minus a marginal amount, ε. Defendant is willing to accept theoffer, given that €60 000 – ε < €60 000. Similarly, if Defendant were the first mover, he would acquire all of the bargaining surplus of

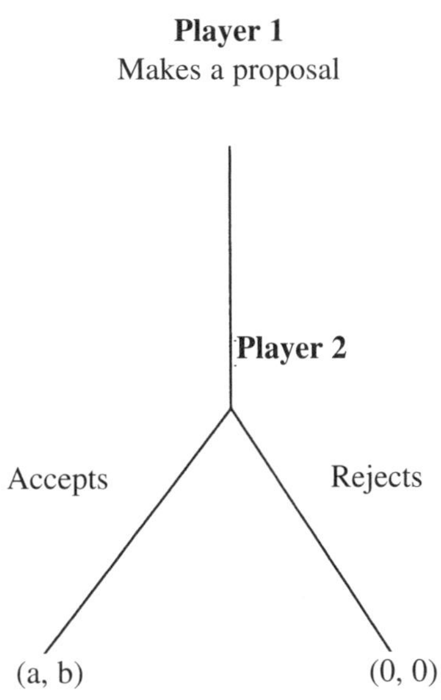

Figure 4.2 Settlement under take-it-or-leave-it offer

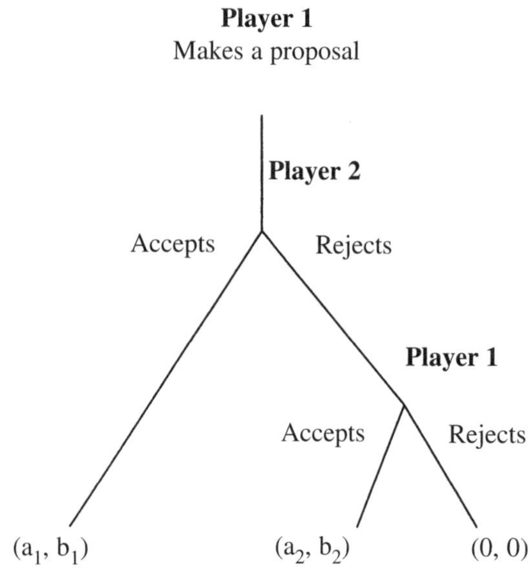

Figure 4.3 Alternating offers game

€20 000 – ε, by making a settlement offer of €40 000 + ε. We can see from this simple example that the division of the surplus depends on the rules of the game, that is, how the bargaining process is structured.[27]

Now consider an alternating offers game with two rounds (see Figure 4.3), where Player 1 makes a proposal (a_1, b_1), $a1$ is his proposed share of the bargaining surplus, and $b1$ the proposed share for his adversary. Note $a_1 + b_1 = S$ $(a_1 \geq 0$ and $b_1 \geq 0)$. Player 2 can either reject or accept this proposal. If Player 2 rejects this proposal he will make a counter-proposal (a_2, b_2), again $a_2 + b_2 = S$.[28] Player 1 will accept any offer where $(a_2 > 0)$. The only outcome to this game is for Player 2 to acquire all of the bargaining surplus less some marginal amount ε. In these types of finite alternating offers games, the player who can make the final offer is able to accrue all of the surplus. One could

[27] One may, of course, argue that Player 2 would reject any offer that was only marginally higher than what he would get out of trial, due to vindicativeness. This may, of course, be a possibility, and may be factored into the offer made by Player 1. Moreover, one may argue that a sense of fairness may persuade Player 1 to make a more generous offer. This argument in the context of litigation should not, however, be exaggerated, given the parties are most definitely on acrimonious terms.

[28] For the moment, we assume that the bargaining surplus is constant and does not diminish.

extend the analysis to any number of finite rounds until T – 1, where T = trial. In this case, the party who makes the last offer still acquires almost all of the cooperative surplus and parties remain indifferent between settling early or late in the game (provided the person who makes the last offer does not change).

Consider another numerical example. As in the above the EC_d of going to court are equal to €60 000 and the EB_p of going to court are equal to €40 000. The bargaining surplus remains €20 000. If Defendant makes the first move, then any settlement offer of less than €60 000 – ε will be rejected by Plaintiff. Where an offer of less than €60 000 – ε is made, Plaintiff will respond with a settlement proposal of €60 000 – ε. Defendant will accept this offer given that it is less than €60 000, his expected costs of going to trial. The parties are indifferent between accepting this offer in the first and the second round.[29] We can repeat the same analysis with Plaintiff going first. The analysis is the same, but with the settlement amount = €40 000 + ε, and Defendant acquiring practically the entire surplus.

There are two other important factors that affect the size and distribution of the bargaining surplus that we have not yet mentioned. The first is what is known as the patience of the players. This refers to how much importance the parties place on money in the present. One euro today is not the same for a player as one euro a year from now. A player is said to discount the value of future income. If a plaintiff expects his benefit from trial, which may take place on year from now, to be equal to €40 000 – as in the above example – he will settle for a value of less than €40 000 at present.[30] Where he is in real need of money, he may heavily discount the future award from trial and be willing to settle for a substantially lower amount. For example, if a plaintiff is willing to settle for €36 000, as opposed to waiting for trial one year from now with expected benefits of €40 000, we say that the plaintiff's subjective discount factor[31] is 0.9. If he is willing to accept €32 000, we say that his subjective

---

[29] There are two equilibria in the game, both of which are Nash and subgame perfect equilbria, with the same payoffs: Round 1 (a_1 = ε, b_1 = S – ε), and Round 2 (a_2 = ε, b_2 = S – ε).

[30] The discount rate we refer to here is the subjective discount rate that measures how much a certain person values the availability of a certain amount of money tomorrow in comparison with the same amount of money today. It is not to be confused with the discount rate computed using the market interest rate (which measures how much a certain amount of money tomorrow is evaluated on the market in comparison with a certain amount of money today). It can be shown that if financial markets are frictionless and everybody has the same subjective discount rate, then the subjective discount rate and the market equilibrium discount rate will coincide.

[31] The subjective discount factor, r, is equal to 1/(1 + δ), where δ is called subjective discount rate. If r = 0.9, for instance, then δ = 1/9.

discount factor is 0.8, and so on. Similarly, a defendant whose expected costs of trial are €60 000 one year from now is not willing to offer up to €60 000 at the present time. He will also discount the value of these future costs. The defendant may be willing to offer up to €54 000. Assuming for a moment that he pays all of these costs upon completion of trial, this represents a discount factor of 0.9. If a defendant is only willing to offer up to €48 000 currently, his discount factor is 0.8. One can clearly see how the patience of the players, therefore, can greatly affect settlement negotiations. Plaintiffs who are in need of money will be willing to accept substantially less than those that can signal their willingness to wait. Defendants who highly value money in the present are less willing to make generous offers.

Courts, by varying the interest rate of damages, may influence the bargaining position of parties in settlements. Where courts only give modest interest rates, plaintiffs may wish to settle earlier given that they are losing money by waiting. Where courts, however, offer high interest rates, plaintiffs may consider their future award as a type of investment, which can strengthen their bargaining position vis-à-vis defendants. They may signal their willingness to prolong proceedings in order to acquire a larger share of the cooperative surplus.

The second factor that was missing in our above discussion was cost. In our examples above, we assumed that bargaining was costless. In truth, in negotiations parties have to pay costs and these are incurred throughout the negotiation period; the bargaining surplus is, therefore, getting smaller with every round. The principle costs are, of course, legal fees. This gives incentives to the parties to agree early. In alternating offers games of the nature we discussed above, parties are indifferent between settling in the first round and settling many rounds later. Once we introduce costs, however, and these are distributed throughout the negotiation, parties have incentives to settle in Round 1.[32] So, why do parties not settle early and what factors can lead to settlement breaking down altogether? This is the focus of our attention in the next section.

4.2 The Information Problem

When parties pay costs throughout negotiations, the size of the bargaining surplus available must be getting smaller. It is therefore in their interests to strike a deal as quickly as possible. This may not happen for a number of reasons.

32 This is a unique subgame perfect equilibrium. See Bebchuk (1996).

One reason is that time is not important to the parties – as discussed above – and there are no real costs associated with waiting. Where one party is in need of funds, he is in a weaker bargaining position and is willing to settle earlier. Where both parties are not impatient, or wish to suggest that they are not impatient, negotiations can drag on. A second reason for parties not striking an early deal concerns reputation-building, where parties – or, one of the parties – are operating in a repeated setting. For instance, in this case a defendant may be interested in establishing a reputation for toughness, indicating that he is willing to accrue costs to fend off future suits. What may at first seem unreasonable may actually be part of a rational, long-term strategy aimed at reputation-building.

In this section we shall be examining a third reason, concerned with *information problems*.

Information about values is often lacking at early stages of negotiation. Parties frequently have not yet formed their beliefs on the important parameters that compose either their expected benefits or their expected costs of trial, or those of their opponent. They may be unaware of their own legal costs involved in prolonging the process, and will, most probably, be unaware of their opponent's costs, his willingness to bear risk, or his need for funds.[33] Defendants may not know how strong a plaintiff's case is. In some cases information asymmetries may enable parties with negative expected value suits to extract a settlement offer, where defendants are uncertain of how strong a plaintiff's case is and plaintiffs can credibly threaten to be willing to go to trial.[34] Moreover, where parties miscalculate each other's subjective discount factors, or underestimate the legal costs of an adversary, this may result in consistently low settlement offers, thereby preventing early settlement or even leading to trial.

---

33 Bargainers may pretend to be patient, even if they are not, showing a greater willingness to prolong the process than they actually have in order to acquire a better settlement.

34 Bebchuk (1988, 1996). Another reason for negative value suits is not related to information asymmetries, but to whether or not it is worthwhile for a defendant to spend on defending his case. If a claimant's costs of bringing a suit are lower than the costs of a defendant mounting a defence, an individual may launch a groundless suit that has no possibility of success, because he knows that it is cheaper for a defendant to settle than go to trial. We should make three comments here. First, under the European rule, a defendant would recover his legal costs if he won, so he would have greater incentives to fight a negative value claim and could credibly signal his willingness to go to trial. Negative value suits should, therefore, be less common under the European rule. Second, the court can mitigate the likelihood of claimants bringing groundless claims by penalizing those that bring them. This could take the form of fines, or cost shifting. Third, predatory suits are not necessarily the same as negative value suits. The former are groundless in nature, the latter may have some merit. If the costs of litigation are high for a plaintiff, and the harm he has suffered low, then a case may still have merit despite being of negative value.

To acquire information on values, several rounds may therefore be necessary, as parties form their beliefs and engage in a process of screening their opponents. Viewing settlement as a series of negotiations with alternating offers – where parties are interested in realizing their highest expected payoffs, subject to information problems – one can easily see how parties begin to accumulate information regarding the value of specific parameters. As information accumulates, parties evolve more specific beliefs, and conditions for settlement may become 'ripe'.

As in any strategic situation, in each round parties attempt to follow their own best strategy, depending on what strategy is being pursued – or is perceived to be pursued – by their adversary. The bargaining strategies chosen by adversaries allow parties to learn something about their opponent's position and form better beliefs on possible outcomes, that is, acquire more information on the (perceived) strengths of their opponent's case. Plaintiffs with strong cases have strong incentives to share this private information with defendants. It may be difficult, however, for parties to share this information in a credible way. For instance, the true damages may only appear with time, as in the case of a construction project. Moreover, there may be a problem of adverse selection, because people with bad cases may try to pool themselves with people with good cases. Another reason why information may not be revealed is that it could be used by an opponent strategically in the next round of negotiations, or at trial. As we shall see below, rules of discovery in litigation serve as indicative of the problems associated with informational disparities and the laws' response to overcome them.

An additional factor we would like to point out is that bargaining strategies chosen by adversaries allow parties to acquire information not just on the values of parameters but also on the 'type of player' an opponent is. Even where parties are fully informed on the expected outcome of trial, to acquire more of the bargaining surplus players might still try to play tough, giving out the impression that they will are unwilling to 'back down'. This scenario is typical of anti-coordination games such as Chicken and Hawk–Dove, where it is preferable not to yield to the opponent if he yields, but if neither yields then the outcome is the worst possible for both players. In our case this is trial.

Figure 4.4 reflects the general form of a Hawk–Dove Game. For simplicity we have assumed asymmetry of payoffs. W stands for win, that is, where a party receives most of the bargaining surplus; T stands for tie, that is, where the parties share the surplus equally; L stands for loss, that is, where a party receives only a small portion of the bargaining surplus; and C stands for collision, that is, where neither party yields and the bargaining surplus is eaten up by trial. In these anti-coordination games, a resource is rivalrous, and sharing comes at a cost. Given that the potential costs of trial may be very high for the parties, however, the reasonable strategy would appear to be to settle before

		Player 2	
		Does not yield	Yields
Player 1	Does not yield	C,C	W,L
	Yields	L,W	T,T

where W > T > L > C

Figure 4.4 Hawk–Dove Game

trial. Nevertheless, considering that the other party is reasonable, one may decide to play tough, in the belief that the other will yield in order to avoid potentially crippling costs.[35] It is very difficult for parties to credibly commit to playing tough, however, given the consequences for both parties of doing so. (We are excluding the possibility of repeated games – mentioned above – where the costs of playing tough and eventually ending up in trial may not be so high vis-à-vis the potential benefits of warding off future attacks. Parties in effect signal their pre-commitment to playing Hawk in the future by doing so in the present). The potential costs of playing various rounds and ending in trial allows parties to 'call someone's bluff'. How serious one is about playing Hawk depends on one's ability to credibly commit to this strategy, which is reflected by the costs one is willing to bear.

A problem normally overlooked in analysis on settlement negotiations is that parties making offers based on their private estimate of trial judgment must also be willing to accept the fact that these offers will be accepted. Where a defendant makes a settlement offer and it is accepted, it is highly unlikely that he offered the minimum amount that a plaintiff was willing to accept. Similarly, where a plaintiff makes an offer and it is accepted, it is highly unlikely that he exploited the opponent's willingness to pay. This problem is known as the winner's curse, a factor that has been subjected to extensive analysis in auction theory.[36] Given this possibility, there are incentives for

[35] There are three Nash equilbria in these types of games: two pure strategy equilibria, (1) where Player 1 yields and Player 2 does not yield and (2) where Player 2 yields and Player 1 does not yield; and a mixed strategy equilibrium (3) where each player probablistically chooses one of the two pure strategies.

[36] See Wilson (1996). On auction theory in general and the winner's curse in particular, see Klemperer (2004).

defendants to intentionally undervalue their settlement offers, and for plaintiffs to exaggerate the minimum settlement offer they are willing to accept.

Given the potential for litigants to arrive at an uncooperative outcome, one can easily see that lawyers play a key role in overcoming these dangers. To wit, lawyers, who are in the litigation game for the long haul, are interested in arriving at cooperative outcomes in order to further their own reputations. Moreover, as repeat players they often come up against each other. Recent empirical work suggests that lawyers who litigate frequently against one another are more likely to pursue cooperative strategies and avoid trial.[37] This is not to suggest that lawyers are not prone to optimism, which as we have seen can lead to trial. Indeed, there is some evidence that lawyers and litigants may be 'systematically optimistic' regarding potential trial outcome. Viewing it from an evolutionary game theoretical framework, Bar Gill (2006) has argued that the persistence of this phenomenon is due to its success as a commitment device in negotiation. By being systematically optimistic, lawyers can credibly threaten to go to trial and therefore extract better settlement offers.

Summing up, informational disparities can be a key reason for prolonged negotiations and for settlement breaking down, thus leading to trial. Parties learn to form beliefs through a series of rounds of negotiation and infer a great deal about the type of player an adversary is, as well as the strength of their case, through actions taken at each round.

4.3 Procedural Rules and Settlement

Procedural rules can have a substantial impact on the likelihood of settlement rather than trial. In the United States and other common law jurisdictions, for instance, the process of discovery serves the purpose of overcoming informational disparities between parties, thus allowing them to better assess future trial outcome. Whilst the costs of discovery are often the subject of much debate,[38] they can be justified to the extent that they allow the parties to settle and thus save the costs of trial. Disparities between parties' beliefs are reduced as they acquire information on the parameters that influence expected trial outcome. Moreover, disclosure reduces the possibilities of surprise at trial. As we mentioned above, individuals with strong cases have strong incentives to voluntarily disclose their private information in order to avoid adverse inferences that could be drawn from their remaining silent and to separate themselves from those with weak cases. Where this system works well those with

---

37 See Johnston and Waldfogel (2002).

38 Cooter and Rubinfeld (1994).

weaker cases will remain silent and thus receive a lower settlement offer. Parties therefore have incentives to disclose all credible information, as long as it is not too expensive to do so.[39]

Procedural rules can facilitate the court in achieving greater cooperation between the parties. In this respect, some of the most interesting developments have been taking place in England. Prior to reforms in civil procedure, parties had no duty to cooperate. As Zuckerman (2003) identifies,

> they were free to refrain from responding to questions from their opponent, free to withhold information unless and until they came under disclosure duty, free to resist settlement negotiations and free to treat any approach from an opponent with disdain. If they engaged in negotiations, they remained free to drag out the talks to no end other than to make their opponent's life difficult.[40]

As discussed earlier, the basis for the Civil Procedure Rules (CPR) was Lord Woolf's *Access to Justice* report. Completely dissatisfied with the state of civil litigation, Woolf suggested a series of wide-reaching measures to improve the system. Prior to the CPR, the English judge was far more standoffish than his continental opposite. Case management became one of the key components of English civil procedure. The judge and his staff are now responsible for making sure that a balance is kept between the complexity of a case and procedural techniques that are employed and the costs of the case (see Box 4.1). Different procedural tracks based on the complexity of cases are one of the techniques to facilitate this effort, as are the greater restrictions placed on permission to appeal.

Lord Woolf indicated in his report that courts should facilitate parties to a dispute 'to embark on meaningful negotiations as soon as the possibility of litigation is identified, and ensure that as early as possible they have the relevant information to define their claims and to make realistic offers to settle.'[41] Courts are now required to look for means for parties to settle. Court resolution is only a last resort, to be implemented where parties are unable to resolve their dispute otherwise, a fact reflected in CPR 1.4(2)(e) and (f).

Lord Woolf proposed the use of pre-action protocols, to 'reverse the culture of litigant warfare'. These pre-action protocols he identified were 'intended to build on and increase the benefits of early but well-informed settlements which genuinely satisfy both parties to a dispute'. These protocols have since become an inherent part of English civil procedure. The aims of such protocols are:

---

39 For comprehesive analyses of disclosure, see Cooter and Rubinfeld (1994), Shavell (1989, 2004).

40 Zuckerman (2003), p. 44.

41 Woolf (1996), Chapter 10.

BOX 4.1 CASE MANAGEMENT IN ENGLAND

Active case management includes:

- encouraging the parties to cooperate with each other in the conduct of the proceedings;
- identifying the issues at an early stage;
- deciding promptly which issues need full investigation and trial and accordingly disposing summarily of the others;
- deciding the order in which issues are to be resolved;
- encouraging the parties to use an alternative dispute resolution (ADR) procedure, if the court considers that appropriate, and facilitating the use of such procedure;
- helping the parties to settle the whole or part of the case;
- fixing timetables or otherwise controlling the progress of the case;
- considering whether the likely benefits of taking a particular step justify the cost of taking it;
- dealing with as many aspects of the case as possible on the same occasion;
- dealing with the case without the parties needing to attend at court;
- making use of technology;
- giving directions to ensure that the trial of a case proceeds quickly and efficiently

Source: CPR 1.4(2)

1. to focus the attention of litigants on the desirability of resolving disputes without litigation;
2. to enable them to obtain the information they reasonably need in order to enter into an appropriate settlement; or
3. to make an appropriate offer (of a kind which can have costs consequences if litigation ensues); and
4. if a pre-action settlement is not achievable, to lay the ground for expeditious conduct of proceedings.[42]

---

42 Ibid.

In addition to promoting cooperation, the CPR provides clear economic incentives for settlement. Whilst use of ADR is voluntary, it is recognized that failure to accept its use at the behest of either the courts or an opponent can have economic consequences. CPR 44.3(4) and CPR 44.5 indicate that the court may take into account the behaviour of a party and its unresponsiveness to offers of negotiation or the court's reference to the use of ADR. Moreover, a successful litigant may be denied his costs if the court considers that acceptance of an ADR invitation may have brought about settlement.

Very persuasive incentives for settlement are established by CPR 36, which refers to 'Offers to Settle and Payments into Court'.[43] As was previously the case, a binding offer to settle can be made by the defendant paying money into the court. A claimant who rejects this offer, and at trial does not obtain a better judgment, will – subject to the court's discretion – normally be ordered to pay the costs incurred by the defendant, starting 21 days after the payment was made. Under CPR 36, however, claimants can also make offers to settle. Where a defendant rejects a claimant's offer to settle and the latter obtains a more favourable judgment, the defendant will – subject to the court's discretion – generally be ordered to pay enhanced costs plus higher interest. With such high stakes, litigants have strong incentives to settle. If the stakes are increased, the risk-averse plaintiff will have very strong incentives to settle.[44]

It is interesting to note that these reforms in English civil procedure – with emphasis now on furthering cooperation and case management by the judge – would appear to have narrowed the divide between the English common law and its European civil law counterparts. There remain of course substantial differences in terminology and role, given that the 'active' English judge refers only to increased procedural powers, whereas judges in civil law jurisdictions are very active both procedurally and in the substance of the case (fact finding and the law).[45]

---

43 Zuckerman (2003), pp. 49–50.

44 There is a substantial economics literature on the impact of offer-of-settlement rules; see Miller (1986), Spier (1994), Bebchuk and Chang (1999). One of the conclusions generally is that offer-of-settlement rules tend to discipline aggressive settlement tactics, deterring extreme offers. They may therefore induce parties to act in good faith and offer more credible signals of their belief. On the other hand, their impact on settlement tends to be strongly influenced by the design of these rules. In some cases, as with Rule 68 of the Federal Rules of Civil Procedure in the United States, only defendants are able to make offers. Allowing one-sided offers may give the offeror a competitive advantage over the offeree. Where only one party can make an offer, as is the case of Rule 68, benefits can be skewed in his favour.

45 van Rhee (2005), pp. 21–2.

4.4 Is Settlement Socially Desirable?

Some may confess non-compatibility between, on the one hand, a court's duty to deal with cases according to their substantive merits and, on the other, efforts to further settlement. In this vein, Fiss (1984) has argued that settlement may be unfair to the weaker party, forcing him to accept less than he is entitled to, and that authoritative decision making goes beyond the resolution of private disputes. Settlement in civil actions, he professes, is 'a capitulation to the conditions of mass society'. But, does settlement really go against the will of litigants? When settlement is concluded voluntarily and parties decide what is in their own best interests, settlement cannot be seen as weak on substantive merits. Settlement allows parties to avoid their litigation costs and where they are risk-averse, the risk premium that comes with trials.[46] As Zuckerman identifies,

> What is important is to ensure that encouragement to settle does not impinge on a litigant's right to insist on court determination of the dispute. It should also be borne in mind that no matter how much we may value compromise, there will always be a need for a legal process where rights, entitlements, and claims can be tested and determined by a court.[47]

Those cases that do go to trial, however, are not representative of the total population of cases.[48] Rather they are characterized by uncertainty in the dispute outcome. The fact that courts tend to litigate those cases where uncertainty prevails may be considered socially efficient, given that other cases tend to settle. On the other hand, however, one cannot draw accurate inferences from the cases that go to trial, a factor which may affect policy recommendations. In a well-known paper on the subject of the selection of cases for trial, Priest and Klein proposed 'the 50 percent rule', according to which the cases that went to trial would be won 50 per cent of the time by plaintiffs.[49] This paper has been the subject of extensive empirical testing. The literature seems to suggest that in tort law and civil rights cases the plaintiffs' rate of prevailing at trial is substantially less than 50 per cent. On the other hand, as the fraction of cases going to trial approaches zero, the rate at which plaintiffs win does appear to approach 50 per cent.[50]

Settlement is, however, not socially beneficial per se, given that litigants' incentives to settle are not perfectly aligned with that which is socially opti-

---

46 Spier (forthcoming), p. 4.
47 Zuckerman (2003), p. 47.
48 Priest and Klein (1984).
49 Ibid.
50 For an overview, see Waldfogel (1998).

mal. As Spier suggests, '*All else equal*, private settlement serves society's interest. What makes this topic more interesting – and sometimes exceptionally challenging – is that *all else is not equal*.' (italic in original) The first major problem with settlement is related to deterrence and the defendant's incentives to avoid harm. As with the decision to file a suit, any decision to settle by a plaintiff will generally not factor in the benefits of deterrence. Clearly, where an injurer knows that he can settle at a lower cost than at trial, he has less incentive to take care in order to avoid an accident.[51] This may – in theory – not be such a problem, given that the total social costs of accidents (costs of precaution + costs of accidents) are now reduced, as society does not have to pay for trial. The optimal level of precaution taken by the defendant should, therefore, be lower. The second major problem with settlement is that plaintiffs are now more likely to bring cases, given that their expected benefit from initiating a suit is now higher. The overall volume of suits filed should then increase, due to settlement. As we have seen in earlier discussion, this factor may be either positive or negative, depending on whether the level of cases is socially excessive or socially inadequate.

5. USER FEES

The state has basically two means to finance its services, through taxation and user fees.[52] There is a continuum between these two factors, with some services finding more weight given to the former and others to the latter. Recent developments in public administration and political debate are clearly encouraging a shift away from the use of taxation to finance services towards a greater utilization of user fees. A general advantage of user fees is that recipients of a product or service who obtain a private benefit pay for such, and these services can be subjected to the laws of supply and demand as found in the market. A secondary advantage of user fees from a policy perspective is that they can be politically popular, as taxes do not need to be raised and state spending does not need to be increased. Very often, however, user fees – like direct taxes – can be politically very unpopular, given that prices are more transparent and are passed directly on to a small group rather than spread out over a much larger population. (Think for instance of the reaction of many users to toll roads, particularly where such systems were previously not found in a jurisdiction.)

---

51 Moreover, given that settlement often occurs in secrecy, the deterrent effect of harmful behaviour may be reduced substantially.

52 One may also include state bonds and interest on investments.

From an economic perspective, this prompts the question: should we shift towards a system of user fees in order to finance the courts? After all, should not users of a good or service pay for that service? When we consume regular goods and services our private benefits of consumption resemble the social benefits. When it comes to court services, however, this may not be the case. The reason that the private benefit of court services does not approximate the public benefit is that court services produce substantial external benefits (positive externalities). The most important benefit provided by litigation is deterrence. As we indicated above, only in very exceptional cases does behaviour lead to litigation, and parties generally try to avoid the courts if they can. But people generally go about their daily business in the 'shadow of the law'. Where parties stray from agreed-upon norms of behaviour and harm others in the process, they face the prospect of facing a sanction and ending up in court. Courts as an inherent component of the system of justice provide a credible threat that unlawful behaviour will be sanctioned. When parties or the state bring cases to the courts, they are making this threat of sanction for future unlawful behaviour credible, the benefits of which are derived by the population as a whole. The second externality provided by litigation is that in some cases it can lead to precedents and help clarify the law on specific points. These benefits assist in the guidance of future behaviour, not just for litigants but for society at large.

The main effect of not subsidizing fees at all would be a reduction in litigation to a sub-optimal level. This is an effect common to most positive externalities, as is shown in Figure 4.5. The basic distinction here is between private and social marginal benefits, the latter being the sum of private marginal benefits and the externality represented in the graph as the vertical distance between the marginal benefit curves. If subsidies to users were zero, then the level of litigation would be Lj, which is lower than the optimal level L*. Only if positive externalities are taken into account will litigation rise to the optimal level. The problem is, of course, in determining how large the difference is between private and social benefits; that is, the social benefits of deterrence, clarification of the law and creating precedents that can reduce future litigation.

For the aforementioned reasons pure reliance on court fees is imprudent from an economic perspective. Clearly, with a shift towards pure reliance on user fees, the fundamental divergence between private incentives to litigate and that which is socially optimal will be increased. This raises the question, what are the pros and cons of a greater reliance on user fees? After all, most court users still only pay nominal fees, so queues have become a means to ration supply even in the most efficiently run courts.[53]

---

[53] This was already identified by Landes (1971).

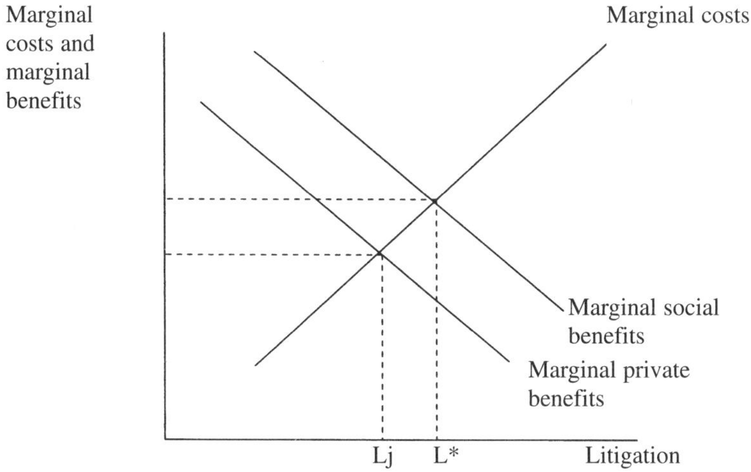

Figure 4.5 Subsidizing legal fees

One of the primary impacts of greater reliance on user fees may be distributional. Greater reliance on user fees will result in a shift in the composition of court users. We shall return to this discussion below. Moreover, increasing court fees may not necessarily have the desired impact of reduction of delay. If all courts implement this measure equally, then arguably fewer cases of low economic value will be brought to court. On the other hand, where this measure is only included for higher courts, procedure permitting, lower courts may witness an increase in demand for their services. An increase in price may not have a very large impact on delay, where demand – at current levels – for adjudication is inelastic. Moreover, legal fees – with only modest rises in court fees – would potentially still soak up most of the costs of litigation for parties. The impact of a rise in court fees, therefore, further depends on how much of an increase this would be on the overall costs of litigation.

Where the increase in court fees is relatively large, it may result in less access to justice on the one hand, but on the other it may lead to greater substantial justice for the cases that are brought. Arguably the cases that remain in the courts will be of greater monetary value, which generally leads to greater investment by clients in the costs of litigation, and therefore better-quality decisions and better precedent. Raising the costs of litigation via court fees may also have an undesired effect on liability standards. For instance, liability standards for optimal deterrence may be set for a certain level of litigation. A decrease in the level of litigation may lead to under-deterrence. This may, however, only be short-term, as individuals and law enforcement bodies modify their behaviour to take this change into account.

As always, the impact of increasing court fees and the expected impact on demand for court services must be weighed against the alternatives available for dispute resolution. Where these alternatives are functioning unsatisfactorily, a decrease in access to courts will be socially more harmful than in the case of realistic substitutes.

6. LEGAL AID

A striking difference between litigation in Europe and litigation in the United States is the degree of government subsidies available in the former in the shape of legal assistance. Access to legal services is considered a right, no different from other rights in societies in Western Europe.[54] Some countries, such as Italy, Spain and Portugal, have included it in their constitutions. The 1947 Italian Constitution, for instance, provides that: 'Everyone can take judicial action to protect individual rights and legitimate interests', and that 'The right to defence is inviolable at every stage and moment of the proceedings.' This right – in theory – should afford all citizens, including the indigent, the right to a lawyer at all times during proceedings. Likewise, the 1978 Spanish Constitution states that 'all persons have the right to the effective protection of the judges and courts in the exercise of their rights and legitimate interests, and in no case may there be a lack of defence . . . all have the right to . . . defence and assistance of an attorney.' Where European countries have failed to make it a constitutional entitlement, these rights can generally be found in legislative acts. As early as 1949, the Legal Aid and Advice Act established a comprehensive and statutory system for legal aid in England and Wales. Today legal aid in England and Wales is set out in the Access to Justice Act 1999.

These entitlements contrast greatly with those found in the United States, where legal services are only guaranteed as a right in criminal matters. The Sixth Amendment to the US Constitution provides: 'In all criminal prosecutions, the accused shall enjoy the right to . . . be informed of the nature and cause of the accusation; to be confronted with the witnesses against him . . . and to have the Assistance of Counsel for his defence.' Gideon *v.* Wainwright [1963] would ensure that defendants have a right to counsel in all criminal trials. The civil context contrasts sharply with the criminal, whereby 'no poor U.S. citizen has a constitutional or statutory right to the assistance of counsel for civil litigation in either U.S. Federal or state courts.'[55]

---

54 Again, we are looking at civil cases, unless otherwise indicated. For a good overview of the subject, see Rhode (2004), Yuille (2004), Johnson (2000).

55 Johnson (2000), p. 87.

Of course where legal aid is a right governments have had to foot the bill for these services. To wit, it is estimated that Western European countries invest between 2.5 times (Germany and France) and 17 times (England) as much of their GNP in civil legal aid as the United States.[56] Greater reliance is placed on contingent fees and other fee structures in the US. Moreover, private lawyers are sometimes engaged in pro bono activities and public interest law firms and institutions have evolved to represent specific groups and causes. This situation has led one commentator to argue that it is 'a national disgrace that civil legal aid programs now reflect less than 1 percent of the nation's legal expenditures and that a majority of Americans have a justice system that they cannot afford to use.'[57] Furthermore, she states that 'it is a shameful irony that the nation with the world's most lawyers has one of the least adequate systems for legal assistance. It is more shameful still that the inequities attract so little concern.'[58]

There is an enormous gap between the legal entitlements guaranteed on paper, and those provided in practice in Europe – though, as always, with substantial differences between the countries. Generally a distinction is made in most countries between assistance outside court proceedings (legal advice) and assistance in court proceedings. Almost all European countries have developed some form of assistance in both categories, with Italy being a notable exception; that is, in Italy legal assistance does not cover legal advice outside court proceedings.

There are substantial differences between the threshold incomes for receiving some type of subsidy. In countries such as Italy and Spain, only the very poor are entitled to assistance, leaving the great majority of the population outside the scope of entitlements. In Spain, for instance, where legal assistance does cover advice outside court, the threshold monthly income level for assistance was €482.80 in 2000. This contrasts sharply with other countries, such as Sweden, where the threshold to receive legal aid was set at 2347 euros, subject to certain other requisites.[59]

There are also substantial differences in the scope of legal aid, that is, its application to various types of cases. In Italy, legal aid covers the entire scope of cases, being 'available without any exception for all jurisdictions and for all proceedings, civil or administrative, where it is necessary to be assisted by a lawyer'. In Germany, legal aid 'is granted in matters under civil law, including labour law, administrative law, constitutional law and social law'. Legal aid in proceedings 'is granted for all sorts of civil procedure disputes, for

---

56 Yuille (2004), p. 911.
57 Rhode (2004), p. 22.
58 Rhode (2001), p. 1786.
59 See Council of Europe, Access to Justice and Legal Aid website, Sweden.

proceedings of non-contentious jurisdiction, for labour, administrative, social and finance court proceedings . . . Debtors in insolvency proceedings are granted respite in respect of the procedural costs.'[60] This situation contrasts with that found in England and Wales, where legal representation is *not* usually available in the following:[61]

- most personal injury cases (other than clinical negligence). These cases should instead normally be pursued under 'no win no fee' agreements.
- most cases arising out of the carrying on of a business
- cases involving disputes about a partnership, company or trust
- boundary disputes
- libel and slander.

The most notable exception from the perspective of litigation rates is undoubtedly personal injury cases. Note, legal aid is generally also available on appeal, subject to re-application or amendment of entitlement certificates. It has been alleged, however, that some High Courts may look unfavourably upon granting legal aid for their proceedings, such as in France, where up to 80 per cent of all applications are refused.[62]

Table 4.1 offers an overview of legal aid spending in Europe, as documented by the European Commission for the Efficiency of Justice (CEPEJ). As with all comparative data, these figures should be treated with caution and numerous qualifications should be made in their interpretation.[63] One can see from the figures the legal aid bill is far higher in all three legal entities of the United Kingdom. In England and Wales, it composes 0.235 per cent of GDP, in Northern Ireland 0.216 per cent and in Scotland 0.173 per cent. A great distance behind one finds the Netherlands at 0.077 per cent, followed by Norway at 0.068 per cent, Liechtenstein at 0.035 per cent, and then Germany at 0.021 per cent. Italy, which has constitutionally proclaimed the right of access to legal services only spends 0.005 per cent of its GDP on legal aid.

The economic argument that can be made in support of legal aid echoes that of the above discussion on user fees. Namely, the private benefit of court services does not approximate the public benefit, as court services may produce substantial external benefits, known as positive externalities. As we have seen above, the most important benefit provided by litigation is deterrence, and the second benefit of litigation is clarifications in the law and precedents. These

---

60 See Council of Europe, Access to Justice and Legal Aid website, Germany.

61 See Council of Europe, Access to Justice and Legal Aid website, England and Wales.

62 Yuille (2004), p. 888.

63 On these points, we encourage the reader to look at the original study.

Table 4.1 Annual public budget allocated to legal aid (2004) (in euros)

Country	Annual public budget spent on legal aid	Annual budget allocated to legal aid per inhabitant	Annual budget allocated to legal aid as percentage of GDP
Austria*	24 100 000	2.937	0.010
Belgium	30 750 000	2.944	0.011
France	291 200 000	4.683	0.018
Germany*	4 684 000 000	5.678	0.021
Ireland	47 649 000	11.794	0.032
Italy	66 060 256	1.129	0.005
Liechtenstein	1 292 008	37.341	0.035
Netherlands	378 358 000	23.224	0.077
Norway	137 528 000	29.856	0.068
Spain	95 455 900	2.773	0.014
UK			
England and Wales	3 070 000 0 00	57.874	0.235
Northern Ireland	93 630 000	54.745	0.216
Scotland	216 000 000	42.533	0.173

Note: * estimated budget or calculated budget

Source: European Commission for the Efficiency of Justice (CEPEJ), *European Judicial Systems*, 2006 (data 2004), pp. 28–9.

benefits to some extent may be enjoyed by society as a whole. Legal aid, therefore, ensures that some socially desirable cases will be brought that would otherwise have gone unheeded.

This should clearly not be interpreted as a call to expand or restrict legal aid, but rather as a factor to focus the discussion. To wit, the desirability of legal aid depends on the alternatives available. From a public policy perspective, the debate rests on the *optimal allocation of risk* between taxpayers, lawyers, private individuals and the rest of the market (notably, insurance companies).

It is clear that where poorer individuals assume too much risk numerous socially desirable cases will not be litigated. But the level of socially desirable cases that would fail to be brought were it not for legal aid depends on the allocation of risk among all the aforementioned actors. Moreover, there are strategic concerns with legal aid. For instance, there is some evidence that those receiving legal aid are less likely to settle than those who do not receive legal aid, given that they can shift litigation costs (partially) on to the state. Moreover, many types of litigation are socially undesirable, as we have seen above, so legal aid could be considered to be promoting these types of suits.[64] Whilst the right to legal aid reflects the *Zeitgeist* of the welfare state, governments in countries such as England and Wales have tended to assume much of the risk without looking at the possibilities of shifting this on to other actors. Whilst many governments, such as Italy, never really ensured that the letter of the law would be translated into practice, probably because of the costs of doing so, other governments have explicitly identified these goals as unsustainable.[65]

The sheer size of the legal bill has forced the United Kingdom to face the realities of government as risk bearer and one can notice a shift away from universality towards targeting those who need the services most.[66] The government has therefore sought to reallocate this risk, enjoying only modest success in doing so.[67] Lessons from the United Kingdom clearly indicate the difficulties governments face in shifting this risk on to other parties. Government has aimed to shift risk on to lawyers through the use of conditional fee arrangements, and has strongly encouraged insurance and claims companies to take upon themselves a greater role in the civil justice scheme.

Though, in theory, the government had the right idea about shifting risk on to other actors, the design of these mechanisms has been poor, at best. Much of the problem with the design of the system lies in the incentives of litigants and especially their lawyers. Pursuant to efforts to promote conditional fee arrangements in the Access to Justice Act, lawyers are now encouraged to accept clients on a conditional basis. Unlike their American counterparts, however, they do not claim a percentage of the damages, but a success fee from the losing side, which can be an increase in their costs of up to 100 per cent. This gives them increased incentives to increase their fees. Moreover, the issue does not seem to trouble victims of injury too much, given the possibility of taking out 'after the event' legal insurance, the cost of which may be transferred on to the losing side if they win. As one commentator has put it,

---

[64] We are only looking at civil litigation here. On the impact of legal aid in criminal matters, from the perspective of optimal law enforcement, see Garoupa and Stephen (2004).

[65] In England and Wales, this culminated in the Access to Justice Act.

[66] Moorhead and Pleasance (2003), p. 2.

[67] See Rickman et al. (1999) for an economic analysis of these measures.

'Before the conditional fees, they did not understand what their lawyers were up to; now they simply do not care.'[68]

The ability to shift risk on to lawyers depends on costs arrangements and legal fee structures. We shall return to this as part of our discussion on lawyers' incentives in the next chapter. The ability to shift risk on to insurance companies – as is commonly the case in Europe – depends on the level of predictability for insurers, as well as their ability to pool risk. It is estimated that the German population spends nearly eight times more on legal expense insurance (LEI) than the government spent on legal aid; in England and Wales, by contrast, recent estimates were that the government spent 28 times as much on legal aid as its people paid out on LEI premiums. Clearly, in the German case, legal expense insurance has assumed much of the risk and costs of litigation, alleviating the need for further public funding.[69] The main area not covered by legal expense insurance is family law and for this reason much of the legal aid budget in Germany is allocated to these cases. As with the case of legal aid where parties do assume their personal costs of litigation, it should come as little surprise that parties with LEI are more likely to litigate. This issue was the subject of a comprehensive study commissioned by the Department of Justice in Germany. It was found that LEI increased litigation by 4 to 8 per cent. However, much of this was due to litigation based on parking violations. As a result of this study, parking violations have been removed from insurance policies. Excluding these cases, the difference in litigation rates was found to be modest.[70]

As indicated above, the ability to shift risk on to the insurance market depends on whether or not conditions are attractive to the insurance market. Conditions in Germany are well suited to the insurance market, given that legal fees are predictable (which may not be the case in other environments, such as the UK). This is due in large part to the fact that fees are regulated according to the Federal Law on Lawyers' Remuneration (*Bundesrechtsanwaltsgebührenordnung* – BRAGO) and depend upon the value of a dispute (more on this in the next chapter). Moreover, all types of speculative funding in Germany are prohibited (including contingent fees, conditional fees, and success fees).[71]

---

68 *The Economist* (2005a).

69 Kilian (2003), p. 41. Kilian suggests that LEI policies provide funding for 3.6 million cases each year (at an average of 540 euros per case), and in the process allocate 1.5 billion in lawyers' fees (15 000 per lawyer), representing 25 per cent of all fees earned by lawyers (ibid., pp. 38–9).

70 See Kilian (2003), pp. 45–6.

71 See The Legal Profession Act (*Bundesrechtsanwaltsordnung* – BRAO) s. 49b II.

As the above discussion has indicated, efforts to shift the allocation of risk between taxpayers, lawyers, litigants and insurers will be strongly influenced by local conditions. There remain strong economic arguments in favour of *some* role for taxpayers in subsidizing the legal costs of poorer litigants, but the optimal nature and scale of these subsidies depends upon realizing the potential of available alternatives.

7. CLASS ACTIONS

In January 2005 the former President of France, Jacques Chirac, asked his government to study formulas that would allow certain consumer groups – and associations that represent them – the possibility of presenting collective claims before courts, as a means to combat abuses he claimed had arisen excessively frequently in some markets. The proposal has had deeper ramifications than first apparent, given that it put back on the table a theme traditionally considered taboo in continental European countries – the introduction of a version of North American 'class action' in continental legal systems.

A class action is a mechanism that facilitates one or more persons to sue (or be sued)[72] as representative of a large group of people with similar interests in a legal matter.[73] It affords the courts the possibility of broadening their jurisdiction and binding everyone with covered claims, including claims by those who are not named as parties and would otherwise not normally be bound. In doing so claims that meet the class definition are extinguished, and not just those of the named parties, as is normally the case.[74]

The court in whose jurisdiction a suit is filed determines whether or not to recognize the claim as a class action. Several requirements must be met. For example, the class must be so numerous that actual joinder of all individuals would be impractical; there must be questions of law and fact common to the class, and these must outweigh any individual questions; and the named parties may sue or be sued as representatives of the class if their claims or defences are typical of those of the class. Moreover they must fairly and adequately protect the interests of their class. The attorney appointed to act for the class, known as the class counsel, should try to notify, in the best way

[72] Though it is far less common – with estimates of less than 1 per cent – a defendant can be certified as representative of a class.

[73] In the United States, class actions are governed by Rule 23 of the Federal Rules of Civil Procedure. Whilst Rule 23 governs class actions in Federal Courts, most states have enacted procedures along these lines. See Cooper Alexander (2000).

[74] See Silver (2000).

possible, all other persons implicated that they have opened this procedure, for example, via newspaper, broadcast media or mail. These persons may then accept to be part of these procedures or expressly exclude themselves from them, with the peculiarity that, with frequency, silence is considered to be a form of implicit acceptance. A person who is not named as a party but falls within the definition of a class is called an absent class member or absent plaintiff. Generally, all members of the class are bound by the decision, unless they opted out of the action at the beginning of the lawsuit. Once the case is resolved – and provided there is monetary compensation for the members of the class – it is the job of the court to identify those who will obtain benefits from the outcome, with judges assuming the role of guardian for absent class members.

In the United States, class actions do not generally compose a large part of a court's civil docket. Silver points out that of the 272 027 civil lawsuits filed at the US federal district courts in 1997 only 1475 (0.5 per cent) were class action lawsuits. Dispersed over all 647 judgeships, this represents only slightly more than two new class action cases a year per judge.[75] It has been estimated that judges spend approximately 11 times as many hours on certified class actions than non-class civil cases.[76] Class action settlements can be enormous: $145 billion was awarded by a Florida jury on behalf of all American smokers in 2000, but was later overturned.[77] In February 2007, a federal appeals court affirmed class certification, giving effectively the go-ahead to what could become one of the biggest class action suits in history: a gender discrimination claim against Wal-Mart on behalf of some two million past and present female employees (see Box 4.2). The WorldCom and Enron litigations are still pending, but have reportedly already reached settlement agreements of $6.128 billion and $2.760 billion respectively.[78] In 2006, 110 securities class actions were filed in America, down from 178 filings in 2005, and well below the ten-year historical average of 193. Though the number of filings for these cases has decreased in recent years, the average settlement has increased substantially, reaching $65 million dollars in 2006.

---

[75] See Silver (2000), p. 195. This number would appear to be on the increase since the passing of the Class Action Fairness Act of 2005. The law, aimed at removing class action lawsuits from state to federal courts, gives federal courts jurisdiction over cases in which individual claims number more than 100 and total more than $5 million in value, and in which any individual plaintiff is a resident of a state different from any defendant.

[76] Ibid.

[77] *The Economist* (2007).

[78] See Stanford Law School Securities Class Action Clearinghouse, at http://securities.stanford.edu/.

BOX 4.2 ADVERTISING A CLASS ACTION SUIT

– Attention –
present and former *female employees* of **Wal-Mart** or **Sam's Club**

- Have you been denied *career opportunities* in management?
- Have you been denied equal pay for equal work?
- Have you been getting the run-around about promotions or raises?
- Have you hit the *glass ceiling*?
- If you worked for Wal-Mart at any time since 26 December 1998, you may have legal claims in a class action sex discrimination lawsuit against Wal-Mart. *Learn more*!

Source: Wal-Mart Class website, see http://www.walmartclass.com/public_home.html

Class actions are applied to several broad and varied types of cases.[79] One of the most common types of class actions relates to consumer rights. These claims are based on economic losses as opposed to personal injuries, and generally involve losses that are too small to justify individual suits. Commonly these claims are associated with allegations of excessive fees or fraudulent business practices and product defects. Another category of cases refers to securities and antitrust. These cases usually involve a smaller class member size and may include institutional investors as representatives. The substantive law is specialized, as are both the plaintiff and defence attorneys. Environmental laws may occasionally be enforced via class actions but this is not particularly common, given that the desired remedy may be injunctive rather than money damages. Mass torts make up the most rapidly growing and controversial category of class action suits. As is the case with consumer class actions, these cases pit individuals against corporations for harms caused by business products or business practice. However, these cases involve very substantial claims for personal injuries – as opposed to claims for pure economic loss. In some cases, the claims may be sufficiently large to justify individual litigation. Finally, civil rights cases – such as school segregation, prisoners' rights, voting rights and employment rights of civil servants – may

[79] See Cooper Alexander (2000).

be brought as class actions, but these are less common. In these cases the parties normally seek injunctive relief.

Civil law systems, particularly those of the continental European tradition, have followed a completely different path.[80] Whilst every system has sought to provide some protection against the, what Cappelletti has referred to as, 'massification' and the abuses of 'mass economy' and big government,[81] judicial protection 'of so-called collective, diffuse, or fragmented interests and concerns about the access to courts of people vested with such interests only began to slowly emerge in the late 1960s and throughout the 1970s'. Even where some form of specialized group litigation developed, one feature that strikes the attention of any reader familiar with the common law tradition has been the aversion shown towards awarding damages for individuals. Group litigation in continental Europe has developed not as a compensatory goal but as a very specialized type of action designed as a means of policy oriented judicial remedy.[82] Consider, for example, the German *Verbandsklage*, which is similar to devices found in other continental European countries. The *Verbandsklage* is an action aimed at obtaining the judicial nullification of illegal clauses in mass contracts for the purpose of protecting consumers against the use of illegal, unconscionable, or unfair clauses in contracts by large companies.[83] In these types of cases, associations are granting standing although they do not suffer an individual grievance.[84] They may, however, only seek injunctions and cannot sue for damages. Damages are restricted to suits by the individual victims.[85]

Class action procedures clearly are easier to apply in the US than in Europe for various reasons. First, the US market for legal services is generally less regulated, wherein lawyers can advertise relatively freely and specifically offer their services for these types of cases. It is often the lawyers that approach the potential client, and not the other way round. In America, moreover, the system of paying lawyers according to the outcome of a case (contingent fees or *quota litis*) is commonplace, which is not the case in Europe. Another important factor is that in the United States the dominant costs rule is that both of the parties pay their own legal costs and only in very special cases will a claimant be obliged to pay those incurred by the other party. This

---

80 See Taruffo (2001) for an excellent overview of these developments.

81 Cappelletti (1989), Chapter 1.

82 Taruffo (2001), p. 412.

83 Ibid.

84 See Walter (2001).

85 In Germany, the number of these cases brought by consumer assocations is still quite small, but they are considered to have been relatively successful in improving conditions for consumers.

reduces the risks for claimants, given that if they lose a case, in addition to not having to pay their own lawyers, they do not need to cover the costs incurred by the defendant. Furthermore, these types of cases are often associated with another typical practice in North American law: punitive damages, that is, compensation that is greater than the harm suffered by the defendant, with the intent of preventing future abusive conduct in cases where there are many potential victims.

Despite these differences, the idea that it would be interesting to introduce these types of collective claims procedures in Europe has been discussed for a number of years and there have been some recent developments in the direction of class action litigation. In France, as we have seen above, President Chirac urged for greater protection to be afforded to consumers in areas where he considered market abuse to be common. Pursuant to his call for greater protection, a draft bill was proposed in April 2006 with the aim of setting up a *recours collectif*. According to the proposal, the court shall decide at the beginning of proceedings whether or not an action can be brought by an association on behalf of consumers (comprising at least two individuals). Thereafter, the association is entitled to a one-month period in which to identify additional consumers. Damages would be limited to 2000 euros for those consumers who have opted into the proceedings. A contingent fee arrangement would not be permitted. The bill would appear to have been sidelined until after the 2007 elections. Interestingly, the bill made reference only to consumer protection and did not press for shareholder or investor protection.

France has not been alone in taking further steps towards class actions. In the Netherlands, the Collective Settlement of Mass Damages Claims Act became effective on 1 August 2005. According to this law, one or two plaintiffs pursue their claim through the courts, and their award is then used as the basis for a settlement for the whole group. Though injured parties are prevented from suing collectively, associations representing the injured parties can negotiate on their behalf. Settlement is then approved by the courts, and is binding for all injured parties who meet certain prerequisites and have not opted out.

In November 2005, Germany passed the Capital Markets Model Case Act (*Kapitalanleger-Musterverfahrensgesetz* – KapMuG)[86] which allows 'sample' proceedings to be brought before the courts in litigation arising from mass capital market transactions. These are representative test cases in securities actions, which become binding on the rest of the class. The law does not, however, allow a claim to be brought in the name of an unknown group of claimants. These measures towards class actions have allowed Deutsche

86 http://www.bmj.bund.de/kapmug.

Telekom to handle approximately 2500 lawsuits brought by 17 000 shareholders seeking damages related to a steep drop in share price. Without this new possibility, it is estimated that litigation could have lasted around 15 years.[87]

In Spain, recent changes to civil procedure rules give certain consumer organizations the right to claim damages on behalf of unidentified classes of consumers. These associations must represent a large number of diffuse consumers who have suffered similar losses. Injured parties are provided with an opt-in mechanism, but there is no opt-out mechanism for affected parties to initiate a separate action on their own if they meet the conditions laid down in the judgment. These associations must notify implicated persons that the procedure has been opened via media communications. Where the injured parties are identifiable or easily identified, they must have been informed of the proceedings before initiation of the suit. In judgment, the courts – where possible – identify a list of individual beneficiaries. Where this is not possible, the courts stipulate the necessary conditions for any party to benefit from a judgment.

Though Italy still does not have class action type legislation, its parliament is reportedly considering no fewer than nine bills on class actions.[88]

7.1 The Case for Class Actions

By allowing individuals with a common grievance to share costs, class actions make the law more affordable for many citizens, thus furthering the goals of access to justice. They allow a great number of persons that have suffered individual harm by specific firms the possibility to receive compensation that otherwise they may never have received, had they been obliged to file individual suits, given the costs – both monetary and non-monetary – incurred in doing so.

Consider, for example, the case of environmental accidents which involve multiple victims. Total damage as a result of environmental accidents is generally very large but the costs to any one individual may be too small to warrant filing suit against the injurer. In this case, where regulation is absent, injurers do not have incentives to internalize the costs associated with their actions and take sub-optimal levels of care. Bundling suits together overcomes the disincentives of individual victims to sue, given that the costs of suit may be shared over the entire group. From the perspective of deterrence, it is easy to see that class actions potentially provide incentives to corporations to internalize the

---

87 *The Economist* (2007).

88 Ibid.

costs of their behaviour, which would have been missing without appropriate regulation.

There are also potential benefits to be had from the perspective of judicial resources. Class actions may economize on judicial resources by eliminating duplicative trials over the same set of factual and legal issues, thereby substantially reducing the amount of time that is necessary to hear cases. Though classes have been certified with as few as 35 members in the United States, it is not uncommon for the number to run into the hundreds, thousands or even millions. It is clear that class actions, because they can include such a large number of claimants, can yield extraordinary economies of scale. Though they typically require judges to invest a substantially greater amount of time into proceedings than other civil cases, the sheer numbers involved far outweigh this investment in terms of court hours.

Businesses can also profit from class actions, given that it affords them the possibility to save time and money on endless petty lawsuits and avoid years of ominous legal uncertainty. Moreover, when cases are heard at different courts, defendants are forced to retain local counsel in each venue, pay experts to testify on the basis of the same evidence, cover the costs of repetitive depositions, and so on.[89]

7.2 The Dangers of Class Actions

Class actions – it is often suggested – may lead to meritless and opportunistic suits for the sole purpose of extracting a benefit. Given that only the most obvious instances of abuse are observable, it is unlikely that the courts can screen out these cases. Faced with even a remote chance of insolvency through a single trial, firms may have substantial incentives to settle cases. Even where a firm is almost 100 per cent sure that it is going to win the case, given the potential reputation loss associated with litigation it may have incentives to settle. Moreover, in a legal fees structure such as that found in the United States, where each party pays its own legal fees in all but exceptional cases, it may choose to avoid the costs of making a defence. Though this argument is plausible, one should not exaggerate the frequency of its relevance. Empirical evidence does not seem to suggest that judges' decisions to certify a class forces innocent defendants to settle (Priest 1997).

Another problem associated with class actions, it is argued, is that they increase the level of litigation. It is clear that where litigants reduce the costs of bringing a suit substantially the likelihood that their expected benefits from litigation will exceed their expected costs increases. Claims that were formerly

---

89 Silver (2000), p. 205.

too small to cover the monetary and non-monetary costs of litigation may now be pursued. Moreover, lawyers paid on a contingent fee basis – given that they represent so many clients – have incentives to initiate claims that otherwise would not have been filed. Let us assume that a lawyer is paid on a contingent fee basis, receiving 30 per cent of the award. The personal cost for the lawyer of representing one client is 100 and the damages sought are 500. Let the probability of success be equal to 0.2. It is clear that the lawyer would not have incentives to accept a case under these terms ($0.2 \times 0.3 \times 500 = 30 < 100$). Now assume that the lawyer has the possibility of representing not only one plaintiff but 1000 plaintiffs. For simplicity, let us consider that the cost of representing all of these plaintiffs is one hundred times higher for the lawyer, that is, 10 000. In this case the lawyer has incentives to accept the case, given that his expected benefit is greater than his expected cost ($0.2 \times 0.3 \times 500\,000 = 30\,000 > 10\,000$).

We remind the reader, however, that an increase in the level of litigation per se is not bad. As should be clear, the social desirability of a lawsuit is not determined by whether the redistributive amount that flows from the defendant to the plaintiff is higher than the total cost of litigation, but rather whether the additional lawsuit will induce a change in behaviour that decreases the social sum of damages and prevention costs vis-à-vis litigation costs in the future.[90] There would appear to be a real danger of class actions promoting the filing of weaker suits – based on the above – that could potentially lead to overdeterrence. However, this risk must be weighed against the benefits of deterring misconduct that adversely affects the interests of multiple parties and that otherwise would go unchecked. Moreover, as we indicated above, class actions also potentially *reduce* the level of litigation by achieving substantial economies of scale, particularly in those instances where legal claims would still have been brought. This can substantially free up the court docket and lead to notable savings for society.

It is clear that class actions in the US have become dominated by entrepreneurial attorneys who essentially control all stages of litigation.[91] This has even led to calls to dispense with the representative plaintiff as a 'meaningless figurehead'. The value of a case lies for the greater part with the absent members' claims – individuals that lawyers have never met. It is clear that this can lead to conflicts of interest. In some instances, such as in securities class action, a large institutional investor may assume the role of class representative, thereby mitigating the conflict that exists between lawyers and members of the class. Commonly, however, a class may be composed of numerous small

90 Calabresi (1970).
91 Epstein (2004).

members, each with only a fraction of the entire economic value of the claim. This factor, coupled with the fact that class counsel generally has the largest economic stake in the claim, converts the lawyer into the 'primary decision-maker'.[92]

As highlighted at length below,[93] legal services are commonly considered credence goods, where it is difficult to assess the value of legal effort not just before but also commonly after a service has been performed. Lawyers operate in complex environments where their actions are not easily observable and cannot be evaluated properly, even ex post. These factors afford lawyers the possibility to pursue their own interests. Plaintiffs normally use contracts to assist in mitigating these problems. Where litigation groups are formed on a voluntary basis – albeit in the face of high transaction costs – plaintiffs can select attorneys, decide upon their compensation and expenses, set up procedures to govern individual and group-wide decision making and devise other structures to try to direct the lawyer to act in the group's interests.[94] Absent plaintiffs, however, cannot influence the aforementioned, nor can they fire an attorney who performs badly. It is the court that certifies the class action and decides how the parties should operate. To wit, in line with other developments in civil law procedure, judges have acquired a more active role in class action cases in recent years. Given that the judge's time and information is limited, however, court employees and outside lawyers may be appointed to monitor lawyers' conduct as well as assist in the facilitation and evaluation of settlements.[95] There may be reason to believe that judicial supervision might be more effective in civil law jurisdictions with an investigative judicial tradition, given the different role the judge enjoys.

7.3 Weighing up the Alternatives

In today's world, with sophisticated and inter-related market economies, it is recognized that numerous individuals can be harmed in similar ways by products made en masse and standardized corporate practices.[96] The potential harm caused by this behaviour can be very substantial, even though individual claims may be small, diffuse and fragmented. Class actions are, however, only one means of dealing with these concerns. There are two other clear alternatives for mitigating these types of harms, the political process (regulation) and the market. The market will work well as a tool for correcting harmful behav-

92 Silver (2000), p. 200.
93 See Chapter 5.
94 Silver (2000), p. 201.
95 Cooper Alexander (2000), p. 19.
96 Ibid., p. 1.

iour where the firms lose business and see the price of their product lowered as a consequence. The market will serve as a corrective mechanism, however, only where consumers learn about the nature of product defects, where they are willing to react to these defects and where they can identify the product and its manufacturer. Reliance on self-regulation depends on an industry having the incentives to discipline its members and being coherent and organized enough to ensure that members comply with the regulation.[97]

The political process is another possibility, based namely on regulation and legislation. The problems associated with government regulation that must be weighed against the possibility of class actions are, of course, the costs and risks associated with bureaucracy and public financing. As a general rule, government regulation may be preferable where a market failure exists, but the costs of inefficiency and bureaucracy can be very high. More specifically, government agencies may not have the tools or resources to identify harms occurring in cases of the nature described above. As Alexander notes, 'Even the US Securities and Exchange Commission, a venerable and respected regulatory agency, has consistently stated that private class actions are essential to enforcement of the securities laws because the agency lacks resources to provide effective enforcement on its own.'[98] Moreover, agencies are often subject to the priorities of political and administrative staff and are also subject to the possibility of regulatory capture by industry. Civil law countries have traditionally been relatively sceptical of relying on courts for policy-making decisions.

Legislation has, therefore, unsurprisingly been the preferred means of dealing with mass torts. When the link between birth defects from a drug named Contergan was recognized and action was taken, the German parliament enacted a statute that created a fund for the victims. The law ordered the drug's manufacturers to pay certain amounts into the fund and developed a distribution scheme similar to those found in fund solutions in US class action settlements.[99] The difficulties are similar in many ways to those associated with agencies. Legislators can yield to special interest groups – just like agencies – and can also engage in acts of blatant populism. These measures are often reactionary, based on a scandal erupting. Moreover, parliament hardly enjoys the time, knowledge or incentives to search for and react to the majority of individual claims, which may in aggregate be very substantial but individually are small and diffuse.

There is, of course, the possibility of relying on other legal alternatives, such as the joinder of parties' claims. But areas where class actions enjoy a comparative advantage over joinder claims are precisely where the transaction

---

97 Ibid.
98 Ibid., p. 2.
99 Walter (2001), p. 397.

costs of getting all the individuals who have suffered harm to come together are exceptionally high. To wit, in the United States, a requirement of certification is that a class be so numerous that actual joinder of all individuals would be impractical. As we have seen, awarding associations the right to sue on behalf of consumers as a means to prevent such harms suffers from the problem that these bodies generally cannot seek damages, or if they can do so may not re-compensate those that have suffered harm. Injured parties, therefore, have little incentive to come forward and highlight the problems.

Current initiatives towards class action should be studied carefully. The business world has not received the suggestion with special enthusiasm, because of the economic implication that these types of cases could have in the future. Within the legal world, there is what Taruffo has termed 'the continuing force of traditional concepts' – manifesting itself in the usual resistance to the introduction of a foreign legal institution, on the basis that it is incompatible with and would damage a national legal tradition.

But class actions have certainly more positive than negative aspects. And some of the most criticized peculiarities of the North American system – for example, the determination of compensation by juries, not by professional judges, and the abusive use of punitive damages – are not basic features of the procedures. Conserving its essential characteristics, it could be adapted to multiple settings in the continental law tradition.

5. Lawyers

1. INTRODUCTION

The market for legal services is large and increasing. In 2006 the two largest firms by revenue in the world, Clifford Chance and Linklaters – both British based – had turnovers of £1030.2 million and £935.2 million respectively.[1] Global revenue for the top 25 firms was £14 813.7 million. Four law firms, Wachtell Lipton Rosen, Cravath Swaine and Moore, Sullivan and Cromwell, and Paul Weiss (all American based), generated revenue per partner of over £3 000 000 in 2005.[2] And law firms are getting larger and going global; in 2006, for instance, Clifford Chance had 3695 lawyers operating in 29 global offices.[3]

In practically every developed country, one can observe a substantial increase in the number of lawyers in recent decades. This has often led to lawyers receiving an uneasy welcome in society. This is not new. Comments on the legal profession throughout history have often reflected its uneasy reception among contemporaries in society. Most American and British lawyers have at one time or another heard Shakespeare's reference to their profession in *Henry the Sixth, Part II*:

Dick: The first thing we do, let's kill all the lawyers.
Cade: Nay, that I mean to do.

Bentham was rather short in the flattery department when he commented that 'Lawyers are the only persons in whom ignorance of the law is not punished.'

Today, complaints generally emphasize the role of lawyers in promoting litigiousness as well as their often significant role in both increasing costs and excessive delays in litigation. One of the most important recent books on the subject must surely be Zuckerman's *Civil Justice in Crisis* (1999). Focusing on three common law countries and ten from the civil law tradition, it was identified that, though a sense of crisis in the workings of the courts is not

---

1 The Lawyer (2006) (see Appendix).
2 Ibid.
3 Legal500.com.

universal, courts in most countries are falling short in fulfilling their stated roles. Zuckerman apportioned a great part of the blame for this position to lawyers, contending:

> One of the clearest conclusions of the survey is that, unless the incentives possessed by the legal system to complicate and protract civil litigation are reversed, and unless the profession's monopoly is weakened, the system of justice will continue to provide poor service to the community.[4]

Historically, the legal profession has proposed ethics over self-interest as a means to separate itself from the market. As Abel suggests,

> Traditional professions justify the privileges of wealth, status, and power by proclaiming their paternalism as a warrant against market temptations to pursue self-interest at the expense of clients. They mandate such paternalism as an expression of noblesse oblige associated with a feudal past and pretensions of aristocratic lineage.[5]

Though the legal profession may emphasize ethics over self-interest, this is a normative ideal and lawyers are no different from other individuals in that they respond to the incentives found in the structure of the market in which they operate.[6] Lawyers, like all others, try to maximize their own utility subject to certain constraints. However, far from operating in an environment reminiscent of perfect markets – characterized by perfect information, homogeneous products and the absence of regulation – lawyers operate in an environment that greatly deviates from this ideal, which we shall explore below.[7] The nature of the market for legal services, as we shall see in the following section, affords possibilities for rent and opportunism not available in many other markets.

2. COMPLEXITY OF THE LAW AND THE PROVISION OF LEGAL SERVICES

Numerous restrictions and prerequisites exist in every country that limit the volume and nature of cases within formal adjudicatory systems, as we have

---

4 Zuckerman (1999), p. 45.

5 Abel (2003), p. 493.

6 Hadfield (2000), p. 956.

7 In perfectly competitive markets goods are distributed by sellers who are unable to influence market price, price is set equal to marginal costs, and output is the quantity demanded at that price.

seen in earlier discussion.[8] The formalities and complex nature of using the litigation process oblige parties in most cases to turn to a lawyer.[9]

To acquire the necessary skills to provide this function, lawyers must have typically undertaken substantial personal investment and shown their cognitive ability to legally reason complex issues of the law.[10] A high level of compensation may, then, seem understandable given the complex nature of legal reasoning and the personal investment made to acquire the necessary skills for working effectively in the profession. As Rosen points out, Adam Smith himself put forth this explanation for the high costs of legal services, stating: 'High wages in a profession are necessary to compensate an entrant when great expenses must be incurred for learning the trade.'[11]

To understand the relationship between legal fees, formality and the complexity of the law, however, we must look far beyond investments in training and expertise towards a whole other series of factors.[12]

An economic justification in favour of formality is based on error reduction in the adjudication process. A requirement to have a will authenticated by a notary, for instance, allows the courts – in case of dispute – to more easily identify the will of a testator.[13] Formalities, naturally, also come at a cost, particularly in the form of increased transaction costs. Clearly, those providing legal services acquire most of the benefit of formalities – given that it increases demand for their services – but internalize little of the cost. This factor strongly motivates them to promote excessive, non-optimal levels of formalities.

Complexity has a similar economic purpose. The more complex a contract or law becomes, the more precisely one can narrow down the actions of parties and ensure they behave according to an intended outcome. On the other hand, however, the more complex a law or procedure becomes, the greater the amount of time (and expertise) that may be needed to resolve the matter. Societies must, therefore, address whether the increase in complexity (and

---

8 See above, Chapter 2, Section 2.

9 Lawyers in the American sense, as a single type of general purpose legal services provider, do not exist in Europe. In most countries, particularly civil law countries, there has been a tradition of giving many legal tasks to a variety of persons (notaries, clerks, and so on). Legal professions consist of a large number of law trained persons known as jurists, of whom only some are advocates who are licensed to practise in courts.

10 A law degree is generally not enough to practise law (with the exception of Spain). Substantial mandatory training periods upon completion of a law degree followed by examination are the norm. This can range from 12 months in England and Wales to 60 months in Austria. Licences are not subject to continued training. See Garoupa (2004) for an overview.

11 Rosen (1992).

12 See Hadfield (2000).

13 Ogus (2002), p. 427.

therefore in the demand for lawyers' services and also in lawyer fees) is more beneficial than the reduction in error.

The inclination of those in the legal profession towards complexity is apparent in manifold areas of legal activities. In transactional legal work, owing to the principal–agent problem, clients are impeded from determining the optimal level of complexity in contracts, and hence cannot identify lawyer over-zealousness. In the litigation process, complexity raises the total cost of resolving a matter, which leads to fewer claims gaining access to courts and lawyers. On a policy level, professional associations, owing to their homogeneity and low coordination costs, can be highly effective in lobbying governments and legislatures for complex statutory provisions, thus necessitating further demand for their services.[14] It is principally lawyers who profit from increased complexity.

On a more subtle level, lawyers may encourage the development of a more complex and conceptual structure of law.[15] On the one hand, precise language can reduce communication and error costs, because lawyers and the legal profession know relatively easily what a term refers to. On the other hand, however, the more complex the linguistic nature of the law, the more difficult it is for non-specialists to follow. Lawyers thus have strong incentives to develop over-complex 'lawyer speak', given that they do not internalize the costs of further complexity and further demand for their own services.

In litigation, if paid by the hour, lawyers have incentives to prolong cases. They can do this by creatively utilizing rules of civil procedure or through creative advocacy, emphasizing the complexity and uniqueness of a case.[16] Judges should be and indeed are called into play to curb their enthusiasm. In particular, rulings on procedure and substantive law – particularly in jurisdictions adhering to precedent – can greatly influence the complexity of the law and lawyers' ability to 'play' the system.[17] Even in jurisdictions that do not strictly adhere to precedence, former decisions inevitably influence future actions by shaping expectations and standardizing behaviour within a court. Developments in case management (discussed above) would appear to be a useful and necessary step to curb the aforementioned tendencies. One of the limitations of case management as a tool, however, is precisely related to the incentives facing judges themselves. Judges make decisions but do not internalize the costs of their decisions. If the costs of opportunism on the part of lawyers are that they raise the costs of proceedings as well as delay, thus preventing others from accessing the courts, then why should judges necessarily have strong incentives to mitigate this behaviour?

---

14 Ibid., p. 428.
15 Ibid., p. 429.
16 Hadfield (2000), pp. 996–7.
17 Ibid.

3. CREDENCE GOODS AND THE ASYMMETRY PROBLEM

One of the characteristics of legal services is they are credence goods. A credence good is a good whose utility is difficult – if not impossible – to measure. Even after consumption, in contrast to experience goods, the utility gain or loss associated with credence goods is difficult to ascertain. These features are found in other markets as well, such as car repairs, many types of medical treatment, home maintenance services and even education. Empirical studies have highlighted numerous examples of fraudulent behaviour in markets associated with credence goods.[18]

Lawyers not only provide the service in question but also determine how much of the service is necessary. Ex post the value of the service cannot be accurately determined, due to the complexity of the law and the plurality of factors that affect a dispute's outcome. This prohibits a client from determining the value added from legal services. Moreover, the legal process is so complex that not only is it difficult for lay persons to determine the quality or value of services, but it is also difficult for legal experts to do so.[19] There is, therefore, an acute problem of information asymmetry which creates strong incentives for opportunistic behaviour on the part of the lawyer.

Professional ethics in theory recognizes the problem of credence goods, and obliges lawyers to act in the furtherance of the interests of their clients.[20] In the United States, for instance, a lawyer is expected to keep the client informed,[21] safeguard the client's secrets,[22] provide competent and diligent services at a reasonable fee,[23] and abide by the client's wishes concerning the purposes of the attorney–client relationship.[24]

The market has developed some mechanisms for mitigating this problem, but these are largely at the disposal of corporate clients. Corporations on the whole accumulate substantial knowledge based on their experiences with individual lawyers, and given the financial resources at their disposal can incur substantial search costs. Moreover, they are repeat customers in the market for legal services. In-house lawyers can help to identify legal needs, search for

---

18 See Emons (2003) for a look at some of these studies.

19 See Hadfield (2000), p. 995.

20 Lawyers generally have a two-fold professional duty, one as an advocate for a client, and second as an officer of the court.

21 See American Bar Association Model Rules of Professional Conduct, Rule 1.4.

22 Ibid., Rule 1.6.

23 Ibid., Rule 1.2; Rule 1.3; Rule 1.5.

24 Ibid., Rule 1.2.

legal counsel and monitor their performance. Additionally, these in-house lawyers have taken much of the legal work inside, thus reducing the potential for opportunism. Corporations also get other legal professionals to monitor legal fees. These factors enable them to mitigate the information asymmetry and align lawyer–client interests.

The regulation of lawyer misconduct is commonly through disciplinary controls that rely on others including judges and other lawyers to report undesirable behaviour. It is clear that such mechanisms suffer from the weakness that peers generally have no incentives in the form of tangible rewards to report misconduct, and may run the risk of retaliatory responses. Lawyers are more likely to turn to more informal mechanisms, such as 'complain to the judge, file a retaliatory motion, withhold cooperation or spread negative information among other lawyers and clients'.[25] The vast majority of the claims coming before the disciplinary system are filed by clients, but it is difficult for these claims to be successful, given the complexity of the law and the information asymmetry associated with numerous legal decisions. Moreover, clients only have incentives to report such actions by lawyers that do not benefit them.

Theoretically, litigation based on malpractice liability may be a means to mitigate the problem. The first limitation of such a system is that clients do not necessarily know when they have been harmed. The second limitation of this mechanism as a means of aligning lawyer–client interests is again related to the complexity of the law, which hinders ex post evaluation of lawyers' actions, making it almost impossible for clients to show that they have been harmed by the specific actions of their lawyers. Lawyers who are, after all, trained in litigation usually find it easy to cover their tracks. Once more, these liability controls seem to benefit corporate clients more given that they have greater means and resources to bring such a claim. Another limitation is related again to the costs of litigation. Though in an ideal world an efficiently designed system of malpractice liability would deter professionals from engaging in unwanted behaviour in the first place, in reality one must not neglect the costs associated with litigation as a measure to deter undesired behaviour, as we have been discussing throughout this book.

The complexity of the law and the nature of dispute resolution in all but the most routine of matters generally means that outcomes are the result of an accumulation of numerous factors, thus leading to high levels of unpredictability.[26] Even the most ethical lawyer often cannot provide any guarantees on outcomes, time required, and so on. (For this reason, lawyers may

---

25 Wilkins (1992), p. 823 fn. 89.

26 Hadfield (2000), p. 986.

rationally be unwilling to offer a flat rate for services.) This makes ex post evaluation extremely difficult. In a market characterized by uncertainty, clients will look for some other mechanisms or signals that may help estimate quality. As generally one-shot players in the litigation process, they may ask friends about their experiences and accumulate impressions based on word of mouth. Again these impressions are subject to the aforementioned limitations on assessing the performance of lawyers. Further, though clients may only be involved in litigation on a one-shot basis, they may belong to associations or institutions where members of the association as a whole are involved repeatedly. This may allow individuals to accrue certain benefits associated with repeated play that can lead to desirable, cooperative outcomes, such as the desire not to forfeit future payoffs or reputation.

In estimating beliefs on quality, litigants may consider factors such as price, academic credentials, the list of other clients, and the office building. In markets where it is difficult to establish the quality of goods, potentially low-quality goods may undercut those of higher quality. This does not seem to happen in the market for legal services. Hadfield provides the following explanation. Legal work is conducted in a tournament-like setting.[27] In litigation the outcome of a case depends not on the absolute quality of a lawyer, but rather on his *relative* quality when compared with the lawyer on the other side, as well as the judge. The difference between a lawyer who is good and one that is only marginally better can be the difference between winning and losing a case. Whilst it is difficult, as we have seen above, to determine which 'moves' in the legal game may actually win or lose a case, it is clear that outcome depends on the ability of legal representation on one side vis-à-vis the other.

Even with difficulties in evaluating the quality of lawyers, clients are still willing to pay substantially higher prices for those who are only slightly better. This dynamic holds in systems of both the common and civil law traditions. Whilst litigation in the Anglo-American system is widely recognized as adversarial, litigation in all legal systems is by its very nature rivalrous, given opposed interests on litigation outcome. Whereas legal processes may be designed with more or less emphasis on the adversarial approach, this does not change the fact that interests are rivalrous, as emphasized in the parallel drawn between litigation and warfare in Chapter 4, section 4.[28] Parallels have been drawn with winner-take-all markets where there are high stakes and small differences in quality greatly affect the rewards. For instance, a gold medal winner at the Olympics generally receives far superior endorsement than a silver medal winner in the same discipline.

27 Ibid., pp. 972–6.

28 See above, Chapter 4, Section 4.

This dynamic is present not only in litigation but also in transactional legal work.[29] The benefits that may be accrued by having a better lawyer in complex contracting can be substantial, particularly where there is a dispute and the threat of litigation. As one would expect, it is not present in those aspects of legal services which are not rivalrous in nature. Standardized transactions, such as authenticating a will, do not have this characteristic. As a result of this, we can expect competition among lawyers in these services to lead to flat fees.[30]

4. THE STRATEGIC ADVANTAGE OF HAVING LEGAL COUNSEL

In some situations lawyers are hired not because it is in both parties' interests to do so, but rather because the parties perceive a strategic advantage in having counsel. This factor boosts demand for legal counsel. In these scenarios, failure to hire a lawyer by one party offers the other party a strategic advantage should he hire a lawyer. This situation is typical of a Prisoners' Dilemma, and evidence of its occurrence has been documented in the empirical literature on negotiation.[31] The familiar outcome of the Prisoners' Dilemma is that parties may arrive at a noncooperative solution, that is, where both hire counsel though it would be in their interests should neither do so.

Let us consider a numerical illustration (Figure 5.1). The gain from winning a dispute is 100. The cost of hiring a lawyer is 30, for both sides. Where neither party hires a lawyer they have an equal probability of winning a dispute, so the expected gain for both parties is 50 each. Where one party hires a lawyer and the other fails to do so, it wins with a probability of 1. Its expected gain in this case is 100 – 30 = 70. Failure to hire a lawyer when the other party does so means that one party has zero probability of winning, and thus has an expected payoff of 0. Where both parties have legal representation, again the probability of winning a dispute is equal to 0.5 for both sides. The expected gain in this case for both players is thus 50 – 30 = 20 each. In this situation, we can see that both would be better off if neither hired a lawyer, thus saving on the expense of legal counsel. The dominant strategy for both, however, is to hire a lawyer, given that hiring a lawyer always results in a higher expected payoff for a player regardless of the strategy chosen by the other.

---

29 Hadfield (2000), p. 989.

30 This would appear to be supported in practice. Most standardized legal work is conducted using low, flat fees.

31 See Ashenfelter and Bloom (1993).

		Player 2 Lawyer	No lawyer
Player 1	Lawyer	20, 20	70, 0
	No lawyer	0, 70	50, 50

Figure 5.1 Prisoners' Dilemma

5. SUNK COSTS

Opportunism may be a fact of life in many markets, but in the market for legal services, as we have seen above, these opportunities are rife. Suppliers of legal services not only provide the service in question but also determine the amount of the good required, and ex post evaluation of performance is frustrated by the complexity of the market. There is another factor that furthers possibilities for opportunism; this is related to the nature of the cost structure between a lawyer and his client.

Legal bills are composed of two distinctive elements, legal fees and disbursements. Disbursements are expenses incurred by counsel on behalf of the client in order to proceed with the client's case. These expenses may include the costs of such things as expert reports, as well as photocopying, postage, couriers, and so on. They only include expenses incurred on behalf of a client and do not include the operational costs of a law firm, such as rent or receptionist's salary. These fees are incremental and incurred over time.

Once a client has chosen counsel, it becomes costly to switch.[32] Numerous investments by both lawyers and clients are relationship specific – the costs of which are inevitably passed on to the latter. For example, lawyers take time to get to know clients, conduct investigations, and research into the law. Clients take time searching for a lawyer, explaining their case, overcoming psychological inhibitions, and so on. Switching to another lawyer is therefore very costly, given that most of these activities would have to be undertaken anew. Numerous expenses are actually sunk costs.[33] This means that clients are to a large degree tied to their lawyers, which affords the latter even greater discretion in their actions, opening up further possibilities for opportunism.

In some instances, lawyers can make it even more costly for clients to switch. In Ireland, for example, the Competition Authority has highlighted the

---

32 Hadfield (2000), pp. 977–80.

33 Sunk costs refer to unrecoverable past expenditures.

fact that solicitors frequently withhold the client's file until a bill has been settled, even if the size of the bill is disputed. Moreover, until 2006, the Code of Conduct of the Bar precluded barristers from taking on a case from a colleague where the first barrister had not yet been paid. This practice was reversed only upon the insistence of the Competition Authority.[34]

There is another important factor related to sunk costs in litigation that can be exploited by a lawyer who receives hourly fees. This can be explained by a sunk cost auction, a game that is often used by economists to explain to students the differences between marginal and sunk costs. The structure of the game is as follows.

Students are entitled to bid on a dollar. Each time a player makes a bid, the amount is recorded. Students are allowed to make several bids, where the highest bid by any individual replaces the former. The auction is conducted as an English auction, with the highest bidder receiving the dollar. Unlike in other auctions, however, all parties who place a bid for the dollar actually pay for the dollar equal to their highest bid. Generally bidding starts slowly at 1 or 2 cents, but gradually approaches a dollar. A student who has bid 99 cents for a dollar and is outbid by another for 1 dollar sees that he has lost his 99 cents. He therefore has incentive to bid an amount over the dollar, say 1.01. Spending an additional 2 cents to get a dollar may not be seen as such a bad idea after all, considering that he has already lost the 99 cents. The results of these experiments are generally that dollars sell for well over their amount. In one case a business school professor managed to auction $20 for $4000! (Interestingly, where the game is repeated, students often try to enter into collusive agreements. These agreements often break down as they learn that agreements are unenforceable and a similar result may be reached. Of course, in litigation the parties cannot enter into collusive agreements, given the structure of the game. Moreover, one of the parties, namely the defendant, has been unwillingly drawn into it.)

This scenario is typical of a war of attrition, where both parties keep incurring costs until one is willing to give up, with the winner keeping the prize. Parties can, therefore, end up paying exorbitant legal fees under an hourly fee structure. Under the European rule (loser pays), the costs of backing down may be even higher, so naïve parties can very easily get caught up in the game.

6. CONTINGENT FEES

In the previous chapter we highlighted the fact that fee structures are often seen as a means for increasing access to justice and providing low-cost legal

---

34 See Irish Competition Authority (2006).

services to a large part of the population. One of the most controversial features of the American legal system has been the use of contingent fee arrangements, a practice condoned by the Supreme Court of the United States since 1884. Though they can take many forms, the principle of these arrangements is that the lawyer is not entitled to payment unless the client receives a financial settlement or an award at trial. The lawyer is compensated on the basis of a percentage of the payment awarded to the plaintiff. In the case where the plaintiff does not receive any compensation, the lawyer thus walks away empty-handed. Contingent fees are therefore only applicable where plaintiffs seek to recover damages.

The attractiveness of contingent fees from the perspective of access to justice is clear: where individuals do not have the financial means to pay for lawyers on an hourly basis, contingent fees allow them the possibility to press forward with legal claims and avail of the civil justice system. In economic jargon, economists see contingent fees as a means to finance cases where plaintiffs are liquidity constrained and capital markets function imperfectly. Standard credit markets fail in this case because lenders lack the knowledge or experience to properly price the loan. One justification for contingent fee arrangements is, therefore, that socially beneficial cases may otherwise not be brought before the courts for litigation.

A second characteristic of contingent fees is that they serve as a risk-sharing device. This is two-fold. First, these types of arrangements shift risk between the public purse and lawyers. This is primarily due to the costs of legal aid. Governments, through contingent fee type arrangements, substitute the need to grant legal aid in many cases and can still promote access to justice. The conditional fee arrangement that has emerged in the United Kingdom is a manifestation of these efforts. (Of course, this only works in cases where plaintiffs seek damages.) Second, these contingent fees shift risk away from clients and on to lawyers. One can assume that lawyers are less risk-averse than clients, given their ability to diversify risks associated with lawsuits among numerous cases. Moreover, lawyers on account of their expertise can better assess the prospects of success and discourage meritless claims. Under hourly fees, lawyers bear little risk relative to what they bear under outcome-based contingency risks and may accept cases that are largely meritless.

Economists have devoted much attention to contingency fees, however, from another perspective, namely the conflicts of interest that occur between a client and his lawyer, due to information asymmetry. Where a client is informed about the law and can easily observe the value of litigation effort, he could get a lawyer to perform in his best interests by paying him on an hourly basis.[35] The fact remains, however, that clients are less informed than their

---

35 Polinsky and Rubinfeld (2003).

lawyers about the law and the strength of their claims, as well as the value of litigation effort. Under an hourly or fixed fee arrangement lawyers internalize the costs of their efforts but not the benefit, giving them little incentive to work hard.[36] Interests are, therefore, not aligned and there is a principal–agent problem. By granting lawyers a stake in the outcome of a case, a contingent fee arrangement may mitigate this problem. This can be seen in the following simple illustration (Figure 5.2).

Let a plaintiff's probability of success at trial depend on the effort his lawyer devotes to his case. The lawyer's effort level is denoted by x. Then using our earlier notation, the expected value of trial for plaintiff is APp(x) – Cp(x), where both Pp(x) and Cp(x) are increasing in x.[37] The costs at trial are those incurred by the lawyer. The optimal effort level occurs as x^*, the point where the difference between costs and the expected value of trial is greatest.

Under an hourly or fixed fee arrangement, the lawyer will get paid regardless of effort level, so he has incentives to minimize the efforts he devotes to a case. Under a contingent fee arrangement, however, the lawyer has a stake in the outcome of a case, denoted by b, which is a fraction of the award at trial.

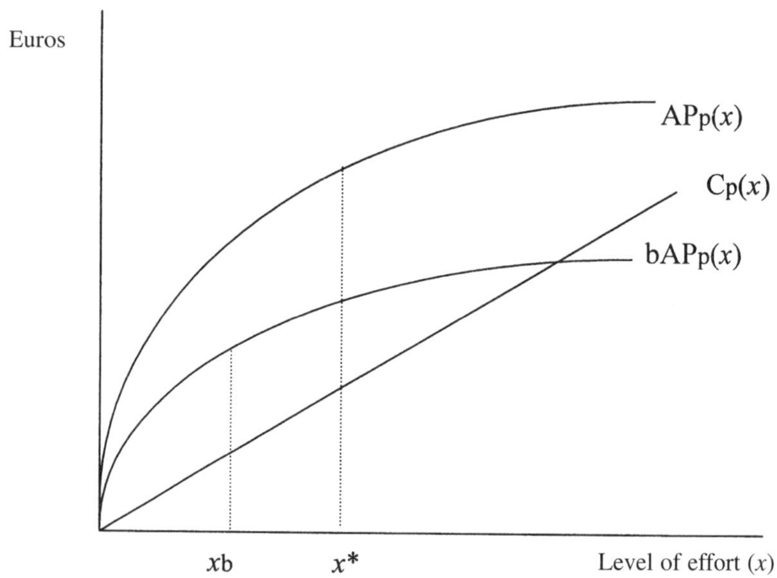

Figure 5.2 Contingent fees and lawyer effort

[36] Miceli (2004), p. 260.

[37] Recall A refers to the 'award', Pp the 'probability with which plaintiff expects to win the case', and Cp 'the costs borne by plaintiff in making case'.

A rational lawyer will select his level of effort to maximize his own returns. He therefore maximizes bAPp(x) – Cp(x), which results in a positive level of effort, xb. This is still less than the optimal effort level, which occurs at x^*.

Contingent fee arrangements, however, create other conflicts of their own. Let us take a close look at lawyers' incentives at the stage of accepting a case, at settlement negotiations and at trial.

Incentives for accepting a case

Lawyers, if paid by the hour for time devoted to a case, have incentives to accept a case even where the expected legal costs exceed the expected award for clients, given that they will be paid regardless of the outcome. Numerous cases may be accepted that are of questionable merit.[38] This contrasts somewhat with contingency fees, whereby if a case is not promising, a lawyer will not want to spend time on it for a low expected fee. Contingent fees may, therefore, reduce the number of frivolous suits, given that where the lawyer has a financial stake in the claim he is unwilling to take them on in the first place. Given the fact, however, that lawyers only receive a percentage of the gains from suit but bear most (or all) of the costs, it is likely that some cases with expected net gains will not be accepted.

Contingent fee arrangements, nevertheless, may be difficult to structure due to the substantial uncertainty in the relationship between legal effort and outcome, and the unpredictability of the law.[39] The lawyer, in order to come up with an appropriate fee, therefore, has to produce what he considers a reasonable estimate of the probability of winning. This is especially difficult to do at the beginning of the lawyer–client relationship, before the lawyer has had the chance to investigate the law, the facts, and his client's reliability.[40] These factors will limit the level of competition on contingency percentages between lawyers for clients. On average, the equilibrium contingency percentage must be set so that the expected compensation of similar lawyers under the conventional contingent fee system approximates comparable hourly wages.[41] (For similar lawyers in fact these fees should probably be slightly higher, as a form of risk premium.) The fee paid to the lawyer in the event of a win, therefore, has to be superior to the fee received where he works on an hourly basis, given

---

[38] Despite the fact that obligations exist upon lawyers in most countries not to file frivolous claims or defences, it is notoriously costly to screen out such actions, primarily because of the issues discussed above, such as the complexity of the law and the fact that it is difficult – even for experts – ex post to establish the value of lawyers' actions.

[39] Hadfield (2000), p. 979.

[40] Ibid.

[41] Polinsky and Rubinfeld (2003), p. 172.

that the lawyer is only going to be remunerated where the plaintiff does not lose a case. If the probability of losing a case were 0.5, then a rational lawyer would charge at least double what he could expect under an hourly or fixed fee arrangement for the same case.

Incentives in settlement negotiations

Lawyers who are paid by the hour may have strong incentives to prolong settlement negotiations in order to clock up more hours. Plaintiffs on the other hand are willing to settle where the gains from settlement are greater than going to trial; that is, $S \geq APp(x) - Cp$, where S denotes settlement. This conflict of interests may result in trial, depending on the lawyer's opportunity costs and the ability of the plaintiff (and the court) to influence settlement negotiations. Under contingency fee arrangements plaintiffs, however, will opt for trial too often, given that they do not factor the legal fees borne by the lawyer into their decision to go to trial; that is, $S \geq APp(x)$. For lawyers on the other hand the incentive to go to trial is too low under contingent fees, given that they bear the costs of litigation but obtain only a percentage of the award; that is, $bS \geq bAPp(x) - Cp$. Switching to contingent fees, therefore, creates a conflict of interests between clients and their lawyers at the settlement stage. This problem can be mitigated, however, where the fraction of the settlement offered to lawyers is lower than the fraction awarded at trial.

Incentives at trial

Lawyers paid on an hourly fee basis have incentives to drag cases out in order to create more work for themselves. Under a contingent fee system, however, as was the case for settlement negotiations, lawyers have incentives to work less given that they bear the entire costs of trial and only obtain a fraction of the award.

Lawyers' purchase claims

Economists have often suggested that the optimal scenario would be to completely sell the case to a lawyer. The reasoning behind this position is that it would create efficient incentives for lawyers to maximize their efforts (that is, to x* in our graph) because they would internalize the costs and benefits of the claims, and it may also lead to allocation of risk to a superior risk bearer. This type of contract is forbidden in every legal system that we are aware of.[42]

[42] In the United States, this is barred by the doctrine of champerty, according to which it is considered unethical for a lawyer to pursue a claim in consideration for receiving all or a substantial portion of the financial rewards from the case. See 14 Am. Jur. 2d, Champerty and Maintenance, sections 1–15 (2000).

One reason put forward for this is that it may lead to lawyers stirring up litigation.[43] Another is related to the fact that plaintiffs may be exploited because they do not have sufficient information to evaluate claims, which could lead to the market breaking down.[44] Another reason may be moral hazard on the part of plaintiffs. Once a suit is purchased, they have little incentive to optimize the interests of lawyers. Whilst the purchasing of contracts would solve the former principal–agent problem (with lawyers as agents and litigants as principals), it may create a different principal–agent problem, based on the familiar factors of information asymmetry and moral hazard, this time on the side of the plaintiff.

6.1 Conditional Fees versus Contingent Fee Arrangements

Now let us consider conditional fee arrangements, which have acquired some footing in Europe. Though they may take many forms, essentially under a conditional fee type arrangement a lawyer receives a mark-up on his legal fee if his client wins a case. This mark-up may reach 100 per cent of his fee. The lawyer is paid on a 'no win, no fee' basis. If he loses the case, he receives no compensation.

Incentives for accepting a case

Do conditional fees encourage low-quality suits? The simple answer to this, as in the case of contingent fees, is no. Plaintiffs will be interested in bringing lower-quality cases, but, given that lawyers do not get paid unless they win a case, they have strong incentives to weed out weak cases. This can be illustrated with a simple example.

Recall that under the European rule the condition to sue was $A.Pp - (1 - Pp)(Cd + Cp) > 0$. Let us assume that it is the successful plaintiff that pays the mark-up on legal fees and not the losing defendant. Under a conditional fee type arrangement, this looks like $(A - d)Pp - (1 - Pp)(Cd)$, where d is the cost based on the mark up for the lawyer's fee when successful.

Let us imagine a case where the amount in dispute, A, is equal to €100 000. The costs for the plaintiff of presenting the case, Cp, are equal to €20 000 and the costs for the defendant in presenting his case, Cd, are equal to €20 000. The probability of a successful claim is 0.25. Under the European rule (loser pays), the plaintiff has no incentive to bring a case forward under a normal fee-paying arrangement: $EBp = (€100\,000 \times 0.25) - (0.75 \times €40\,000) = -€5000$. The plaintiff would not bring suit. Now consider the case with conditional

43 Miceli (2004), p. 260.

44 Ibid.

fees. EBp = (€100 000 – €20 000) × 0.25 – (0.75 × €20 000) = €5000. The plaintiff therefore has incentives to bring low-value cases forward, where he formerly did not. (Recall that the same thing occurs under contingent payments.) However, we have left lawyers' incentives out of the equation. A lawyer under conditional fee arrangements, as with contingent fee arrangements will be less willing to take a case if it is not promising, as he would be doing so for a low expected fee. Conditional fees, like contingent fees, may, therefore, reduce the number of frivolous suits, given that where the lawyer has a financial stake in the claim he is unwilling to take them on in the first place. In the aforementioned example, lawyer's compensation under a conditional fee arrangement is €40 000 × 0.25 = €10 000, which is less than the €20 000 he would have received on an hourly fee basis.

For stronger claims, where Pp is high, the benefits for plaintiffs of using conditional fees will be reduced unless the size of d, based on the mark up on legal fees, is reduced. Consider the following. As in the above, let the amount in dispute, A, be equal to €100 000. Again, the costs for the plaintiff of presenting the case, Cp, are equal to €20 000 and the costs for the defendant in presenting his case, Cd, are equal to €20 000. Let the probability of being successful, however, be 0.6. Under the European rule (loser pays), the expected payoffs (under normal fee-paying arrangements) for plaintiff in bringing a suit are equal to (€100 000 × 0.6) – (0.4 × €40 000) = €44 000. Under a conditional fee arrangement, however, the expected benefits for plaintiff of bringing a suit are equal to (€100 000 – €20 000) × 0.6 – (0.5 × €20 000) = €38 000, with d = 100 per cent. The plaintiff would therefore receive higher compensation under a regular hourly fee arrangement.

Incentives for settlement

Under a conditional fee arrangement, the lawyer has less incentive to settle than was the case under contingent fees. This is hardly surprising given that the lawyer's income is not tied to the award, but is once again based upon the number of hours worked. Lawyers – provided they are confident of having a positive value claim – have incentives to clock up the hours, as was the case on an hourly fee basis. Allowing successful plaintiffs to receive the mark-up on lawyer fees from losing defendants, as has been the case in England and Wales subject to regulations introduced in 2000, makes the problem even worse.

Inventives at trial

As in settlement negotiations, there are clear incentives for confident lawyers to prolong cases under conditional fee arrangements, given that they are still paid by the hour and even receive a mark-up on their fees. Reforms in the UK now allow success fees to be passed on to the losing side and victims to take out after-the-event insurance, which can be passed on to the losing side if they win. Any incentives plaintiffs had to control their lawyers are clearly out the window. Moreover, in relation to the sunk cost auction game discussed in Section 5, once the parties are actually at the trial stage we can expect them to fight even harder, as the stakes have been raised for the defendant, as well as for the plaintiff's lawyers should they lose a case.

7. RESTRICTIVE PRACTICES IN THE PROVISION OF LEGAL SERVICES

The notion of anti-competitive practices and monopolies in the legal profession has found its way into academic and – more importantly – policy circles in recent years. One of the key characteristics of legal services is that they are generally delivered by a self-regulated body. The literature in law and economics has highlighted several features commonly supported by the profession that restrict competition and may damage public welfare: (1) restrictions on entry to the profession are quite common as are (2) restrictions on who can provide legal services; (3) commonplace also are limits placed on advertising and the promotion of competition within the profession; (4) organizational form is often highly regulated and (5) there are restrictions on fee competition and/or fee contracts between clients and their lawyers.

7.1 Entry to the Legal Profession

Restrictions on entry to markets are one of the most studied areas of microeconomics. The dangers highlighted by these studies are clear: barriers to entry can lead to supply shortages and economic rents for suppliers. Moreover, this generally leads to high prices and low quality, which are passed on to the consumers of these goods and services. In a competitive market, the response to high incomes is that others enter the market offering the same good or service, thus correcting the aforementioned. In markets characterized by restrictive barriers to entry, this occurs less. Moreover, restrictive practices have tended to affect women and minorities to a greater extent.

One of the clearest developments in the legal profession in recent years is that it has not been very successful in controlling admissions. Numbers have continued to grow. Consider Germany, for instance (Figure 5.3). In 1970, there were 23 599 lawyers (data published by German Federal Bar Association (*Bundesrechtsanwallskammer*), see http://www.brak.de.). By 1980 this number had increased to 37 314. In 1990, there were 59 455 and by 2003 there were 126 793 lawyers in Germany. Between 1970 and 1991 (the last year for statistics prior to unification), the absolute number of lawyers increased by 4.6

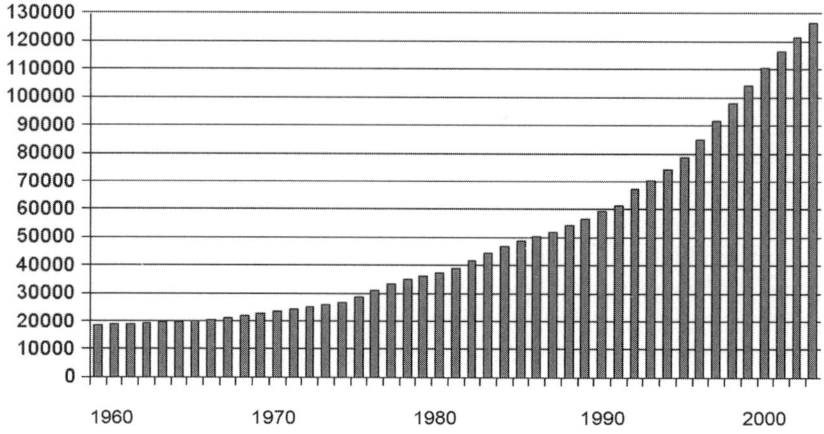

Source: German Federal Bar Association

Figure 5.3 Growth in number of lawyers in Germany

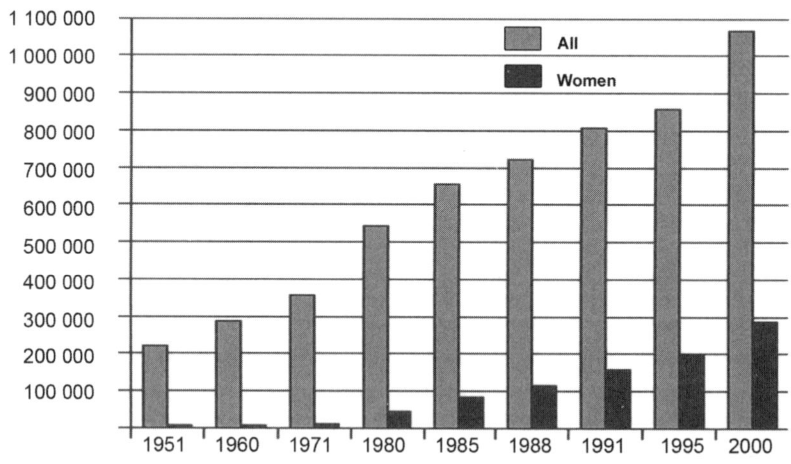

Sources: Curran et al. (1985); Curran and Carson (1994, 2004)

Figure 5.4 Growth in number of lawyers in the United States

per cent per year. Between 1993 and 2003, the absolute number of lawyers increased on average by 5.96 per cent per year. The number of women entering the profession has continued to increase substantially. Whilst the proportion of female trainee lawyers (*Referendarinnen*) was 28.93 per cent in 1982, by 2004 this number had reached 47.5 per cent, or approximately half of all trainees.

The American Bar Association has not been capable of controlling entrance to the profession in recent years (see Figure 5.4). Current American Bar Association (ABA) statistics indicate that there are 1 116 967 lawyers (year 2006). ABA-accredited law schools have an estimated 148 698 students, with 49 920 JDs or LLBs awarded (year 2006). In 1980, 92 per cent of all lawyers in the US were male. By 1991, the number of female lawyers had risen from 8 to 20 per cent. By 2000, it had reached 27 per cent. In 2003–04, 49 per cent of JD enrolled students were female, 51 per cent male, and 20.6 per cent from ethnic minorities.[45] In 2000, 74 per cent of lawyers were working in private practice, with 8 per cent in government and a further 8 per cent in private industry; 5 per cent were retired/inactive and a further 3 per cent were active in the judiciary; 1 per cent of lawyers were active in education, the legal aid/public defender sector and private associations.[46]

As of 31 July 2006, there were some 104 543 practising solicitors in England and Wales, which represented a 234.5 per cent increase over 1976

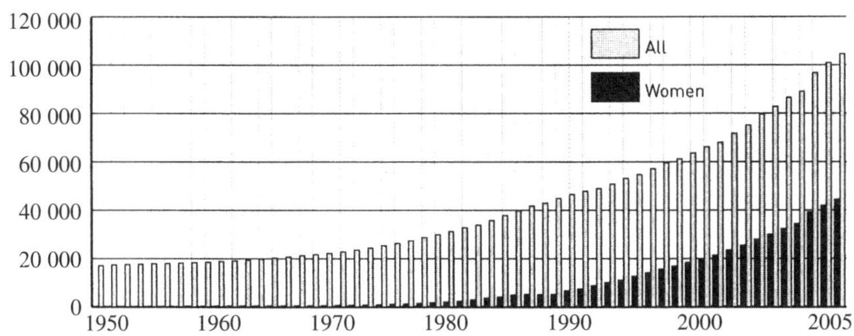

Source: Cole (2006)

Figure 5.5 Growth in number of solicitors with practicing certificates in England

[45] See ABA, Section of Legal Education and Admissions to the Bar, available at http://www.abanet.org/legaled/statistics/stats.html.

[46] See Curran and Carson (2004).

(4.1 per cent on average per year) (see Figure 5.5). Of these, 77.1 per cent work in private practice, with 8.2 per cent working in commerce and industry, 3.5 per cent in government, and 2.2 per cent for the Crown Prosecution Service. A further 7.2 per cent are not attached to any organization, and are composed in large part by the young and recently qualified. Women now account for 42.8 per cent of solicitors that practise the profession. Whilst the number of solicitors holding practising certificates has grown by 53.7 per cent since 1996, the number of women who can practise has more than doubled, having increased by 107.9 per cent.[47] As of July 2005, there were 14 623 practising barristers in England and Wales, 67.1 per cent of whom were male and 32.9 per cent female. Ethnic minorities represented approximately 11 per cent. In 2005, 527 persons received pupillage, of whom 50.9 per cent were men and 49.1 per cent women.[48] There were 11 818 self-employed members of the bar and 2805 employed barristers.

Clearly, one of the most striking features in the market for lawyers is that the numbers of men and women entering the profession are roughly equal in most developed countries, but the number of women that actually reach the level of partner in important law firms is very modest. If we examine the largest European law firms in terms of revenue generated, there are surprisingly few women in the upper echelons of these organizations. In the top three firms by revenue in Europe, Freshfields Bruckhaus Deringer, Clifford Chance and Linklaters – all headquartered in the UK – the percentage of female partners in 2005 was 13.3, 19.2 and 15.2 per cent respectively.[49] Only 7.75 per cent of partners in the largest law firm in France, Fidal, were female. In Garrigues, the largest law firm in Spain and continental Europe, female partners were only 11.4 per cent of total partners. Whilst attrition rates for women in the profession are generally higher, this does not seem to fully explain the gap. Other restrictive practices seem to be at work and deserve further study.

Another feature of the market for legal services is that, while entry restrictions to the legal profession do seem to be on the decline globally, some countries still seem to be lagging behind. The moral hazard of having the legal profession control entry to the market for legal services is clear. Entry in Ireland is monopolized by those in the profession, with the Law Society controlling who may train to be a solicitor and the Honourable Society of King's Inns controlling who may train to be a barrister. They also decide both the location and format of training. Potential solicitors and barristers must

---

47 See Cole (2007), p. 14.
48 Davies (2005), p. 5.
49 All calculations are based on The Lawyer (2005).

accept the format of the training (full-time/part-time/weekends), as there is only one choice on offer. This arrangement excludes many individuals from entering the profession. Unlike in many other common law jurisdictions, there is thus only one accredited institution for each type of legal training. A new report by the Irish Competition Authority recommends transferring the setting of standards of legal education from the aforementioned to a Legal Services Commission, which would confer rights upon various institutions for the training of solicitors and barristers.[50]

Restrictions on entry to the profession may have been weakened, but competition in specific service markets has not necessarily been the result. Professional service markets are still often subject to inefficient demarcations; for example, in many countries existing members of the legal profession are not entitled to appear before courts outside the local area in which they have been admitted. In some cases, entry barriers may be more subtle. For instance, in Ireland in the past individuals wishing to practise as a solicitor or barrister were subjected to an Irish language test, despite the fact that Irish is rarely the language of the courts and all matters are generally conducted in English. These types of measures clearly potentially disadvantage foreigners wishing to practise as lawyers and solicitors. Moreover, acquiring permission to practise as a legal professional is clearly not a guarantee of entry into the legal market, particularly where much of the work is still done at a local level, restrictions to advertising still exist and firms do not compete on fees.

7.2 Who Can Provide Legal Services?

Lawyers often enjoy a monopoly on the provision of various services for which there may be no justification. Specialists working in different markets, such as accountancy, conveyancing and insurance are frequently sufficiently informed to offer advice in their areas of expertise.

England and Wales revoked the sole right of solicitors to provide conveyancing services as professionals in the 1980s. The results on the whole have been rather disappointing. Conveyancers have only secured around 5 per cent of the value of the market for conveyancing. (The UK Department for Constitutional Affairs does point out that the cost of conveyancing a £65 000 house fell on average by 25 per cent between 1989 and 1998.) Whilst competition on the whole produced a drop in price in those areas where it took hold, after a few years the gains were substantially reduced. One explanation may be that conveyancers have similar interests to solicitors in keeping the price up. As Stephen and Love suggest, 'the limited effects of

[50] Irish Competition Authority (2006).

removing a monopoly in a restricted field, as in this case, may not carry over to a more general removal of monopoly rights.'[51]

Societies that have introduced much more competition in the provision of services would appear to have been far more successful in reducing costs for legal services (as well as delays in litigation). In the Netherlands, for example, where lawyers may charge what they wish and by the hour, legal advice may be provided by persons and organizations other than lawyers. Insurance companies provide clients with dispute resolution services and lawyers employed by companies and other bodies are able to represent their employers in court.[52] Trade unions and similar organizations offer legal advice as part of their membership services, and legal cost insurers offer their own consultation and representation in lower courts. Zuckerman argues:

> The fact that lawyers do not have a complete monopoly over legal services has two effects. First, it has kept down the cost of litigation. Second, it has prompted the legal profession to develop skills and services which compete favourably with other providers of services.[53]

Blankenburg conducted a study of traffic accidents and ensuing litigation as a result of their occurrence in North-Rhine Westphalia and the Netherlands.[54] He found not only that fewer reported traffic-related injuries reached the courts in the Netherlands compared with Germany (0.1–0.2 per cent compared with 1–2 per cent) but also that there were fewer disputes regarding traffic accidents. The explanation put forward for this lies with the practice of legal advice and negotiations by insurance companies. In Germany, lawyers enjoy a monopoly right on the provision of legal advice as established by the law, whilst in the Netherlands various professions and institutions provide this service. Intervention by attorneys in the settlement of traffic-related disputes is the exception rather than the rule. Injuries resulting from traffic accidents are generally resolved by employees of insurance companies, who may offer legal advice to the parties, rather than having claims formulated by attorneys.

7.3 Advertising

The legal profession has traditionally sought to limit or place an outright ban on other factors promoting competition, such as advertising and quoting fees

51 Stephen and Love (2000), p. 996.
52 Zuckerman (1999), p. 45.
53 Ibid.
54 Blankenburg (1994).

in advance of work. The arguments are often along the lines that advertising and other measures that promote competition lead to the commercialization of the profession, thus lowering ethical standards and the quality of legal service. Recent deregulation reforms have seen restrictions on advertising relaxed to varying degrees (see Table 5.1).

The economic argument in support of advertising is that it is an information provider and as such can reduce information costs and the costs of using the market. Advertising can thus reduce price dispersions and enhance quality. Price advertising generally should be welfare enhancing because it improves customer choice.[55] The nature of the market for legal services, however, limits the positive impacts normally associated with price advertising in other markets.[56] This is due to the fact that legal services are credence goods, as we have seen above, which makes it difficult to assess their quality and value. Clients might believe lawyers differ in quality, but it is very difficult to determine precisely to what extent. They therefore have to estimate quality on the basis of various inferences, including price, as well as numerous other factors, such as firm size, list of other clients, location, and word of mouth. Lawyers, given the difficulty of signalling quality, may be reticent about offering their services at a low price. It is possible, therefore, that price advertising becomes an adverse signal on quality. Put differently, offering services at a low price may be interpreted by some clients as an indication of low quality, particularly where clients assume the market price is a reflection of information attained by better-informed customers.

Empirical studies on advertising in the legal profession indicate that those firms that advertise charge lower fees on the whole and that fees are lower on average where advertising is allowed.[57] In line with the aforementioned analysis, non-price (quality) advertising is more common than price advertising, with only a few per cent of those who advertise displaying the price of services. Price advertising would appear to work well in markets where the quality of the service is relatively homogeneous. Given the difficulty of measuring the quality of legal services, it is not surprising that empirical studies using various proxies for quality have not been capable of coming up with conclusive answers on whether price advertising increases or decreases quality.

---

55 Stephen and Love (2000), p. 997.

56 Advertising can also lead to collusion. We are all familiar with notices where a store suggests that it guarantees the lowest price to a customer, and if a customer finds an even lower price it will return his money. A store is, in effect, indicating to other stores what it is willing to sell a product for. Should another firm deviate from this price, a customer may return to the store and demand the difference between what they paid and what is available elsewhere. Thus, the customer may actually be enforcing a cartel-like agreement, because it acts as a monitor against price cutting.

57 For a list of these studies, see Stephen and Love (2000) and Garoupa (2004).

Table 5.1 Advertising restrictions

	England and Wales	US	Germany	Belgium	Nether-lands	Spain	Portugal	France	Austria	Norway
Advertising is allowed subject to the same constraints as other services?	NO	NO	NO	NO	NO	NO	NO	NO	NO	NO
The state restricts the advertising of attorneys relative to other services?	NO	YES	YES	YES	NO	NO	NO	NO	YES	YES
The self-regulatory body restricts the advertising of attorneys?	YES	NO	YES	NO	YES	YES	YES	YES	YES	YES
Advertising is very limited (e.g. phone book and the name plate)?	NO	NO	NO	NO	NO	NO	NO	NO	NO	NO
Special expertise can be advertised?	YES	YES	YES	YES	YES	YES	YES	YES	YES	YES
Fee level can be advertised?	YES	YES	NO	NO	YES	NO	YES	NO	NO	YES
Is comparative advertising possible?	NO	YES	NO	NO	NO	NO	NO	NO	NO	NO
Cooperation with other attorneys can be advertised?	YES	YES	YES	YES	YES	YES	YES	YES	YES	YES
Cooperation with foreign attorneys or partners can be advertised?	YES	YES	YES	YES	YES	YES	YES	YES	YES	YES

Source: Garoupa (2004)

7.4 Organizational Forms

Comparing professional businesses with other enterprises active in manufacturing and retail, we see that the latter are often organized as public corporations with shareholders and hired managers. In the former, organizations are structured typically as partnerships. These include not just law firms, but consultancy firms, accountancy firms, medical practices, advertising agencies and architectural practices.[58] Even investment banks were organized as partnerships until recently.[59]

It is common for the organizational structure of legal service providers to be subject to strict restrictions. Incorporation is often restricted, and, even if incorporation is permitted, unlimited liability is maintained and managers are members of the legal profession. Moreover, multi-disciplinary partnerships involving members of more than one profession, such as lawyers and accountants, are often prohibited or limited[60] (see Table 5.2). In England and Wales, for instance, there are strict rules governing outside ownership interests, including:

- rules prohibiting partnership between barristers and between barristers and other professionals (lawyers and non-lawyers). Employed barristers may work for solicitor firms, but may not with re-qualification become partners
- rules prohibiting solicitors from entering partnership with members of other professions (lawyers and non-lawyers)
- rules preventing – in large part – solicitors in the employment of business organizations not owned by solicitors (including banks and insurance companies) from providing services to third parties.[61]

Justifications for restrictions on organizational structure are sometimes made along agency lines. Accordingly, given the difficulty in assessing quality and performance, sole practitioners and professional partnerships are the most likely and least costly form of organization to mitigate agency problems.[62] The General Council of the Bar of England (the Bar Council) adds a different twist to the story.[63] It argues that the prohibition of partnerships between self-employed barristers on the grounds that it widens choice and

---

58 Brealey and Franks (2005).
59 Ibid.
60 Garoupa (2004).
61 Brealey and Franks (2005), p. 6.
62 Garoupa (2004), p. 20.
63 See Bar Council (2001).

Table 5.2 Structure of law firms

	England and Wales	US	Germany	Belgium	Nether-lands	Spain	Portugal	France	Austria	Norway
Can attorneys enter into partnerships?	YES	YES	YES	YES	YES	YES	YES	YES	YES	YES
Can attorneys enter into multidisciplinary partnerships?	NO	NO	YES	YES	YES	YES	NO	NO	NO	NO
Can attorneys incorporate?	YES	YES	YES	NO	YES	NO	NO	YES	NO	YES
With respect to incorporation, do any further restrictions apply?	YES	YES	YES	–	YES	–	–	YES	–	YES

Source: Garoupa (2004)

competition, principally because those within the same firm cannot represent competing parties in a case. It particularly warns against the dangers of partnerships between self-employed barristers who have specialized in the same field of the law, suggesting that this would lead to a restricted choice on the market for these services.

There are numerous costs associated with these types of organizational limitations. For one, benefits associated with economies of scale may not be realized. The provision of legal services through larger groups can further specialization in various aspects of the law, thereby reducing the costs of providing services. Moreover, there may be benefits associated with risk spreading, as specialities may be subject to business cycles and thus income can be spread out among the group.[64] Restrictions on organizational form may also prevent the realization of economies of scope, where multiple services could be provided cost effectively by a single firm and a client could avail of all of these services without having to incur the costs of searching for another firm.

In the United Kingdom and Ireland, the legal profession is divided into two key branches – namely solicitors and barristers. Though the traditionally sharp dichotomy is showing signs of softening around the edges, it still remains rather firm. Solicitors have traditionally been involved in non-contentious aspects of legal service provision, including property conveyancing contracts, wills and estates, trust, and advice/correspondence. The solicitor also deals directly with clients at first instance, giving them advice and engaging a barrister on their behalf, as well as arranging meetings with expert witnesses, medical examinations, and so on. Moreover, they may represent clients before the lower courts. Barristers, on the other hand, have rights of audience before all courts, and represent litigating parties and plead their cases. Is there an economic justification for this dichotomy? A separation between service function (assessing and diagnosing a problem) and the agency function (implementing a correct solution) may assist in the reduction of opportunism and create incentives for the revealing of information. On the other hand, such a prohibition prevents gains that may be derived from vertical integration, including benefits associated with economies of scale and the hold-up problem.[65] The economics literature on the efficiency of this separation is inconclusive.

What are the current tendencies in the organizational structure of law firms? It may be surprising to some but a great number of lawyers are still solo practitioners in the United States. In 1991, 45 per cent were sole practitioners;

---

64 Stephen and Love (2000), p. 1005.

65 Garoupa (2004), Stephen (2003) Emons (1997).

in 2000 this figure had reached 48 per cent. Some 15 per cent are active in law firms composed of between two and five lawyers, and 7 per cent in law firms composed of six to ten lawyers. The number of lawyers working in firms of between 11 and 50 lawyers has remained constant in recent years (13 per cent in 1980 compared with 12 per cent in 2000), while 14 per cent of American lawyers are active in law firms of 101 lawyers or more (year 2000).[66] In 2006, the largest law firm with its main office based in the United States was DLA Piper, with 3623 attorneys; the second largest is Baker and McKenzie, with 3335 lawyers, both of which are Chicago-based. There are 25 law firms in total with their main offices in the US that employ over 1000 attorneys.[67]

In England and Wales, as of 31 July 2006, 8.3 per cent of solicitors working in private practice were sole practitioners; 22.8 per cent were working in firms of two to four solicitors, 15.7 per cent were active in firms of between five and ten solicitors and 14.1 per cent were active in firms of between 11 and 25 solicitors. Like their American counterparts, the number of solicitors that practise in large firms is quite substantial: 17 per cent work in firms of between 26 and 80 solicitors, whilst 22.2 per cent work in firms that employ 81 or more solicitors.[68] In 2006 four of the seven largest law firms by revenue in the world were based in London; these were Clifford Chance, Allen and Overy LLP, Freshfields Bruckhaus Deringer, and Linklaters. Clifford Chance is also the largest law firm in the world in terms of lawyers, employing 3892 attorneys.

Continental Europe seems to be observing similar developments though with differences between the countries. Whilst the number of sole practitioners and small partnerships is still substantial, current trends indicate a shift towards larger partnerships and corporations, as well as multi-disciplinary organizations, where they are permitted. The largest law firm in Spain is Garrigues, which is also the largest law firm in all of continental Europe, with a staff of 1563 lawyers.[69] There are four other law firms of over 100 lawyers.[70] France has 12 firms of over 100 lawyers, the largest of which is Fidal with 1285 lawyers, followed a long way back by Landwell and Associés with 660 lawyers. In Germany the largest law firms are rather small by comparison. The largest law firm operating in Germany is Freshfields Bruckhaus Deringer,

---

66 Curran et al. (1985); Curran and Carson (1994, 2004).

67 As reported in the National Law Journal's 30th Annual Survey of America's 250 largest law firms. For a firm to be included in the survey, it must have more lawyers based in the United States than any other country. Moreover, it does not include contract or temporary lawyers.

68 Cole (2007), p. 22.

69 All data derived from the Legal500.com, available at www.legal500.com.

70 These are Cuatrecasas (654 lawyers), Uría Menéndez (402 lawyers), Gómez-Acebo and Pombo Abogados (216 lawyers) and Clifford Chance (159 lawyers).

which has 594 lawyers on its payroll. This is followed by Clifford Chance and Lovells LLP, which have 594 and 330 lawyers respectively.

7.5 Legal Fees

Legal fees have been subjected to regulation in one form or another in most jurisdictions in Europe. Fees have been subject to regulation by the courts, the states or the profession itself via mandatory fee schedules.[71] Mandatory scales that prevailed over much of Europe have gradually been transformed into recommendations, and in recent years these recommendations have started to be replaced by the market.

Recommended fee scales have proven to be difficult to enforce, as members of the profession can easily sell services at prices below those agreed or recommended by the profession. As we know from cartel theory, this is due in particular to the fact that a large number of members and transactions frustrates monitoring and collusive practices. Where bargaining exists between lawyers and their clients, we can expect scale fees to perhaps best serve as a focal point in negotiations.

Legal fees can thus now be freely negotiated in most Western European countries, and the more competent lawyers generally charge higher fees.[72] The most important exception is contingency fee type arrangements, where lawyers have a stake in the outcome. (This was discussed at length above.) Fees are generally based on hours worked, litigation value and the complexity of the case.[73] The most common arrangement is based on hourly fees or flat fees. Conditional fees were introduced in the 1990s in the UK, and were later introduced in Belgium and the Netherlands. The Netherlands is apparently considering allowing contingent fees.[74] As adumbrated above, fees resulting from legal aid, though generally lower than normal fees, supplement some lawyers' incomes.

---

[71] Stephen and Love (2000).

[72] In Germany, however, lawyers' remuneration may be calculated on the basis either of the Lawyer's Remuneration Act (*Rechtanwaltungsvergütungsgesetz*) or negotiated fees. Negotiated fees which exceed the statutory level are always possible but negotiated fees cannot be lower than those prescribed by statute.

[73] Garoupa (2004), p. 18.

[74] Emons and Garoupa (2004).

8. APPENDIX: TOP LAW FIRMS BY REVENUE

Table 5.3 Law firms by revenue (2005)

Rank	Firm	Turnover (£m)	PEP (£k)	Country	Profit (£m)	Margin (%)
1	Clifford Chance	1030.2	810	UK	309.6	30
2	Linklaters	935.2	1063	UK	375.3	40
3	Skadden ARPS Slate Meagher & Flom	884.6	1049	US	395.6	45
4	Freshfields Bruckhaus Deringer	882.1	830	UK	432.3	49
5	Latham & Watkins	776.1	879	US	356.9	46
6	Baker & Mckenzie	742.9	418	US	251.0	34
7	Allen & Overy	736.3	788	UK	269.7	37
8	Jones Day	706.0	396	US	191.1	27
9	Sidley Austin	617.6	679	US	209.7	34
10	White & Case	574.7	681	US	184.0	32
11	Weil Gotshal & Manges	558.5	1005	US	198.1	35
12	Mayer Brown Rowe & Maw	538.5	525	US	224.1	42
13	Kirkland & Ellis	533.0	1165	US	223.6	42
14	DLA Piper (US)	489.3	549	US	137.4	28
15	Sullivan & Cromwell	480.8	1324	US	209.2	44
16	Greenberg Traurig	472.8	599	US	147.9	31
17	Shearman & Sterling	458.8	761	US	144.6	32
18	WilmerHale	447.8	503	US	163.4	36

19	O'Melveny & Myers	444.0	887	US	193.4	44
20	Morgan Lewis & Bockius	442.0	549	US	137.4	31
21	Mcdermott Will & Emery	439.3	703	US	202.5	46
22	Cleary Gottlieb Steen & Hamilton	417.6	1077	US	183.1	44
23	Gibson Dunn & Crutcher	409.9	898	US	227.3	55
24	Simpson Thacher & Bartlett	399.5	1302	US	201.8	51
25	Lovells	396.2	571	UK	132.6	33

Source: The Lawyer (2006), p. 34

Table 5.4 Law firms by revenue in Europe (2004)

Country	Rank	Firm	Euro revenue (m)	Global revenue (m)	Profit (m)	Margin (%)	PEP (k)	Total equity partners	Total partners	Total lawyers	Global offices partners	Total female	Total female equity partners
UK	1	Freshfields Bruckhaus Deringer	1052.36	1157.01	457.65	43	994.88	460	460	1940	27	61	61
UK	2	Clifford Chance	980.14	1400.21	253.47	26	828.33	306	469	2080	29	90	38
UK	3	Linklaters	912.64	1061.20	341.73	37	993.41	344	415	1730	30	63	50
UK	4	Allen & Overy LLP	843.07	960.98	196.71	23	609.00	323	358	1643	25	51	37
UK	5	Lovells	514.98	555.66	221.75	43	869.60	255	297	1153	27	61	45
UK	6	Eversheds	436.57	436.57	83.66	19	486.39	172	335	1712	29	82	25
US	7	Baker & McKenzie	421.57	987.96	112.94	27	493.18	229	360	1193	69	65	26
US	8	DLA Piper Rudnick Gray Cary	387.34	405.32	77.01	20	700.10	110	310	1330	23	65	11
UK	9	Slaughter and May	328.99	365.53	132.78	40	1207.12	110	117	525	4	19	17
UK	10	Herbert Smith	322.49	358.15	99.05	31	1031.73	96	167	695	10	27	11
US	11	White & Case	285.61	766.72	100.00	35	884.98	113	242	854	38	44	29
UK	12	Ashurst	284.46	290.36	99.83	35	767.90	130	148	601	11	25	5
UK	13	Norton Rose	262.35	302.15	102.67	39	596.93	172	196	754	20	35	28
US	14	Fidal	250.00	250.00	26.71	11	109.00	245	245	1220	100	19	19
UK	15	CMS Cameron McKenna	238.03	246.00	74.01	31	611.67	121	135	537	10	20	20
UK	16	Simmons & Simmons	228.45	262.80	54.72	24	405.32	135	186	628	19	28	15
UK	17	Denton Wilde Sapte	223.89	174.00	56.05	25	479.02	117	189	650	13	55	31
US	18	Shearman & Sterling	221.25	619.49	85.12	38	1134.90	75	75	323	19	30	30
UK	19	Hammonds	199.71	199.71	37.68	19	400.90	94	202	689	17	45	20
NL	20	Loyens & Loeff N.V.	189.00	214.00	60.00	32	600.00	100	100	694	17	7	7
UK	21	Addleshaw Goddard	184.53	184.53	51.10	28	473.12	108	169	514	3	28	13
Sp	22	Garrigues	172.10	172.10	15.41	9	230.00	67	167	1201	26	19	4
US	23	Cleary Gottlieb Steen & Hamilton	160.00	545.34	85.43	53	1355.99	63	63	343	12	21	21
GER	24	Hengeler Mueller	157.85	157.85	65.28	41	859.00	76	76	195	5	3	3
UK	25	Berwin Leighton Paisner	150.33	150.33	35.71	24	626.41	57	125	330	2	26	10

Source: The Lawyer (2005)

6. Other key players in the litigation process

1. CIVIL LAW NOTARIES

Alongside the courts, legal systems have developed institutional mechanisms whose objective is to increment security in economic transactions. These mechanisms raise the guarantees given by parties with respect to the fulfilment of contractual agreements. In this sense, the existence of authenticated public documents and registries lends a hand in increasing levels of certainty in transactions and reducing the expected level of litigation. When we refer to notaries, it is important to be clear that notaries in common law countries exercise a very different role from notaries in civil law systems. In a country such as the United States, a notary is a 'citizen of high moral character and integrity' whose activities consist of witnessing and certifying documents and taking attestations and depositions, but he does not practice law. In fact lawyers are the only people entitled to give legal advice. The civil law notary – often called 'Latin notary' – however is a member of a legal profession who not only witnesses and certifies the validity of documents but also is entitled to give legal advice and, in fact, is often required to do so by law. He writes the documents he certifies, guarantees their legality and sometimes plays a role in the legal system similar to that exercised by judges and lawyers in the common law.[1]

Official authentication grants a weight of 'truthfulness' otherwise non-existent in documents of a strictly private nature. It is a function that is exclusively granted by the state. A significant number of civil servants in any of the branches of public administration grant 'official authentication' to documents. In the legal world, for example, court secretaries are the authenticators of documents pertaining to legal proceedings. In the realm of private law, it is the notaries who in the name of the state confer official authentication to documents.

Notarial activity must be understood in accordance with the basic principle, from an economic perspective, that a judicial system consists of a set of norms

---

[1] See Arruñada (1993).

and institutions that should reduce transaction costs and, as a consequence, increase the efficiency of an economy and the welfare of individuals in a society. Notarial intervention lends itself to these purposes in numerous ways. It serves as a means to reduce the rate of litigation, given that it prevents many cases from entering the adjudicative system that otherwise might have to be resolved by courts if parties' claims were based solely on private documentation. Moreover, in those cases that reach the courts, the existence of these publicly authenticated documents facilitates evidence and ensures that numerous issues covered by the officially authenticated documents are not discussed.

Having described some unquestionable benefits that public authentication by a notary can offer a judicial system, any discussion would be incomplete should we fail to take into consideration the costs involved. Notarial intervention is costly, and a public document is generally more expensive than a private document. If notary intervention is efficient, then it is so not because it does not have any costs but because these costs are inferior to its expected benefits.

Consider the case of a publicly certified mortgage document, utilizing the services of a notary. The intervention of a notary converts this document into a publicly authenticated document, with the privileges afforded to these documents by civil and commercial law. This legal control reinforces the guarantees offered by the parties, but it also imposes higher costs. From the perspective of efficiency, an increase in control of legality will be efficient if the marginal benefits accrued by the requirement are greater than its marginal costs. In this case net social benefits will be created. In Figure 6.1, the marginal benefits curve (MB) is falling because every increment in legal security obtained by greater levels of intervention by notaries and greater legal control implies a smaller increase in social welfare than the former increment, and tends towards zero in situations where legal security has reached a level where its expansion is redundant.

The marginal costs curve (MC) is, on the other hand, rising. Every new increment in security involves a marginal cost that is continuously increasing. As long as the marginal benefit of every increase in legal security is superior to the corresponding marginal cost (that is, for all those points to the left of s*) it will be efficient to assume additional costs that strengthen the legal security of a commercial transaction. But, once this point s* has been reached, any new increase in security will be inefficient, given that the associated costs exceed the benefits. The optimal level of legal security is, therefore, in this case the point represented by s*, that is, the level of legal security where marginal benefits are equal to the marginal costs, and thus marginal net benefits (defined as the difference between marginal benefits and marginal costs for each level of legal security) are equal to zero.

Where the use of a notary is not mandatory, the effect of excess demands

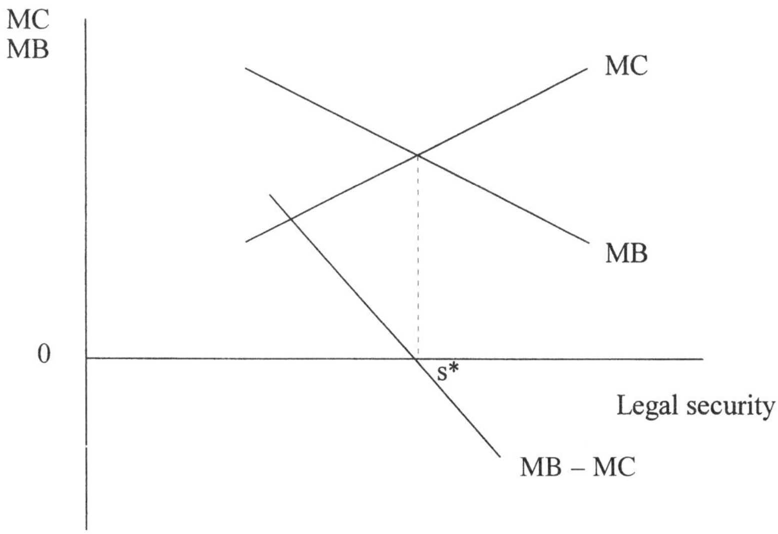

Figure 6.1 Costs and benefits of legal security

on legal security will be that parties turn to notaries less often. This will have adverse social costs, given the positive externalities that public authentication can generate. If official authentication is mandatory, excess legal security will result in an unjustified increase in price in civil and commercial transactions.

1.1 An Analysis of Costs and Benefits

Though from an economic point of view the argument on optimal use of notaries is clear, practical application in the real world is more complicated, primarily due to the difficulty of estimating the value of the variables in play. The costs of using notaries are quite clear, as fees are verifiable. A distinct and much more complex problem is related to the measure of the benefits of notarial activity. On the one hand, this is due to the fact that, for contracting parties, benefits consist of – to a large extent – a reduction in future risks that is difficult to quantify. Legal security acquired by official authentication by notaries reduces the probability of conflict and the need to go to court to a degree that can only be estimated by indirect means and with a substantial margin of error. On the other hand, not all of the benefits associated with public authentication by a notary are internalized by the contracting parties. Given that the resolution of conflicts via judicial means is strongly subsidized by the public sector, the use of public authentication – and the resulting reduction in legal proceedings

– has positive externalities for all of society. Moreover, the social benefits increase once we take into consideration the fact that the costs of legal proceedings are not limited strictly to the monetary costs of litigation to the parties involved. On the contrary, a significant percentage of the costs of litigation are often caused by the fact that judicial procedure obliges either the non-use or sub-optimal use of the goods or resources that are the object of a dispute, as is often the case in bankruptcy proceedings. An instrument that allows for a reduction in the duration of these procedures, therefore, allows for a further reduction in the social costs of litigation.

Despite the existence of these public benefits, however, there can be little doubt that the main beneficiaries of notarial authentication of documents are the economic agents directly involved. There is, then, a need to analyse how notarial intervention benefits each of these parties and how the costs of intervention are distributed among them. Let us return to our discussion on mortgage loan agreements. The first observable effect for those who buy a home is clearly the increase in costs as a result of using a notary. The obligation on a borrower to pay the costs of this intervention does not mean, however, that the real cost falls squarely on him. Though formally the costs of notarial intervention are supported in full by the borrower, this additional cost leads to a drop in demand for loans and credits. The reason for this is that the borrower, at the point of calculating the total price of acquiring a loan, does not merely take into consideration the interest that the bank will charge but considers all of the costs involved in the transaction, including those associated with the use of a notary.

Conventional analysis of this problem is presented in Figure 6.2. Here we have a market for loans, where equilibrium is represented by point A – determined by the intersection of the demand and supply curves. The curve S should, therefore, be understood as representing the supply of loans (by banks), and curve D as representing the demand for credit (by firms and individuals). Let us suppose that in equilibrium A notaries do not exist and, therefore, the costs of notarial intervention are zero. The interest rate at equilibrium i_1 represents the interest charged by banks.

Let us now introduce the notary into our analysis. The first effect of notarial activity is that loans become more expensive. The supply curve, therefore, shifts upwards relative to the costs of the intervention. Given that the marginal utility of receiving a loan by borrowers has not changed for firms and owners, the demand curve does not change. The result of the aforementioned is that we now have a new equilibrium B, which differs from A in two respects. First, the interest rate on a loan has now moved from i_1 to i_2. Second, there is a reduction in the volume of loans awarded, from L_1 to L_2.

It is easily observable that the distance that separates these two interest rates is inferior to the distance between both supply curves. The reason for this

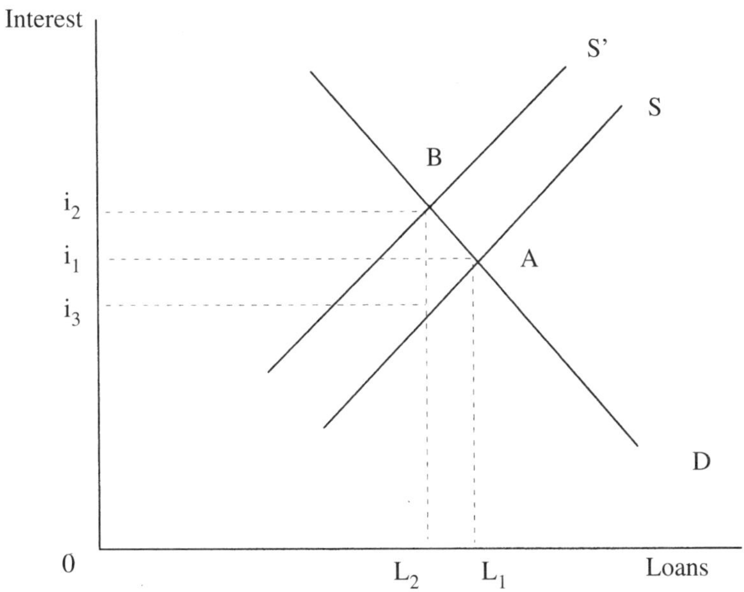

Figure 6.2 The distribution of costs in publicly certified documents (1)

is the following: given that the demand curve is falling borrowers reduce their demand for loans, and a part of the costs of intervention, represented by the distance between i_1 (the original equilibrium rate of interest) and i_3 (the rate of interest actually received by the banks in the new equilibrium), will be supported by the lenders. Conventional analysis of our case leads us then to the conclusion that the costs of intervention are divided between borrowers and lenders, depending on the elasticity of demand for loans. Banking institutions do support, nevertheless, a part of the costs of using a notary as a consequence of the reduced demand for loans brought about by intervention.[2] Conventional analysis is insufficient, however, for the case that we are looking at here, because notarial intervention that shifts the supply curve benefits the contracting parties.

Although the costs of notarial intervention were represented by a shift upwards in the supply curve, its impact has the opposite effect, since it reduces the interest rates charged by banks to borrowers. To understand the idea, one must disaggregate the various elements that constitute the rate of interest paid

2 Only in the most extreme case – which is difficult to imagine – in the presence of a perfectly inelastic demand for loans would banks support none of the costs of notarial intervention, and these would be borne entirely by borrowers.

on loans. First, there are the costs of using capital in the present, which depend fundamentally on temporary preferences in the market. Second, there are the costs of depreciation associated with money when inflation rates are positive. Third, there are the costs of intermediation of the financial entity. Last, but not least, there are the costs associated with the risk of a borrower defaulting on paying interest on the loan, and the costs of attempting to recover the loan where this is possible. The final effect is of greatest relevance to us here.

Formalizing a loan or credit in an official notarial document has two positive effects for banks. First, it reduces the costs of banking since, in the case of non-payment, the privileges afforded by the publicly certified document vis-à-vis a private document reduce the costs for the bank in recovering its loan. And second, the probability of recovering a loan is higher in bankruptcy cases if the credit has been publicly certified. The effect of these two factors is clearly the reduction of interest rates levied by banks on their clients. In the case of a reduction in transaction costs in debt collection, the effect is clearly positive, not only for the banks but also for the economic system as a whole. The second factor related to an increase in the probability of recuperating a loan vis-à-vis other creditors' causes is more complex for society as a whole, given that the increase in probability for banks of recovering a loan may be accompanied by a decrease in probability for other creditors who do not have an officially certified document. Most arguments, however, indicate that there will also in this case be an increase in social welfare, and bankruptcy laws maintain the privileges of these credits in most countries.[3]

If an increment in costs for a given volume of loans leads to an upward shift in the supply curve, a reduction in costs obviously entails a downward shift. We then find ourselves in a situation where there are two effects pushing in opposite directions, as is shown in Figure 6.3. Here we show both effects. In this figure we begin at the same equilibrium A, as defined in Figure 6.2. For reasons outlined above – reduced transaction costs and a significant reduction in the risk of non-repayment of a loan – it is reasonable to assume that the net result will be a supply curve S'' situated not just below S' but also below S. This curve S'' is what represents, therefore, the supply of loans by banks once they have taken into consideration the costs of intervention by notaries and the benefits related to the reduction in transaction costs and the risk of non-repayment. Our new equilibrium occurs at point E, where the volume of loans increases to L_3 and the total rate of interest paid by borrowers is reduced to i_4. Both the borrowers and lenders, therefore, benefit from the guarantees offered by officially authenticated documents.

[3] The classic article on the subject of creditor privileges is Schwartz, A. (1981). For an up-to-date bibliography on the subject, see Bowers (2000).

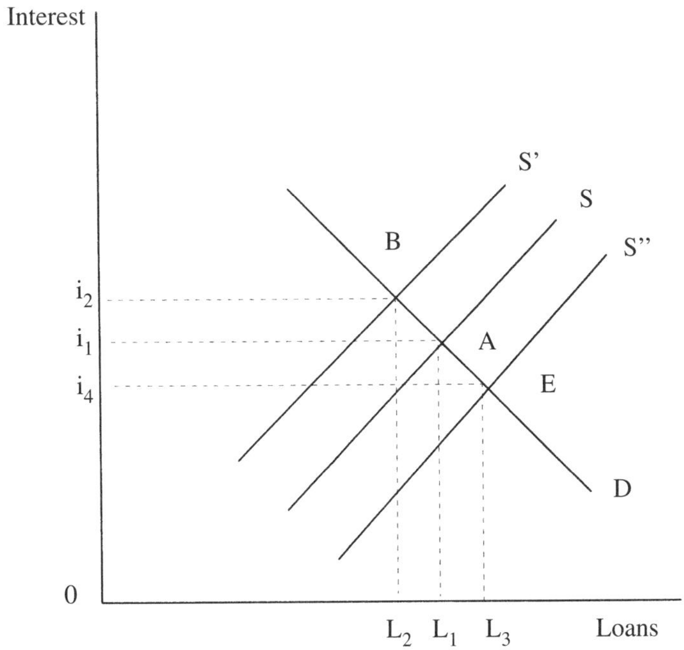

Figure 6.3 The distribution of costs in publicly certified documents (2)

1.2 Notaries and Competition

An important question in systems using the Latin notary is the cost of lack of competition among notaries. To wit, the European Commission has voiced its concern about the low level of competition among notaries in Europe. In 1999 a new Dutch Notary Act introduced important changes in the regulation of the notary profession in the Netherlands, with the main objectives being to allow competition on fees and a greater freedom of establishment. It is not surprising that the Dutch reforms are being carefully watched on the continent. Notary services are still a monopoly in the Netherlands but, pursuant to these reforms, Dutch notaries operate in a less regulated environment than their counterparts in other European countries. The basic issue can be traced back to the compatibility of the dual nature of notaries who act as both civil servants and professionals. With regard to their strict role as civil servants, the rules of competition are hardly applicable. What is relevant, however, is the regulation of notaries' activity as professionals. The regulation of officially recognized professions is based on the criterion of partial submission of the professions to the rules of antitrust. There are still specific provisions in many countries which accept restrictions on competition – such as obligatory association membership and the prohibition of new professional associations – and which would not be permitted in other sectors.

In European countries the organization of professions such as those of lawyer and doctor is traditional and some features of guild corporatism still remain. For many such professionals, free competition in the practice of their activities is not desirable. Most of the arguments against competition, however, are weak and simply reflect old-fashioned prejudice or the defence of monopoly rents on the part of the professionals involved. This is the case of all the arguments based, for example, on the need to reduce competition because of the high social function of the members of a specific profession, or the advisability of maintaining the 'dignity' of certain professions, which, in some people's opinion, might be harmed by having to compete in the search for customers. Other arguments carry more weight and justify the regulation of professions in terms of efficiency. But a different matter, as we shall see below, is the degree to which these arguments really support the regulation that exists today.

There is one sound argument for regulating the activities of professionals, namely the one based on information asymmetry between those offering the services – the professionals – and those requiring them – their customers.[4] There is fairly wide consensus amongst economists regarding the advisability of establishing a specific entry requirement in order to guarantee a minimum of quality in the practice of certain professions, restricting the activity to those people who have proved they have appropriate technical qualifications. Requirements for an academic qualification or the passing of competitive examinations in order to practise certain professions clearly constitute an entry barrier to a specific market but may form the basis for a system that will efficiently guarantee service quality.

However, certain comments should be made here. Firstly, the need for entry barriers is debatable for any type of profession. Companies are often happy to take on the services of business consultants who are not qualified economists but engineers or lawyers, for example. The degree of information asymmetry in such cases is much smaller than in other relations between professionals and their customers, so there is less need for regulation and it may be convenient to apply different regulations for different customers, with stricter regulation for individual customers and greater flexibility for companies. When companies require a specific professional service, they are more able than private persons to judge the competence of possible candidates. The conclusion here

[4] The seminal article on the effects of information assymmetries is Akerlof (1970).

would be that information asymmetry plays a much less important role in relations between professionals and companies than in relations between professionals and private persons. This, in turn, would justify a greater degree of regulation in the latter case than in the former.

Secondly, reservation of the activity does not necessarily mean that the administration or a professional association has to set fixed fees. The idea that a reduction in professional fees would lead to poor-quality services does not necessarily follow from the above model of information asymmetry. On the contrary, once a minimal level of quality has been guaranteed by the reservation of the activity, it would be reasonable to encourage competition amongst professionals. In many sectors, market functioning shows that price control does not always guarantee better product quality and in this case would serve, rather, just to push up revenue for the professionals involved.

To what degree can such considerations be applied to notaries? There are substantial differences in the industrial organization of notaries in civil law countries. While in countries like the Netherlands and Quebec effective competition among notaries exists and fees charged to consumers are determined by demand and supply in the market, in most civil law countries supply and prices are strictly controlled by public regulation. This makes the analysis of competition for such professionals working as civil servants especially complex because their monopolistic or quasi-monopolistic position is not due to the control of a market share through business strategies but to the fact that they are granted this special situation by the public administration, which sets the number of agents acting in each of the submarkets for notarial services as well as the basic conditions for practising the profession. Any attempt to establish a greater degree of competition in the activity of such professionals must take this basic restriction into account. The idea is to introduce greater competition but always under two conditions. The first is the above-mentioned institutional restriction. The second is that, in return for the advantages the administration offers these professionals, it requires them to carry out certain activities in the public interest as civil servants and these may be completely independent of strict market criteria. Two examples are the existence of fees with cross-subsidies, and non-payment of certain actions relating to elections. Any policy aiming to promote competition must, therefore, take into account the organization of these professions and evaluate the cost of applying regulations to activities that are not market-linked.

This idea takes us to an argument that carries greater weight in favour of more competition amongst notaries – the need to increase business efficiency by reducing transaction costs measured not only in monetary terms but also in terms of opportunity cost. It has been repeatedly stated – and quite rightly so – that one of the main advantages of notaries is that they offer greater guarantees for contracts and reduce transaction costs for economic agents. We should therefore find out what restrictions are needed on competition for the system to work correctly and in what respects competition should be increased to reduce the cost/benefit ratio for those using notaries' services. But there are also two sound arguments in favour of maintaining a degree of regulation in the market for notarial services. In addition to the above-mentioned problem of asymmetrical information, there is another question that has been much less frequently discussed regarding doubts about complete liberalization of the profession, especially increased price competition. This is a result that is well known in economics whereby there may be incompatibility between strong price competition and a market in which there is a large number of service suppliers, as in the notarial market.

The theory of industrial organization has drawn attention to a possible undesired effect of price competition in specific circumstances.[5] Under conditions of sunk costs, an increase in price competition amongst suppliers of a good or service increases the degree of concentration in the sector. The reasoning behind this is as follows. Growing price competition tends to reduce the benefits for each offeror acting in the market. If companies have incurred sunk costs to enter the market, the drop in profit will prevent them from recovering such costs and some companies will disappear. In the medium and long terms, if companies are to survive in the market they will have to raise their operating margins and, since they cannot do this by raising prices, they will have to alter their production structure. This can be done through mergers or purchases of other companies. If such formulae cannot be applied, the strategy will be to increase the size of the company.

In the case that concerns us, notaries could follow similar strategies. On the one hand, they can join up with other notaries to set up larger offices. On the other, they can try to increase the size of their office, at least in the case of notaries who have a potential market share that is larger than the existent one. Note that such an increase in the size of a notarial office may be efficient with regard to the provision of quality services and the prices at which these are offered. But, if we want a market in which many operators can act simultaneously, this objective may be incompatible with full price competition.

Although price reductions are one of the basic tools for competition amongst economic agents, competition amongst notaries can be increased using other tools. And the most important one would be to increase the number of people offering notarial services in the market. As with the number of judges, the number of notaries is very different in the various civil law countries. Moreover, it is difficult to make direct comparisons because in countries like France and Spain notaries usually work full-time in their profession, but

5 See Sutton (1991).

in others – Germany, for example – not all notaries practise this profession exclusively, with many of them also working as lawyers. It is extremely complicated to determine the optimal number of notaries in a specific country and there may be no clear solution to this problem. As is common in such cases, opinions vary. Consumers of notarial services favour a substantial increase in the number of notaries in order to speed up processes and facilitate the search for notaries prepared to provide urgent services outside their offices, such as recording minutes or drafting a last-minute will. Notaries, on the other hand, feel that an increase in their number would cut back their income, making certain notary offices unprofitable, and reduce incentives for the large investments in human capital needed to qualify for the profession, dragging down the high technical level of notaries.

Regarding the first of these arguments, this is more a problem of demarcating districts and allocating a specific number of notaries to each of them. The second argument is more relevant. It is true that there is usually a direct link between expected remuneration and the intellectual and technical qualifications of people hoping to enter a specific area of public administration. If such high remuneration cannot be expected, outstanding potential candidates might prefer to work as lawyers, for example. But two problems arise with this argument. Firstly, the remuneration is not the only reason why some people choose to become notaries – other attractions include independence and security within the legal profession. It is impossible to calculate the degree to which lower remuneration would exclude possible candidates from the profession but it would definitely be the case to some extent. Secondly, notaries enjoy large quasi-rents and one of the basic characteristics of such quasi-rents is precisely that, if they decrease, this will not necessarily lead to expulsion of the market agents, provided the expected remuneration offers higher returns than could be obtained in a competitive market for a specific investment in human capital.

A second method for increasing competition is related to the demarcation of districts. When we talk about the market for notarial services, it would be more accurate to refer to the submarkets created within each of the notarial districts. There may be large differences in the number of notaries in such submarkets. In some cases, at least as far as the number of notaries is concerned, the markets may be very competitive, as is the case in big cities. The opposite extreme can be found in towns which the demarcation system determines should be covered by a single notary working in a monopoly type situation, although the monopoly is to some extent limited by potential competition from notaries in other districts. Though laws often limit the practice of the profession to the district to which the notary has been assigned, the sharp reduction in transport costs in recent years means that, in some cases, there may be very little difference in consumers' transaction costs between using the services of the notary in their home town and going to one in a neighbouring district. In some districts, notaries have many clients from other locations. This indicates that expanding the districts might be one of the best methods for introducing greater competition in areas where there is only a single notary or a small number of them.

One last way in which competition might be enhanced would be by eliminating, or substantially reducing, the existing limitations on advertising by notaries. Such a measure would affect none of the notary's functions either as a civil servant or as a professional. And it might serve to reduce the information asymmetry which is one of the arguments we have used to justify the public regulation of the notarial profession. There is not much sense in claiming that, because of consumers' insufficient information, it is necessary to regulate both professional practice and the prices notaries charge their customers while, at the same time, making it difficult for customers to obtain more information on what each notary can offer them. There is widespread opposition to advertising based on the idea that it serves mainly to deceive customers into buying a specific product or, in this case, to persuade them to go to a specific notary. But it is often forgotten that, rather than moulding consumer taste or guiding consumers towards a specific supplier, advertising transmits information on the characteristics of a product or service which may help to distinguish it from its competitors. From this point of view, any measure to restrict advertising – except for that which is deceptive or goes against the basic values of society – would be very damaging for market efficiency: firstly, because it would make it more difficult to establish a reputation in the market and, secondly, because it would increase the cost of obtaining information on a large number of products. With regard to notaries, advertising would be especially beneficial for younger notaries and for those who are transferred to a new location and who therefore start out at a clear disadvantage in relation to those already established there.

The results of the Dutch reform are mixed. It is clear that competition is today higher than it was in 1999. But price competition seems to be lower than expected. As predicted, the reform has reduced cross-subsidies, with the effect of a reduction in the price of documents related to real estate and an increase in the price of documents related to family law, such as wills. As was also to be expected, the size of notary offices increased and this has made it difficult to have a wider geographical distribution of notarial services over the country. The main problem, however, seems to be a deterioration in the quality of services, measured in terms of perceptions by clients and other indicators.[6]

In summary, the regulation of competition in a sector that has so many

6 See Kuijpers et al. (2005); Nahuis and Noailly (2005).

special characteristics is very complex because the figure of notary is a hybrid one, falling somewhere between civil servant and private professional. Greater price freedom would probably reduce the prices to be paid by some users but at the cost of raising other prices – since incentives to cross-subsidize are reduced. Concentration indices may also rise. Any possible reform should take both of these variables into account. However, other measures to increase competition could be adopted without obvious negative effects, namely an increase in the number of professionals, enlargement of districts and the authorization of advertising.

2. JURIES

Since ancient times juries have played an important role in the administration of justice. The principal idea that serves as a basis for this institution is that it offers guarantees to a person that he will be judged by his peers and that his case will not be left solely to a judge – a person who, particularly in times past, could be considered as someone whose lifestyle was very different to the social values of the group to which the accused belonged. It is interesting to note that the jury is not the only organ that pursues this objective within the administration of justice. Numerous institutions are based on the same principle. This is the case, for instance, of commerical courts in some countries, ecclesiastic courts and professional disciplinary organs. Although – in large part – these courts have disappeared and have been substituted by courts manned by professional judges, they have served an important purpose throughout the passage of history and are still very relevant in some cases.

The jury was an important organ in the administration of justice in Athenian democracy. In the Middle Ages it would acquire strength in England and, with time, would be adopted in those countries in which British expansion introduced the system of common law. In continental Europe, though not unknown in former times, it received a strong push following the French Revolution and the influence of Napoleonic law. Currently juries exercise an important role in the administration of justice in many countries, but their importance varies greatly. Whilst in some civil law countries it simply does not exist, or is of limited importance, the jury is a very relevant institution in common law countries. This is particularly the case in the United States, where juries are not limited in use to criminal law cases, but are also used in civil cases, and even establish the size of compensation in some tort cases. One should not exaggerate, nevertheless, the importance of the jury in countries such as the United States. Given the frequency with which plea bargaining type procedures are used, it is estimated that only 3 per cent of criminal cases end in trial, and only half of those are ever resolved by a jury.

The importance attached to the role of the jury has differed greatly throughout history. Opinions have ranged from affording it a position as a key institution in guaranteeing an equitable administration of justice to considering it a main factor of many problems in the administration of justice. In the 18th century, Blackstone professed that this institution was 'the glory of the English Law' and 'the most transcendent privilege any subject can enjoy' (quoted in Lieberman 1998).

But in the England of these times it was also possible to encounter opinions and commentaries far more sceptical of the jury, such as those presented by Adam Smith in his Glasgow Lectures.[7] Smith argued that the jury was not an institution characteristic of English law, but one shared by tradition with many European countries which had used them in the past. Smith further raised serious doubts concerning their efficiency, especially due to the rule of unanimity in making decisions, a theme we shall look at again later. He certainly accepted that English law guaranteed the impartiality of the jury and through that the institution contributed towards guaranteeing the liberty of citizens; he was convinced, however, that it was far from being an ideal institution, highlighting what he considered to be serious defects and recommending reform towards the Scottish system, which used the rule of qualified majority.

This criticism has been frequent among many economists who have studied the efficiency of the jury as a decision-making organ in civil and criminal cases. 'The jury is not a good technique and personally I would prefer to be tried by a professional judge if I were falsely accused', concluded Gorden Tullock.[8] Diverse studies that have been conducted in countries utilizing this institution reflect a similar lack of confidence by citizens facing the possibility of being judged by a jury, as well as a reluctance to become a member of one. This does not appear, however, to be the only position found in the world of administration of justice; and it is certainly not the position of a multitude of lawyers, particularly in the United States, where jury trial is an authentic speciality requiring certain skills, particularly in advocacy.

Juries have been defended, principally, as a guarantee of the rights of those who must appear before a court. But there is also an old efficiency argument known as the Condorcet jury theorem.[9] Modern literature on juries and decision making has started to give it increasing relevance.[10] The theorem essen-

---

[7] Smith (1762–66/[1978]).

[8] Tullock (1998), p. 399.

[9] The origin of the theorem can be found in Marquis de Condorcet (1785 [1972]).

[10] In connection with the modern literature on the theme and its application to the economic analysis of law, see for example Edelman (2002).

tially establishes that in a decision-making process in which x persons intervene, and in which each party has a probability superior to 0.5 of voting for the correct solution, the probability of a decision being adopted that is the correct one will be higher, the larger the number of persons involved in the decision. As a result, as this number tends towards infinity, the probability that the correct decision is adopted will tend towards 1.

This theorem has been applied to diverse areas, from testing the superiority of a democratic system in the adoption of efficient collective decisions to the composition of committees, of which the jury is a good example. The problem associated therewith, as is often the case with theorems, is whether these assumptions are borne out in the real world, a question which in the case of decisions made by juries is highly debatable. One may certainly argue that the probability of a juror arriving at a correct decision is superior to 0.5. The reasoning is quite simple. The probability of arriving at a correct decision in random binary cases – such as tossing a coin – is 0.5. If one takes as a starting point that members of a jury act in good faith, without prejudice, and invest some time in obtaining information on a case that they have to decide (evidence, information administered by a judge, lawyers' arguments, and so on), then it is reasonable to think that the probability of reaching a correct decision is superior to 0.5. A more complex issue, however, is what may be understood as a 'correct solution' in the decision of a jury. The question is straightforward if the mission of the jury is simply to decide, say, whether the accused committed a murder or not. But it is more difficult if it is a question of determining how one must interpret specific behaviour, what is the adequate sanction in the case of torts, or whether punitive damages should be applied. On the other hand, one may also argue that, as the number of members in a committee increases, individual members are likely to reduce their investment in information gathering, given that they are conscious that the importance of their decision to the final result decreases as the number of members increases. In juries, however, the rules of unanimity or qualified majority substantially reduce this risk. Particularly relevant is also the problem of independence in the position adopted by each member of the jury in relation to those chosen by other members. In the model it is assumed that each member votes independently of how others vote, a factor which excludes – among other things – the design of strategies to achieve a decision closer to one's preferences. This, as we shall see below, may not be accurate, as a member of a jury may not defend the position he considers to be most just or adequate but the position that – given the opinions of others – is closest to their preferences.

There is ample empirical literature – particularly in the United States – on jury behaviour, decision-making strategies and the possible differences that exist between professional judges and juries. For four decades the classical study on American juries was that conducted by H. Kalven and H. Zeisel.[11] The study is relevant not just because it constituted in its day an important new development in jury studies but also because it served to reinforce the idea that juries act rationally and that their decisions do not differ much from those taken by professional judges in similar cases. Using a sample of 7000 cases – approximately half civil and half criminal – Kalven and Zeisel analysed what judges would have done in cases decided by juries. The result was that in the vast majority of cases – around 78 per cent of civil and criminal cases – judges suggested that their decision would have coincided with that taken by juries, if they had been the ones that had to emit a verdict. The number of criminal cases in which the judge would have acquitted the defendant where the jury found him guilty was only 3 per cent. The major differences were in those cases in which the judge would have found the accused guilty but the jury acquitted the accused, and in those cases where the jury could not arrive at a verdict (hung jury) – 19 per cent of the total of such cases. With regard to civil cases, judges affirmed that they would have awarded lower damages in a large number of cases (52 per cent). They would, however, have awarded higher compensation in 39 per cent of cases, which indcates that juries were more generous, but not to a very high degree. It is interesting to note that a recent study (Eisenberg 2005) seems to confirm these results; finding that in 75 per cent of cases the decisions reached by juries and professional judges would have coincided.[12]

Other studies, however, arrive at different conclusions, particularly in the case of damages which must be set by juries, both compensatory and punitive damages. Sunstein et al. (2002) have strongly attacked the capacity of juries to determine in a rational manner the awarding of punitive damages. Their thesis is that members of the jury are frequently ‘intuitive retributionists’, more influenced by opinions based on moral character than rational calculation, and that they frequently act in an erratic manner. On the basis of empirical analysis of 63 cases in which punitive damages were awarded equal to or above 100 million dollars, Hersch and Viscusi (2004) show that juries often act very differently from judges. Their results indicate that it was juries in 95 per cent of these cases that awarded compensation. Their conclusions are that juries award punitive damages far more frequently than judges; that the amounts fixed by them are significantly higher than those fixed by judges; and that these awards in the case of juries bear less relation to compensatory damages than in the case of judges.

---

11 Kalven and Zeisel (1966)

12 The number of empirical studies on jury verdicts is quite substantial. For a survey of these studies, see Robbennolt (2005).

2.1 Composition and Selection of Juries

The composition of juries varies according to national legal systems and case types. The most common model is that formed by groups of persons without knowledge of the law, selected randomly. This is, however, not the only possibility. One alternative option is to have a mixed jury of judges and persons without knowledge of the law. There is also the possibility of combining both models, allocating to the non-professional jury decisions on culpability and to a mixed jury the determination of sentence. The advantages of one or the other have been the object of many studies, especially in those countries where the jury has been installed *de novo* or re-established after many years of non-use, as in the case of Spain.[13] The main advantageous of mixed juries is that they allow decisions to be made with greater knowledge of the law, whilst ensuring that decisions remain in the hands of citizens that represent society. The principal problem, however, is that the opinions of those who are legal professionals tend to prevail over those of non-professionals, distorting the basic logic behind the use of the jury.

Juries formed entirely by persons without knowledge of the law have a diverse number of members, normally between 6 and 12, even more in some cases. In the case of 'grand juries' – which in some North American states decide whether there is enough evidence for a trial – this number can even exceed 20 members.[14] It is interesting to note that traditionally in common law countries juries are composed of an even number of persons, at least in criminal law cases. The reason for this is not clear. One must bear in mind, however, that problems typically associated with even numbers in the adoption of decisions are not present in juries, given that decisions usually require a qualified majority or even unanimity in some cases.

One important aspect of the formation of a judiciary is the efforts made to ensure that members are representative of society as a whole. An accused should be judged by his peers, but clearly not all his peers can assume this role. It is important then to design a model that guarantees in some way a representation of his peers, in a manner similar to that in which a survey sample or a statistical study attempts to represent the population as a whole. The most common means, and surely the most simple, is the random selection of members of a jury. In practice this method can cause serious problems. Juries are formed by a reduced number of persons, which can lead to the situation

---

[13] Spain stopped using juries in 1936 and returned to using them in 1995, opting for a lay jury model, without the intervention of professional judges.

[14] In England the institution of grand jury, which was made up of 23 laymen and a magistrate who served as president and decided whether or not to open a penal case against the accused, was abolished in 1933.

that they are biased and not sufficiently representative of the whole of society. Even where one considers that on aggregate the total composition of all juries is representative of society as a whole, in individual trials this is not the case.

Consequently juries can reflect prejudices against certain groups of persons or institutions. These prejudices can take various forms. For example, they can take the form of persons treating accused of their own race in a favourable manner, or affording unfavourable treatment to persons of different races. Historical examples of this behaviour are numerous, but one should not consider this issue a thing of the past, as these attitudes continue to exist, and lawyers are very aware of them in the selection of juries. Similarly prejudices exist towards foreign companies and in favour of national firms, prejudices that have been observed in antitrust cases when defendants have their headquarters outside the country in which the trial is taking place. There can also be little doubt that prejudices sometimes exist amongst members of juries that have to decide tort cases, where they fix the punitive damages to be paid by a firm that has lost a case.

It is true that these prejudices can also exist among professional judges. Some of the studies referred to above, however, indicate that bias is less amongst judges than juries, especially in civil law cases. Judicial training and experience are clearly the principal reasons for these differences. To find a solution to this problem is not easy, given that what is sought in a jury is precisely this lack of legal knowledge and experience.

The process of selection of members of a jury also raises problems of bias, for two reasons: the strategies selected by lawyers and the particular interests of possible members. The manner in which juries are selected can vary substantially. In the majority of cases, however, juries are selected randomly on the basis of a list – such as official information regarding residents in a certain zone or registered voters in an electoral district – in a process in which lawyers from both sides can intervene. Lawyers can reject a candidate for two types of reasons. First, a candidate can be rejected because of possible impartiality in a case that may be predictable from prior manifestations of personal characteristics. Second, lawyers can reject a candidate for reasons that are arbitrary in nature and which they are under no obligation to justify in court. In the latter case the maximum number of rejected individuals is normally fixed by law. Given that, as we identified above, members of the jury can be substantially biased, each lawyer attempts to have those members selected who would tend to favour his client. The final result depends on the previous list of candidates and on the ability of lawyers to predict the behaviour of each member when the jury comes to a decision at the end of trial.

In the selection process there is a clear information asymmetry between lawyers and potential members of the jury. Whilst the latter have complete information regarding their characteristics and opinions, the lawyers tend to adopt proxy variables in order to estimate their potential attitudes in a case. This problem is similar to that observed in other areas – such as the hiring of workers – where there are information asymmetries. The most efficient strategy for those who have less information is to rely on stereotypes and consider that an individual is going to behave according to the standard practices of a representative group (men or women, white or black, young or old, rich or poor, and so on). This has the effect that, at the moment of reaching a decision on whether or not to reject a member of a jury, lawyers intentionally try to reduce the social representation of juries and look for stereotypes that they consider favourable to the interests of clients.

The utility functions and cost restrictions of each potential member of the jury also contribute to the fact that juries are not adequately representative of society as a whole. Every person that is selected to form part of a jury can realize a previous cost-benefit analysis in deciding whether or not it is convenient to be selected. If he considers the costs to be higher than the benefits he can adopt a strategy to increase his chances of not being selected. There are basically three benefits to being selected for jury membership. The first is moral in nature, whereby individuals consider themselves to be contributing to one of the basic functions of the state, the administration of justice, and in so doing highlight the fact that they are free citizens, a condition in the case of juries that can be traced back to Athenian democracy. The second benefit is the satisfaction obtained by managing to have one's ideas or interests prevail. If a person thinks many firms that contaminate the environment are acting in an immoral fashion or he suffers from the effects of contamination generated by another firm – though not the firm before the court – he may consider it in his interests to be part of the jury and attempt to have the firm sanctioned. The third benefit is the payment a member of a jury receives for his time and dedication. Although this remuneration is generally small, for some individuals (unemployed, retired, and so on) it can be in their interests to receive the additional income.

The costs of forming part of a jury can be high. The most relevant costs are opportunity costs that can be measured in terms of money and time. A professional who has to dedicate several days to jury service can experience a significant loss of income; and a housewife with small children can encounter serious inconvenience in jury activity. As opportunity costs are individual, everybody values them differently. If one applies some objective criteria for measuring the shadow price of jury membership, there can be little doubt that persons with a high level of income pay a significantly larger price that those with a lower income, or those retired. It is worth noting that, in accordance with the principles of benefit, those with a higher income should have greater incentives than those with a lower income in contributing towards having the court act in their interests. Given the low probability, however, that jury activity is relevant for their personal interests, as well as the opportunity costs associated therewith, it is logical that the tendency to avoid being a member of a jury is higher among persons with higher income. This can lead to the effect that those with lower opportunity costs are over-represented in juries.

It is interesting to compare this situation with a result known in political science as the paradox of voting. It is well known that an elector behaving rationally should not vote, given the costs of doing so (obtaining the necessary information, going to the polls, and so on) are almost always greater than the expected gains, defined as the gain in benefit attained if his choice prevails multiplied by the probability that his vote was decisive in the election. Nevertheless, the majority of people continue to vote. It is debatable, however, whether people would behave in a similar fashion if they were given the choice of being put on the list used as the starting point in jury selection. The costs of being a member of a jury are certainly greater than those of voting in an election, and the benefits experienced by a member of a jury – if his position prevails – are far smaller than the benefit obtained if his party wins the election. On the other hand, however, the probability that the vote of a member of the jury is decisive in the making of a decision is very high, especially in those cases where the jury must arrive at a unanimous verdict, which can be an incentive to participate for those persons who value highly the potential to influence and veto a collective decision.

The second cost is based on the inconvenience and annoyance associated with being a member of the jury. Trends in recent years have substantially reduced these costs, given that one of the most important inconveniences – isolation during trial – is rarely applied today. Participation in sessions and deliberations, as well as change of routine, and so on, can be particularly costly for some people. Procedural rules can influence these costs. If the jury acts, for example, according to the rule of unanimity, the pressures placed on a member who is not of the same opinion as the majority are much higher than in the case where the decision is based on qualified majority. This argument is not new. Adam Smith pointed out two-and-a-half centuries ago that he considered this a considerable deficiency in the regulation of juries in England. In his opinion the principle defect of English judiciaries was the rule of unanimity, which potentially placed a member of the jury under great pressure if he had an opinion that differed from the majority. 'In England the whole jury must be unanimous, which renders the office of a juryman a very disagreeable service', he contended, and for this reason persons of better means tried to avoid exercising this function.[15] His conclusion was clear:

15 Smith (1762–66 [1978]), p. 426.

> People of fashion are not fond of meddling in a jury attended with such inconveniences, and therefore only the meaner sort of people attend the judge. A great man would not consent to be often called and returned, and perhaps treated in such a manner as no gentleman would choose to be.[16]

It would appear that things have not changed much since those times.

2.2 Voting Rules

Surely the most discussed topic in relation to jurors has been the voting rules used in the making of their decisions, and many of the reform initiatives aimed at the jury have had voting rules in mind. The tradition in common law countries has always been the requirement of unanimity in criminal cases. It is not clear when precisely this practice began, but it would appear that by the end of the 14th century the rule was well established in England. It continued thus until the 1960s.[17] It has been and continues to be the general rule in the United States. Whilst the United States Supreme Court in Apodaca *v.* Oregon in 1972 concluded that the right to trial by jury in criminal cases does not demand a verdict be unanimous and that individual states could establish majorities of 10–2 or 9–3 in cases that did not require the death penalty, only three states have established the majoritarian rule in criminal cases.

On the other hand, most American states have adopted the majoritarian rule for verdicts in civil law cases. This preference for stricter rules in criminal cases is based on the broad principle that court decisions in criminal cases can have more serious consequences for the accused, thus necessitating a stronger set of guarantees for defendants than in civil cases.[18] Outside the United States, nevertheless, rules of qualified majority are common in criminal cases,[19] and in some countries where absolute majority rules currently exist reforms are being considered.

If unanimity or a required majority is not reached, the jury is hung, and it is necessary to repeat trial with the costs that this generates for the defendant,

---

16 Ibid.

17 English law since 1967 demands majorities of at least ten members in juries composed of twelve persons.

18 It is noteworthy, however, that this has not always been the case. Before modern criminal codes it was common that criminal cases were far more rapid than civil, with fewer guarantees and possibilities for appeal to a higher instance. It was considered that damages/harm incurred as a result of crime demanded immediate amends, which was not the case in litigation related to questions such as contractual or land disputes.

19 Clearly the fact that the death penalty does not exist in Europe – and in many countries that use juries – has facilitated this transition.

on the one hand, and the administration of justice, on the other. The probability of this occurring is logically higher the stricter the voting rule in question. According to data provided by the Public Law Research Institute, 'a 1967 study estimated that the rate of hung juries decreased from 5–6% with unanimous verdicts to only 2.5% with non-unanimous verdicts.'[20]

Unanimous rules and rules that require a large number in qualified majorities, moreover, can bring about a problem in the behaviour of members of the jury that runs contrary to the basic principles of this institution. This strategic behaviour can be found in both civil and criminal cases. In civil cases with a rule demanding a very large majority, a jury may – after deliberations – be presented with two choices: to hang or to compromise in order to reach a verdict. For the aforementioned cost-based reasons hanging a jury may be an undesirable solution and be recognized by the jury as such. Compromising, however, can require some members of the jury to renounce their convictions and vote against that which they hold to be correct.[21] Consider a tort case with a twelve-member jury which applies a qualified majority rule of ten votes in order to reach a verdict. Suppose nine members consider the defendant to be liable for damages and three consider this not to be the case. The nine members in the majority, moreover, unanimously believe that the award should be set at a substantial figure, x. In accordance with the law, if each member were to vote according to his convictions, the jury hangs and the trial would need to be repeated. It is possible, however, that some members of the majority are prepared to accept a substantial reduction in the award and fix it at, say, $^x/_3$ or $^x/_4$ if any member of the minority is willing to change his vote. If this occurs and a majority vote is reached, two undesirable effects may be the result. First, a basic principle behind the use of a jury may be violated, namely that members should vote in a accordance with what their conscience considers correct. Second, the solution may not be efficient in terms of deterrence, in that compensation is set too low to deter similar undesirable behaviour in the future.

In criminal cases we can find jurors influenced in their decision on the guilt of the accused according to the sentence they expect the judge to pass later, should the accused be found guilty. Consider a jury where members unanimously consider, on the basis of the evidence, that a defendant is guilty and that – on the basis of this evidence – it is very probable in the case of a guilty verdict the judge will apply the death penalty. Further suppose that various members of the jury for certain reasons do not believe the death penalty to be an appropriate sanction. In this case it is probable that some members of the

20 Hunter (1996).
21 Schwartz (2005), p. 348.

jury will vote 'not guilty' and that the jury will hang, not because evidence or the belief that a defendant is guilty does not exist, but rather because of disagreement with the sanction seen fit by the judge.

In common law systems a practice known as jury nullification exists that reflects a conflict between what the law establishes – or what a judge interprets as being the law – and the opinion held by members of the jury. Jury nullification has been interpreted in different ways, from the perspective that it serves as a final guarantee to preserve individual rights against unjust laws, to consideration of it being an abusive practice by members of the jury who are clearly not meeting their obligations.

It is possible, therefore, that a jury reaches a unanimous verdict in favour of a defendant who broke the law, because of dissatisfaction with the law. Under a unanimity rule, when just one member of the jury adopts such a strategy, it will have the effect of hanging the jury and necessitating a repetition of trial.

2.3 The Reform of Juries

In recent years there has been a proliferation of studies and proposals regarding the reform of juries and their introduction in some countries. We have already mentioned the case of Spain; and in Russia and other countries formerly belonging to the Soviet Union, juries have started to be utilized. Some countries in Latin America, for their part, are currently discussing the benefits of introducing juries.

At the same time, nevertheless, there is growing distrust of jury use in various European countries – including England – which are studying means to reduce their application. This distrust towards juries has various causes. First, distrust of having one's case heard by a professional judge has been substituted by the distrust of having a group of people without any knowledge of the law decide it. Second, these trials are slower and are significantly more expensive than those decided by professional judges. This factor is worsened by the fact that juries frequently do not reach a verdict – because they do not attain the required majority – and trials need to be repeated. Moreover, the number of appealed verdicts is significantly higher in cases decided by juries than in those decided by judges.

The most discussed issue in reform projects for juries has been the voting rule. A clear tendency exists to shift away from the requirement of unanimity towards qualified majority. What is being discussed here is – in effect – the relative importance of guarantees for a defendant vis-à-vis the efficiency of the system. There can be little doubt that a rule of unanimity offers greater guarantees for a defendant. From the perspective of efficiency, however, a rule of qualified majority is preferable. On the one hand, it would reduce the number of cases in which a jury is unable to reach a verdict. On the other, it would reduce the time necessary to reach a decision, mitigating the use of veto strategies by one or more members of the jury. In short, it would allow for a reduction both in costs and in congestion in the resolution of matters, which are common problems of numerous court systems.

3. ALTERNATIVE DISPUTE RESOLUTION

Alternative dispute resolution (ADR) has recently been championed by access-to-justice advocates, politicians, lawyers and judges themselves, who have seen it as a means to reduce their own caseload.[22] ADR refers to 'a set of practices and techniques aimed at permitting the resolution of legal disputes outside of the courts'.[23] These methods include mediation and arbitration, as well as a mix of 'hybrid processes'.[24] Though particular methods of alternative dispute resolution may differ from one context to another, a common feature they share is the involvement of a neutral third party who offers an opinion or communicates information about the dispute to the parties involved, hence facilitating its resolution without resorting to formal adjudication. [25]

To understand the potential costs and benefits associated with ADR mechanisms, we need to understand what we are comparing them with. Arbitration is normally compared with adjudication (conventional litigation) and mediation with unfacilitated negotiation.[26] Let us first consider litigation vis-à-vis arbitration.

3.1 Arbitration and Litigation

Though substantial differences exist between legal systems, we have seen that a common characteristic of the adjudicative process is that it is extremely formalized, with strict procedures and rigid criteria. Formal obstacles and requirements differ according to jurisdictions, but the stated goal of these requirements is normally the same, namely to guarantee litigants objectivity

---

22 See Rhode (2004). Due to the popular appeal of ADR, it is not surprising that some authors see it as 'a fugitive label attached to a range of disparate and contradictory, but entangled, projects' (Robert 1993, p. 452). To further confound the matter, numerous features associated with ADR, such as mediation, have long been common features within the litigation process.

23 Mnookin (1998), p. 56.

24 Ibid.

25 Shavell (1995b), p. 1.

26 Mnookin (1998).

and impartiality, as a means to achieve a fair and unbiased outcome. The complexity of substantive and procedural rules generally obliges the contracting of persons specialized in the area, with costs that can be highly elevated. Judges are a neutral third party appointed by the state who have the power and responsibility to run legal proceedings and resolve a dispute. They are specialized in the administration of justice to guarantee their independence, the costs of which include those of inferior technical knowledge, when compared with professionals with expertise in a specific area. Judges make decisions based on legal norms, and their decisions are binding on the parties, subject to appeal to a higher court. Decisions are generally made in a transparent and non-confidential process open to the public.

Arbitration resembles traditional litigation in a number of ways. It involves the use of a neutral third party who hears the disputants' arguments and imposes a final and binding decision generally enforceable by the courts. An arbitrator, however, is typically a private person chosen by the parties. He may or may not have legal training, but almost always has specialized expertise in the area of the dispute in question. Parties often include arbitration provisions for the resolution of future disputes in contracts, but in some instances arbitration is selected after the dispute has arisen. In both instances, parties have to agree to arbitration. Moreover, procedural rules may be set by the parties in their arbitration agreement. Proceedings are generally less formal and, unlike court decisions, generally cannot be appealed.

There are several advantages and disadvantages associated with the use of arbitration vis-à-vis traditional adjudication. A clear advantage is that the parties can select an arbitrator of proven expertise in an area. Judges on the other hand are assigned to them by the court. Expertise can ensure that arbitrators do not need to be instructed in an area, thus moving matters on significantly. Moreover, their decisions may be better informed and more predictable, which can result in lower transaction costs and higher-quality results than through traditional adjudication.[27] Another advantage of arbitration is that there is less procedural formality. Where arbitration procedures are optimally designed from the perspective of the level of procedural complexity, they may offer a 'better fit' than general procedures designed to incorporate a far broader range of considerations and case types.

Arbitration is generally much faster than litigation. Courts reduce and allocate their access by queuing (that is, delay), which can be detrimental to a business. Further, arbitration is less adversarial generally than litigation, which can further reduce any harm caused to business relations and assist future business dealings. In addition, arbitration is private, if the parties so

27 Ibid., p. 57.

wish.[28] Secrecy, of course, from an economic perspective is not necessarily good. It may, for instance, prevent other injured parties who have been wronged from coming forward. It may also prevent other parties from acquiring information on the expected value of their claims. These factors can lead to sub-optimal deterrence and prevent firms from taking necessary precautions. The differences, however, may not be as great as expected. We know that most litigated disputes settle before trial and that secrecy itself is often a characteristic of settlement agreements, facilitated by so-called 'gag orders' or private contracts.

Another important benefit of arbitration is that parties may select to avoid the application of state-made law, by agreeing to something in a contract that would otherwise be overturned within the formal court system. Importantly, parties may agree to adhere to business practices or custom as opposed to statutes or precedents applicable in a specific jurisdiction.[29] These business practices constitute the sources of many basic rules under which contracts are drafted and disputes arbitrated within countries. Bernstein has documented the rejection of state-created law by the diamond industry in favour of its own internal rules, which include arbitration institutions and private sanctions. The Board of Arbitrators of the New York diamond merchants does not apply the New York law of contracts and damages, rather it prefers to resolve disputes according to trade custom and usage.[30]

An obvious limitation of arbitration is its cost. Given that courts are heavily subsidized, parties that decide to turn to arbitration may be forced to pay much higher fees. This has the effect of limiting its application to parties with substantial financial resources.

A point often raised about arbitration is that it is limited in use to situations where a contractual agreement already exists or where there are close ties between disputants.[31] Ex post agreements to arbitrate are clearly less common than ex ante agreements. It is argued that defendants commonly refuse to engage in arbitration ex post, because there are no sufficient sanctions that exist as a result of refusal to submit to arbitration. Nevertheless, there are some instances of ex post agreement to arbitration without need for intervention by the court. For example, non-members of the diamond merchants' organization who have a dispute with members often request ex post that the diamond industry's arbitration board hear their cases and this is done if both parties sign an ex post agreement to arbitrate.[32] Moreover, the growth in private for-profit

---

28 Benson (2000), p. 164.
29 Ibid.
30 Bernstein (1992).
31 Landes and Posner (1979), p. 246.
32 Bernstein (1992), p. 126.

courts and the broadening of the scope of arbitration to disputes where parties did not have a contract suggest cases where parties find arbitration a preferable alternative to the regular courts.[33]

The fact that arbitration decisions are generally not subject to appellate review has itself both costs and benefits. A benefit of this feature is that it can reduce substantially the length of time needed to reach a final decision. On the other hand, however, as the discussion on appeals in Chapter 2 has shown, appellate review serves as a means of error correction. We have seen that a fundamental economic argument behind allowing appeals is that litigants who have been wronged form a subset of all cases, and, instead of having to increase the allocation of resources to all cases to mitigate error, gains can be forthcoming by increasing resources over a reduced set of cases. Individuals possess private information on when they have been wronged and appeals can allow courts to access this information. We have also seen that, where appeal is allowed, the optimal level of investment in adjudication without appeal is higher than when there is appeal, given that the expected harm of an egregious error is higher without appeal than with. What this essentially means is that, all other things being equal, in arbitration where there is effectively no appeals process, the level of resources devoted to dispute resolution should be higher than if appeal were possible. There is, however, reason to believe that in most cases the risk of error due to the lack of an appellate structure is more than compensated by other factors. Arbitrators are, after all, specialized in the resolution of specific disputes, which allows them to generally render a decision faster, thereby reducing the costs for disputants, and reduce the likelihood of error.[34] Further reducing the likelihood of error is the fact that arbitrators have robust incentives to develop expertise and render unbiased decisions in line with past decisions, given that they would otherwise find their services unrequested.[35]

3.2 Mediation and (Non-assisted) Negotiation

Parties frequently choose to engage in negotiations directly, on their own initiative, with the aim of achieving a settlement to a dispute. Negotiation does not require the involvement of a neutral third party that influences the structure of the dialogue or the terms of a resolution. The aim of negotiation is to arrive at a mutually beneficial agreement, whereby parties can save time and costs associated with going to trial. Negotiation generally does not adhere to

[33] Benson (2000), p. 167.
[34] Ibid., p. 162.
[35] Ashenfelter (1987).

any formal legal procedure and parties are not obliged to reach a settlement. This is not to suggest that negotiations may not influence expected trial outcome. We have seen, for example, that, according to Rule 68 of the United States Rules of Civil Procedure, a plaintiff who rejects a settlement offer and later receives a judgment that is less favourable is forced to bear the defendant's post-offer costs. In England and Wales, not just plaintiffs but also claimants can now make offers to settle.[36] Should a defendant reject a claimant's offer to settle and the claimant obtain a more favourable judgment, the defendant will – subject to the court's discretion – generally be ordered to pay enhanced costs plus interest. Given that the litigation costs are very considerable, the risk of losing the entitlement to one's own costs, and of having to pay those of the opponent as well, acts as a powerful incentive to settle. With the stakes increased, the risk-averse plaintiff will have very strong incentives to settle. Settlement negotiations are often organized by parties' respective lawyers. Settlement agreements can subsequently be enforced as a contract and are not normally subject to judicial review.

Mediation, like arbitration, utilizes a neutral third party in order to bring about a resolution to a dispute. However, unlike in arbitration, a mediator cannot force an agreement upon the parties; rather, he aims to assist the parties in reaching a mutually agreeable settlement. In doing so, he will rarely exert pressure on the parties to accept a solution. A mediator will generally manage the mediation process, but there are not standard procedures or fixed rules.[37]

There are substantial differences in mediation techniques and areas of application.[38] Mediators may be rather passive, and not be asked to come up with a solution themselves. In some instances, expert clauses inserted in a contract may lead to the appointment of specialists to monitor the implementation of a contract to ensure performance. When difficulties arise, the expert may be asked to develop an independent solution for the parties to take into consideration.[39] Unlike in litigation, mediation may be conducted, in some instances, where parties are not in the presence of counsel. Moreover, mediators may meet privately with one of the parties, where the other is absent, in order to encourage parties to talk more openly and share confidential information, under the premise that this information is not shared with the other party – a practice frowned upon in many legal systems. Some mediators may indicate to the parties the likely outcome of trial; others may emphasize the needs and wants of the parties, encouraging dialogue and concessions outside the legal dispute in question. Parties may therefore emphasize their 'real' as

---

36 Code of Procedural Rules (CPR) 36.

37 Mnookin (1998), pp. 58–9.

38 See Mnookin et al. (2000) for a description of some of these techniques.

39 Cadiet (1999).

opposed to legal interests. As with negotiation, any agreement can generally be enforceable as a contract.

There is no 'single best' platform for dispute resolution. Mediation, like all other forms of dispute resolution, has numerous costs and benefits. The first advantage of mediation is that it may partially serve as a substitute to the formal adjudicative system, where the latter is functioning poorly. Recall that a primary objective of the formal adjudicative process is not to settle as many disputes as possible, but to deter formal adjudication and support informal dispute settlement by proffering the credible threat of effective state enforcement where informal settlement fails. Where the formal adjudicative process works well, it serves in the background as a credible threat and parties contract in 'the shadow of the law'.[40]

In many legal environments, particularly those in developing countries, vast segments of society find themselves divorced from the formal legal system. The gap between the 'law in the books' and 'law in action' is a serious problem.[41] Mediation and other forms of ADR serve as a means of conflict resolution. However, unlike in a well-functioning legal system, parties are not generally contracting in 'the shadow of the law'. We see, therefore, that, on the one hand, the need for mediation and other forms of ADR may be greatest, but, on the other, incentives to accept these forms of conflict resolution are often blunted, given that the formal legal system – which may be the next step – is not a viable or credible threat.

As earlier discussion has identified, economic theory normally considers settlement failure to be a result of divergent expectations regarding trial outcome. One needs therefore to ask whether mediators can mitigate this divergence of expectations more efficiently than traditional methods, that is, negotiations. There would appear to be a difference of opinion in the literature on this issue. Shavell questions whether mediation would do this better than negotiation.[42] He argues:

> Why should ADR result in parties learning more than they would through voluntary exchange of information and the discovery process? It is sometimes said that ADR provides parties new information because they hear the opinion of a neutral outsider, yet it would seem that parties could always consult individually with outsiders without adopting ADR.[43]

Mnookin suggests, however, that this may be the case with strong rationality assumptions and in particular types of theoretical bargaining models, but it

---

40 Mnookin and Kornhauser (1979).
41 See Buscaglia and Stephan (2005).
42 Shavell (1995b).
43 Ibid., p. 21.

fails to take into account either irrational behaviour or the means by which strategic information can prevent the exchange of information that leads to the convergence of expectations.[44]

A substantial literature has developed based on factors that prevent the resolution of conflicts.[45] It is widely documented that bargaining and coming to agreements are seen as an interactive process with inferences not just on the size of the payoffs available but also related to more subtle behavioural factors. Decisions to cooperate or not to cooperate include a reflection of cognitive and motivational processes. There are biases and limitations that necessarily do not arise out of self-interest. Parties may overvalue the opinion of a leader, for instance. Another well-documented phenomenon in conflict resolution is 'reactive devaluation' whereby a proposal is rated less positively if it comes from an adversary rather than from someone who is considered a neutral or beneficial party (see Ross 1995). A respected and skilled neutral may help overcome these biases. In civil law countries, this role may be partially filled by the notary.[46]

One well-recognized problem within economics that may stall dispute resolution is related to the divergence of interests between lawyers and their clients.[47] Clearly, for instance, where lawyers are paid by the hour, they may have incentives to delay the resolution of disputes in order to increase their fees. Other types of principal–agent problems may also exist, for example where accused managers seek vindication but this runs contrary to a firm's interests. Mediation may facilitate settlement in the presence of these strategic problems.

3.3 Other Forms of ADR

Whilst mediation and arbitration are basic alternatives to formal adjudication, several 'hybrid' dispute resolution processes also exist, which represent adjustments to these basic alternatives.[48] In particular, these alternatives represent the possibility of linking together numerous different procedures, with a clear tendency towards placing ADR systems within the formal system of adjudication.

The mini-trial is an example of a hybrid of the basic alternatives, which is being used in large-scale disputes involving questions of mixed law and fact, in such areas as construction disputes, product liability and antitrust cases. In

---

44 Mnookin (1998), p. 60.
45 Arrow et al. (1995).
46 See discussion on notaries in this chapter.
47 See Chapter 5.
48 Mnookin (1998), p. 59.

a mini-trial, parties present a condensed version of their cases, including core legal arguments and evidence, to executives from both sides, normally with the use of a neutral observer, who sits with management and oversees the hearing.

Another form is a process known as court-annexed mediation in the United States, which is similar to preliminary conciliation in Europe. These processes, as their names suggest, involve the use of a neutral person who attempts to facilitate a negotiated agreement at an early stage in a dispute. Parties are generally obliged to submit themselves to an attempt at mediation before they can have their cases decided by a judge.

Preliminary conciliation was a well-established belief of the revolutionary lawmaker in France. Introduced in a restricted form from the revolutionary ideal in the 1806 French Code, the idea of preliminary conciliation before the justice of the peace was later exported to many countries that came under Napoleonic rule. At the early stage of the Revolution it was perceived that citizens could 'find social harmony through the laws and institutions expressing the Nation's general will'.[49] Preliminary proceedings were imposed in most procedures before District Courts and in appeals against the judgments of those courts.[50] The experiment was quickly resented, being considered by many to be time-wasting and expensive. Moreover, the justices of the peace were considered unprofessional.[51] By the time the French Code was drafted, the role of preliminary proceedings was substantially reduced and experience therewith is often considered unsuccessful.[52] In Spain, until reforms in 1984, it was obligatory to try conciliation and as a general rule one could not present a claim without having gone through the conciliation process.[53] Following the reforms, conciliation became optional. This change as a result of the fact that most efforts at conciliation had proven to be useless.[54]

Court-annexed arbitration has become common in the US Federal Courts.[55] It generally entails that parties to a lawsuit are told that before they can get their case tried they must present it to an arbitral panel composed of practising lawyers. It is therefore an involuntary process. The panel's award is not binding and parties do not have to accept it. The award is seen as an information generator which tells parties about the likely outcome of trial, thus

---

49 Wijffels (2005), p. 198.

50 Ibid.

51 Ibid., p. 199.

52 van Rhee (2005), p. 186; Wijffels (2005), p. 197.

53 Giménez (1999), p. 401.

54 In labour cases it remains compulsory to attempt conciliation prior to proceeding to a full trial (ibid., p. 402).

55 Posner (1996), p. 238.

furthering the possibilities of settlement. Theoretically, parties' estimates of outcomes should converge, which makes settlement more likely.[56]

Yet another method is known as a summary trial. In a summary trial, parties are obliged to present their case before a judge and jury in an abridged mock trial (normally without witnesses, just with counsels' arguments).[57] As with court-annexed arbitration, the outcome is not binding, but serves the parties as a generator of information on the likely outcome of a real jury trial, thus furthering the possibilities of settlement.

3.4 Should Courts Mandate the Use of ADR?

Shifts towards mandatory use of ADR are not new, as we have seen above in our discussion on preliminary conciliation, but they are once again the subject of intense debate. Pursuant to reforms in civil procedure in England and Wales, the Civil Procedure Rules (CPR), ADR has become a key component of the philosophy and basic approach taken by the courts.[58] Whilst use of ADR is – in theory – still voluntary, the court disposes of substantial means to encourage the parties to use ADR where it considers it appropriate. The court, according to the Civil Procedure Rules (CPR Part 26.4), can of its own accord decide to stay proceedings to further alternative dispute resolution or other settlement negotiations. It is recognized that failure to accept its use at the request of either the court or an opponent can have substantial economic consequences. It is not just up to the parties to consider the possibilities of using ADR; it is defined as a case-management duty of the court to encourage the parties to use an ADR procedure if the court considers that appropriate, and to facilitate the use of such. Importantly, the courts may take the pre-litigation activities of the parties into consideration when considering the issue of costs.[59] Parties that resist ADR do so at their own peril, and successive case law has seen unreciprocative parties being forced to bear unfavourable legal costs.[60]

Additional support for the use of ADR can be found in the Queen's Bench guide, the Chancery guide and the Commercial Court guide. Contained in the

---

[56] Ibid.

[57] Ibid., p. 239.

[58] Note, in England and Wales, reference to ADR almost invariably means mediation.

[59] If the court thinks proceedings were unjustifiably issued or could at any stage have been dealt with more justly or effectively through ADR, it can penalize the offending party in costs (part 44.5 CPR).

[60] In Dunnett *v*. Railtrack plc (2002) 2 ALL ER 850, Railtrack, which was a successful litigant, forfeited a costs order in its favour because it declined to consider the court's suggestion to mediate.

last is explicit support for the use of an ADR order in an appropriate case.[61] To wit, case law has offered examples of the court ordering reluctant parties to accept ADR despite strong resistence by one of the parties. Even where courts do not impose an ADR order, the economic costs that may be incurred for failure to accept mediation can similarly coerce the parties. Refusal to accept ADR is, in the words of one judge, a high risk strategy.[62] If the court finds that the mediation did have a real prospect of success, then a party that refuses mediation may be severely penalized in costs.

Both economic theory and empirical evidence seem to highlight some dangers associated with mandating (non-binding) ADR. The most obvious danger is that it may result in an unnecessary additional layer in the adjudication process. This would appear to be the case when ADR does not substantially increase the probability of settlement (particularly when most cases settle anyway), thus not justifying the additional time and costs incurred as a result of its use.[63] This would seem to be supported by evidence on the US Federal Courts.[64] Empirical work by Kim Dayton on the Federal Courts in the US found no statistically significant differences in court delay, number of case terminations per judgeship, trials, or other indicators of the efficient dispatch of federal judicial affairs between district courts that employ alternative dispute resolution and those that do not.[65]

Another factor is the possibility that ADR may lead to an increase in the number of suits brought, if it is cheaper.[66] Where the demand for dispute resolution is dependent on costs and is downward sloping, a decrease in the expected costs of dispute resolution may lead to an increase in the number of suits brought. Moreover, where ADR is a cheaper alternative, some parties who would have opted for early settlement may choose to go to ADR, thus prolonging the dispute. ADR may increase the frequency of suits and decrease the probability of immediate settlement.

Furthermore, research seems to indicate a significant difference between use of mandatory and voluntary ADR processes.[67] Mandatory processes do

---

61 CCG paragraph G1.8.

62 Hurst *v.* Leeming [2002] EWHC 1051.

63 Moreover, some ADR procedures make use of judges' time that could be put to better use. Posner has been especially critical of this procedure. He argues: 'That time might be better utilized mediating cases or disposing of contested cases whether by trial or otherwise. Its contribution to reducing judicial workloads may thus be zero or even negative even if, like compulsory pretrial arbitration, it reduced the number of trials slightly' (Posner 1996, p. 239).

64 See Dayton (1991).

65 Posner (1996), p. 239.

66 Shavell (1995b).

67 For examples, see Rhode (2004).

not increase the choice-set of individuals and may in some cases lead to major disparities in power and resources between parties, depending on the institutional design and safeguards inherent in a specific system. The procedural safeguards inherent in formal adjudicative processes designed to further judicial independence and 'accurate' outcomes may be absent. It is clearly unwise to support ADR systems that are biased purely in favour of cost reduction. Clearly, poorly designed ADR institutions, like all poorly designed institutions, will produce undesirable results. We should not, however, exaggerate the weight of this argument in most circumstances. After all, as we have seen above, arbitrators, mediators and other specialists in ADR are valued precisely because of their expertise. Moreover, the costs of poor results in ADR depend on whether the outcome is binding or not binding. Mandatory arbitration procedures are normally not binding, so they do not exclude the litigation option. Further, the same can be said of mediation. Where the parties arrive at a mutually beneficial settlement, they enjoy a contractually enforceable agreement. Where a party is unhappy with the outcome, he cannot be (and most definitely should not be) obliged to come to or accept an agreement.

7. Conclusion: considerations for a reform agenda

1. STRATEGIES FOR REFORM

Poorly functioning courts run contrary to both legal principles of justice and economic principles of social welfare maximization. Courts and the judicial framework are not secondary or complementary to political economy, but play a fundamental role in the well-being of a market economy. Failure to guarantee and enforce legal rights and norms can have disastrous economic and social consequences, a factor now well recognized by economic, legal and political scholars, leading to national and international efforts to further court capacity. Judicial reform has become a popular theme in many countries; as the informed reader will know, the issue is of much greater importance than merely the courts, touching on features that extend to broader state reform.

Whilst a state of general dissatisfaction with the courts is commonplace in many countries, it is not uncommon for populist opinions to shape the debate surrounding causes and recommendations. The term 'litigation crisis' seems to represent the popular ills that have beset many judiciaries,[1] but the situation is far more complex and nuanced than first suggested. In some countries, such as the United States, politicians, celebrities, comedians, media, novelists and mass culture have accepted the idea of litigiousness and the greed of their citizens and lawyers.[2] Similar observations – though generally not as widespread – can be found in other countries.[3]

Shorthand terminology, such as 'litigation crisis' or 'litigation explosion', is not helpful for understanding the general incentive crisis facing many courts and their users. Caseloads have constantly fluctuated throughout history. Changes in societal preferences have always had an impact on the demand for courts. For instance, the increase in the rate of marital break-ups flooded the courts in many countries in the latter part of the 20th century. Courts, however,

---

1 See Fix-Fierro (2003), pp. 9–10.

2 Haltom and McCann (2004).

3 In Spain, for instance, lawyers are sometimes referred to as 'picapleitos', individuals who are fond of pettifoggery, those trying to stir up disputes.

in many countries are learning to cope with these factors by routinizing procedures, and frequently delegate the issues to negotiations outside the court, permitting the judge to assume a notary function and removing the need for litigation in a large number of cases.[4] Similarly, increases in the number of traffic-related cases have resulted in court congestion, with courts' time being consumed by having to attribute fault and determine liability in road accidents. Shifts towards litigation avoidance, particularly in the form of introducing no-fault liability schemes and a greater role being played by insurance companies, have been effective in reducing the burden being placed on the courts.[5]

Experience has shown us that some of these changes may be short-term. Periods of economic boom, such as that which occurred at the beginning of the Industrial Revolution, generally increase the level of litigation. Unsurprisingly, periods of economic crisis, such as that which occurred after the onset of the Great Depression, also cause caseloads to increase substantially. Another factor that greatly affects the level of litigation is the degree of government intervention in the economy. The welfare state, for instance, and the demands it places on both government and business, has undeniably increased the level of litigation in courts.

At the root of understanding the problem and improving the administration of justice is not addressing broad generalizations related to litigation levels but rather an investigation of the incentive structures facing all stakeholders: litigants, judges, lawyers, notaries, juries, and so on. Public sector reformers must always exercise utmost prudence in their endeavours. This is ever more the case in any reforms related to the administration of justice. Objectives must be decided upon explicitly; that is, it must be determined specifically what a system or reform wishes to accomplish and what the precise impediments are to achieving these ends. Importantly, objectives may be conflicting. For instance, reforms aimed at increasing access to justice may not necessarily be compatible with reforms aimed at ensuring efficiency in the justice system, or reforms based upon optimal deterrence. Moreover, reforms generally require certain requisites to be in place; depending on the scale and scope of the measure, these may include political will and support among key stakeholders in the reform process, financial resources and intellectual know-how, leadership from within the judiciary, and so on. The introduction of reforms without looking at the requisites for achieving reforms is a sure-fire means of blunting their effectiveness. New proposals must always be examined carefully and assessed on the basis of their potential capacity to meet well-defined objectives. The institutional environment must be assessed in order to determine

4 Blankenburg (1991), pp. 12–13.
5 Ibid.

both the credibility and feasibility of reforms. Further, reforms may be best introduced gradually, in order to rectify errors and take advantage of an action learning process. Below, we address considerations for a reform agenda.

The need for and practicability of any measure will differ from one jurisdiction to the next. Whilst the suggestions are abstract, in the sense that we do not focus on a specific jurisdiction, they may be locally accommodated to the particular circumstances prevailing in a jurisdiction, according to the credibility and feasibility of the particular measures.

1.1 Review the Scope of the Law

If a society wishes to change the nature and level of demand for court services, and the costs of the administration of justice, it must think in broader terms than the litigation process itself. Demand for court services is not just a function of cost or quality, but also depends on the initial allocation of legal entitlements and obligations. Hence, the first place a society can look in order to reduce or redirect the level of demand for court services is at the initial allocation of legal entitlements and legal obligations. To illustrate, take the case of decriminalization of consensual crimes. An inherent property of consensual crimes is that demand generates its own supply. A famous example of a misguided policy against 'consensual crimes' was that of Prohibition in the United States. It famously backfired, leading to widespread transgression and the rise of organized crime. Alternatively, consider the impact of gambling restrictions, which have been reversed in many countries and jurisdictions throughout the world. This argument may also be extended towards prostitution and drugs. Consider the latter. In some countries, such as the United States, an extremely high percentage of criminal cases are related to drugs. Instituting a process of decriminalization would reduce the caseload of criminal courts and assist in relieving the burden on overcrowded prisons, and the costs associated with incarceration. In short, laws prohibiting consensual practices are notoriously expensive to enforce, and many of them should be looked at again closely.

There are also numerous examples from civil law which are worthy of greater attention. It is not uncommon, for instance, for car accidents to account for a substantial amount of tort litigation. Indeed, in the United States it is estimated that half of all tort litigation is related to car accidents.[6] From an economic perspective, liability should serve to regulate socially inappropriate or costly action, ensuring that certain activities are curtailed and that a socially optimal level of care is taken. Put differently, liability acts as a deterrent to

---

6 Shavell (2004), pp. 395–6.

parties from deviating from what is considered correct (social welfare maximizing) behaviour. The deterrent effect, however, of liability for car accidents is quite low, as parties already have great incentives not to cause accidents, due to the risk of personal injury, fines, or other penalties.[7] Given that this litigation is so costly, sound arguments can therefore be made for a re-examination of liability structures in key areas and a reduction in the scope of the law.

1.2 Recognize Trade-offs between Accuracy, Cost and Delay

As adumbrated above, procedural systems have traditionally only aspired towards accuracy, neglecting the effects of cost and delay.[8] This position not only leaves ample room for strategic behaviour, particularly on the part of lawyers, but leads to great inefficiency and injustice, where parties are commonly left waiting excessively lengthy periods for the resolution of their disputes, and costs (as well as delay) prevent many from turning to the courts in the first place. The blind pursuit of accuracy without attention to costs and time is a gross mismanagement of resources, and a feeding ground for lawyers (and certain clients) to engage in socially pernicious strategic behaviour. The aim of a justice system should be to achieve an acceptable level of accuracy within a reasonable time and at a predictable and reasonable cost.[9]

Cases should be afforded different management rules according to their importance, proxies for which may be developed along the lines of the amount at stake in disputes, social policy goals, urgency, and so on. In this vein, fewer resources should inevitably be directed towards smaller claims – given that societies should endeavour to find an optimal trade-off between the costs of error and the costs of the procedure in use. The obvious cost of small claims courts is the reduction in accuracy associated with their design and hence an increase in the probability of erroneous decisions.[10] But as the costs of error are lower, so too should be the efforts devoted to resolving these disputes. Moreover, not only do more summary procedures for these types of cases generally offer substantial efficiency advantages vis-à-vis regular procedures, but they also increase access to justice for many individuals who otherwise would not have their cases heard. Mindful of these benefits, societies may consider instituting these procedures in a wider range of dispute types, and may consider expanding summary courts' jurisdiction by raising their maximum threshold dispute value level.

---

7 Ibid.

8 See Zuckerman (1999), Chapter 1.

9 Ibid., pp. 11–12.

10 Fast-tracking certain disputes, particularly over small quantities, is generally considered to have been successful in most countries where it has been introduced.

Conscious of these trade-offs, societies may also review rights of appeal. As discussed at length above,[11] appeal structures serve the purpose of error correction as well as harmonization of law. By offering a subset of wronged litigants the possibility of having an erroneous decision rectified, appeals can offer cost savings to society – given that society can afford to reduce the level of resources devoted to arriving at a correct decision at the first instance. Instead of having to increase resources over all cases to arrive at more accurate decisions, societies by having the appeal option can devote resources to a subsection of cases where decisions are contested. One of the problems, however, with appeals as they stand in many countries in Europe is that appeal rights are too generous. Often, cases may be heard *de novo*. The screening process does not work and numerous cases are unnecessarily heard twice. As the number of cases that are appealed increases, the optimal level of investment in court procedures at first instance should be reduced accordingly. This is unlikely to occur in an efficient fashion for several reasons. First, numerous administrative costs are unavoidable. Second, judges generally do not enjoy having their decisions reversed, so they have incentives to dedicate a certain amount of the court's time to a case. Third, many litigants will use the appeal process in a strategic manner. Where appeal is considered a virtual right, it affords excellent possibilities to litigants with weak cases and their lawyers to drag out the process, possibly forcing the other side into a type of brinkmanship. Wide-open doors to appeals may slightly further substantive justice (in the sense that error costs are reduced), but at a rate that cannot justify the substantial increase in procedural expense.

1.3 Simplify the Law

Simplification of the law can have a substantial impact on the nature and level of litigation. Where the law is clear, it becomes easier to monitor actions, and less costly to resolve disputes.[12] Simple rules can assist courts in resolving a controversy at lower costs. Moreover, fewer cases should ever go to trial as parties can more easily assess their expected costs or gains and thus settle.

---

[11] See Chapter 2, Section 8.

[12] Shavell suggests: 'one way to drastically reduce the amount of litigation is to use predetermined schedules or tables to calculate the damages that accident victims can collect rather than making the amount a subject for litigation.' This approach is followed by many countries when determining the compensation for on-the-job injuries. Insurance can assist victims, he notes, who are worried about under-compensation. Furthermore, simplification of the law reduces discretion and therefore the amount of strategic behaviour on the part of clients and their lawyers (Shavell 1999a, p. 3).

Clear and simple rules not only increase predictability but may also reduce corruption in those environments where judicial corruption is an issue, given that judges enjoy less discretion in making decisions. Further, where human capital is a problem, it places less demands on judges if the law in a particular case is clear. Precisely, however, because judges enjoy less discretion in making decisions, simple rules may also come at a cost, given that simple rules are not necessarily 'the best fit'. Because simple rules are not necessarily a best fit, the development of clear and simple rules requires substantial ex ante investment by lawmakers in the determination of what is optimal.

1.4 Simplify Procedures

Complex procedures are an obvious source of delay. Countries such as Spain and especially Italy are notorious for delays due to procedural complexity and the accumulation of largely obsolete formalities. Though there is a trade-off between cost, delay and accuracy, this does not mean that substantial slack does not exist. Many procedures do not favour accuracy, and may even do the opposite. In some instances, they may further opportunities for individuals to 'play' the system and engage in strategic behaviour. Reducing the power of lawyers to dominate the pace of procedures, as well as their ability to file motions and interlocutory applications, can speed up cases and curb strategic behaviour.[13]

1.5 Encourage Early Disclosure

To further expedition in civil litigation parties may be obliged to prepare their cases before the court really gets involved, with minimal court involvement. In England and Wales, for example, pre-action protocols have been introduced

(a) to focus the attention of litigants on the desirability of resolving disputes without litigation;
(b) to enable them to obtain the information they reasonably need in order to enter into an appropriate settlement; or
(c) to make an appropriate offer (of a kind which can have costs consequences if litigation ensues); and

---

[13] One issue that has received considerable attention is the use of oral argument in proceedings, with civil law systems traditionally seen as under-relying on oral argument and common law systems as going too far in the opposite direction. These are sweeping generalizations, however. At the Supreme Court of the United States, for example, the length of oral argument for most cases is only half an hour per side; at the Federal Courts only 40 per cent of appeals are now argued orally (Posner 1996), p. 160.

(d) if a pre-action settlement is not achievable, to lay the ground for expeditious conduct of proceedings.[14]

These protocols encourage litigants to cooperate before the court is involved, assisting in the reduction of the information asymmetry that exists between litigants regarding the strength of cases and the likely outcome of trial. Moreover, even if the courts later get involved, the protocols can save time, given that much information has been generated.

Another method is to oblige plaintiffs to provide as much information as possible in their statement of claim, which can speed up the hearing for an action. In Hungary, van Rhee reports,[15] plaintiffs have to include in their statement of claim the evidence they rely upon. The defendant is obliged to file a response to this statement at the first hearing, and the plaintiff a speedy reply shortly thereafter. In the Netherlands, plaintiffs must include an anticipated defence in their statements of claim.

1.6 Strengthen Obligations to Advance Proceedings

If one of the purposes of judicial administration is, as Posner identifies, 'to enable courts to dispose – justly, expeditiously, and economically – of the disputes brought before them', then the incentives of all key stakeholders (litigants, lawyers, judges, and so on) must be closely examined in accordance with these objectives.

It is now recognized, for instance, that judges in England and Wales are required to consider not just the case before them in exercising their discretion but the impact of their actions on litigation generally.[16] Judges are compelled to ensure that a case uses only its appropriate share of the resources of the court (CPR Part 1.1(2)(e)). Courts must not just take the relative positions of parties into account but also consider the impact of their decisions on the administration of justice in general, including the court's ability to tend to other cases.[17]

Empowering – and importantly requiring – courts to be more active in the management of civil litigation would seem to be an important factor in any environment where strategic behaviour by clients and their lawyers affects the length and pace of litigation. This statement is valid not only for common law but also for civil law systems. Though subject to strong criticism, along the lines that they run contrary to the adversarial tradition, it would appear that

14 Civil Procedure Rules (CPR), Chapter 10.

15 van Rhee (2004), p. 19.

16 See Jones *v.* University of Warwick [2003].

17 Zuckerman (2003), pp. 9–10.

case management methods and the proactive judge are inexorable trends in common law countries, developed as a response to what is seen as abusive practices by litigants and their lawyers. Civil law countries should equally study case management systems as a means to weed out abusive practices. To wit, the civil law tradition and the role of the judge make their utilization less controversial.

One other means to curtail the use of strategic behaviour by lawyers is to review their obligations as officers of the court and reinforce sanctions for violations. Extending judges' power to fine lawyers for strategic behaviour via court orders for abuse of civil process may be a possibility.[18] Similarly courts can raise the costs of not adhering to procedural deadlines, by refusing to accept late submissions.

1.7 Tie Budget to Needs

Without prejudice to judicial independence, the judicial budget should be allocated, in a transparent and accountable manner, according to the requirements of sectors and individual courts. The internal allocation of the judicial budget should reflex caseload, importance and complexity and be clearly linked to a well-designed case management strategy. The budget should be considered a means to increase both judicial capacity and judicial accountability.

Recently some countries have pushed for constitutional reforms to secure fixed funding. El Salvador, Costa Rica and Honduras, for instance, have all changed their constitutions in order to maintain fixed rates of annual funding for the judiciary.[19] In Costa Rica the judicial branch – which includes the judicial police and the prosecution – receives 6 per cent of public funds available. This figure can, however, be reduced to 1.5 per cent of the total after discounting the costs of the latter two.[20] Fixed percentages are not necessarily the answer.[21] Commonly, countries that have legislatively prescribed percentages do not comply with them. Moreover, a minimum percentage – we know – can very easily become a maximum, when it becomes difficult to justify increases. In addition, there may be adverse effects on judicial accountability, efficiency and transparency where courts no longer need to justify their actions or spend-

18 Key obligations faced by lawyers in the United States as officers of the court include the obligations not to assist a client in fraudulent conduct, file frivolous claims or defences, unreasonably delay litigation, intentionally fail to follow the rules of the tribunal, or unnecessarily embarrass or burden third parties.

19 Davis (2002), p. 165.

20 Ibid.

21 USAID (2002), p. 26.

ing to the legislature.[22] A policy of having a fixed percentage of GDP allocated to the judicial budget may be appropriate for countries with sustained economic growth, but it does not satisfy the needs of countries with volatile economies.[23]

In several countries poor management of resources within the judiciary itself presents the main challenge, as opposed to insufficient budgetary allocation. Too often the judicial budget is seen as a recurrent fund without any appraisal of its efficiency.[24] More detailed studies have shown that budgetary increases were particularly effective where the capital budget grew exponentially compared with those budgetary resources used for salaries, benefits and additional staff. The judicial budget can and should be used as a tool for the development of management strategies tied to case management systems. Financial allocations should be tested against well-defined criteria and assessed according to their ability to reduce the caseload and increase economic efficiency.[25] Ring-fenced financial funds may be directed to specific problems, such as clearance rates in specific courts.[26] Increasing salaries of judicial personnel does not seem to have a substantial impact on performance where salaries have already reached a certain level.[27] However, in the long run, higher salaries may attract better-qualified judges.

It is important that the judiciary itself retain – at least – partial control over or have substantial input into the expenditure of its budget. In the US, for example, it is considered imperative for judicial independence that the judiciary administer itself.[28] The judiciary must, however, be responsible for the presentation of its own financial needs in a professional and competent manner, documenting requirements and identifying what it considers to be its priorities for funding.[29] In many European countries, such as France and Germany, the courts are still administered by the ministries of justice. Experience teaches us that whether or not the judiciary is funded through the ministry of justice is not of primary importance, but rather whether the executive can position itself to use the funding mechanism for its own benefit, influencing the activities of the judiciary.[30] Further, the allocation of funding

---

22 Ibid.

23 McEldowney (2001), p. 3.

24 Ibid., p. 5.

25 Ibid., p. 3.

26 Ibid.

27 See Chapter 3, Section 4.

28 See American Bar Association Central European and Eurasian Law Initiative (2001), p. 13

29 Davis (2002), p. 165.

30 See USAID (2002), p. 14.

within the judiciary can be a significant problem. The independence of lower-court judges is seriously compromised when budget allocations are made untransparently, arbitrarily or in a manner to sanction those that do not fall into line.[31]

1.8 Change Court Fee Structures

As we saw earlier, the main effect of not subsidizing court costs for users would be a reduction in litigation to a sub-optimal level.[32] The reason for this is that litigation produces substantial external benefits, or positive externalities – the most important of which is related to deterrence. Similarly, where court fees are relatively large, access to justice may be denied for individuals who cannot afford to go to court.

One possible solution to this problem may be the use of exponential fees. This could take various forms. For instance, the first day of trial could be free or cost a small fee; the second day would be more expensive than the first; the third more expensive than the second, and so on. There are still some worries, of course, from the perspective of access to justice with this measure. Whilst it would still guarantee poorer litigants access to the courts, this access would be restricted as time passes. This is a trade-off perhaps that some will not accept. To limit objections to this measure, the rate of exponential fee growth should not be very steep. Another problem is related to strategic behaviour, particularly by wealthier clients, who could engage in forms of brinkmanship to acquire a better outcome for themselves. This would have to be combated through the use of fines and other sanctions for strategic behaviour. Moreover, it could be combined with measures obliging parties to do much of the preparatory work without court involvement. Where adequate means cannot be found to curb certain types of strategic behaviour, the measure may be best used in scenarios where litigants are financially on a similar footing.

1.9 Review Alternative Means of Dispute Resolution

An obvious means for consideration in reducing the case burden on courts is to deflect cases towards alternative means of dispute resolution. From an efficiency perspective, however, the benefits of ADR are not always clear-cut. It is necessary to consider the comparative gains of ADR vis-à-vis the traditional system.[33] Where the courts are doing a poor job at meeting the demands

---

31 Ibid., p. 25.

32 See Chapter 4, Section 6.

33 ADR is discussed at length above – see Chapter 6, Section 2.

placed upon them, there may be more scope and reason to further the ADR cause.

In many societies, vast segments of the population consider themselves divorced from the formal legal system, so alternatives to the formal adjudicative system for dispute resolution are their preferred means of dispute resolution. Clearly alternative systems in this context may serve as means for parties to redress their grievances and solve conflicts that otherwise are not available.

ADR mechanisms, however, generally require the parties to support the process. Unlike in the formal adjudicative system, mediators and conciliators – for instance – generally do not have the same tools at their disposal to oblige the parties to cooperate and pull their weight. Where societies recognize specific ADR processes, the law can facilitate their use through various means. For instance, it can enforce clauses in contracts for arbitration or mediation if the parties insert such clauses. It may also afford greater legal weight to the outcomes of these dispute resolution processes. Furthermore, it can make it more costly for parties not to turn to ADR. As adumbrated in Chapter 6, for example, in England and Wales refusal to participate in ADR can have serious cost consequences for litigants; successful litigants who have refused to participate in ADR may be obliged to pay part or all of their legal costs.

1.10 Use Professional Administrators

There seems to be little dispute about the fact that staffing courts with professional administrators can assist in improving court performance. The majority of courts, however, are still not staffed by persons with the necessary management skills to tackle these tasks efficiently. These problems are reflected not only within the courts, but often within the broader system of judicial administration.

As it is a conservative profession, most judiciaries will only employ staff with a legal background. Interesting parallels can be drawn with the medical profession in the recent past. While doctors for many years were the only ones allowed to manage hospitals, this has changed over time and professional managers have taken over the administration of large hospitals, freeing up the doctors to do what they have been trained to do. Professional administrators are now used in many parts of the legal system in the United States, but are not as common in Europe. Singapore is another country that has broken with the tradition of solely employing those with law degrees, bringing in professionals without a law degree to build management information systems, performance-based management systems and innovative management techniques similar to those found in advanced private sector organizations.[34] As a result, individual judges are

---

34 See Langseth (2004).

capable of dealing with a substantially larger caseload than was previously the case.

1.11 Create Competition in the Market for Legal Services

Societies that have introduced much more competition in the provision of services often traditionally confined to lawyers would appear to have been far more successful in reducing the costs for legal services, as well as delays in litigation. This is considered, for instance, to be one of the factors behind the success of the Dutch system of civil justice.[35] Legal advice is not provided solely by lawyers but by numerous groups and organizations. Insurance companies furnish clients with dispute resolution services and lawyers working for companies are able to represent their employers in court. As part of their membership services, trade unions and similar organizations offer legal advice, and insurers offer their own consultation and representation in lower courts. This has assisted in keeping down the costs of litigation and induced the legal profession to hone their skills and services towards better performance, by competing with other service providers.[36] Experience teaches us that the market must be freed up on a broad range of services and not just in specific areas, such as conveyancing, where lawyers and their competitors have narrow, concentrated interests.

1.12 Bundle Claims

There are numerous means to bundle claims for compensation in the case of multiple injuries. These range from test cases to joinder of parties in a suit to legal action taken by associations and class actions. By allowing individuals with a common grievance to share costs, bundling claims makes the law more affordable to many persons. Moreover, bundling claims may allow societies to economize on judicial resources by eliminating duplicative trials over the same set of factual and legal issues. To wit, this is the foundation of bankruptcy proceedings. Countries may consider experimenting with different bundling options and seek out disparate areas of application. Class actions as found in the United States may be seen as the greatest extension of the bundling option. Civil law countries should study this mechanism, with a view to addressing the benefits of the model and eliminating – what are considered by many – its negative features. Indeed, many of the difficulties associated with class actions, such as the determination of compensation by juries, not

---

35 Zuckerman (1999), p. 45.
36 Ibid.

professional judges, and the abusive use of punitive damages are not common legal features in civil law countries.

1.13 Consider Contingent Fee Arrangements

As discussed at greater length above, there are substantial benefits associated with the use of contingent fees. Permitting contingent fees can greatly increase access to justice. They allow poorer individuals the possibility to pursue claims, which – under hourly fees – they may not have the possibility of doing. Moreover, they serve as a risk-sharing device. Unlike under hourly fees, where a lawyer gets paid regardless, under contingent fees his payment is outcome-based. This factor can significantly reduce his incentives to accept meritless cases. Additionally, contingent fees – by giving a lawyer a stake in the outcome – encourage lawyers to increase their level of effort.

We know that there are also costs associated with contingent fees, principally in the form of conflicts of interests. Lawyers paid according to this arrangement may be too willing to settle early, given that they bear substantial costs and only a portion of the benefits associated with their effort. Similarly, if a case goes to trial, they have incentives to under-invest in a case. The benefits associated with the use of contingent fees, however, seem to exceed the costs. Moreover, recent experiences in many European countries have caused people to voice their dissatisfaction with the size of the legal aid bill – including the degree to which it is diverting funds from other public services. Permitting the use of contingent fees may substantially reduce the burden placed on the public purse by legal aid, as it shifts some of the costs away from the state and on to the lawyers.

1.14 Promote Transparency in Judicial Proceedings

Increasing the level of transparency and accountability in courts can greatly improve performance. Open court proceedings not just for affected parties but for all interested citizens, the media and civil society are an important safeguard against malfeasance or the appearance of malfeasance. The 'open court' principle has even been described as 'the most important safeguard for an independent judiciary'.[37] In a push to increase transparency, statistics on individual judges and courts should readily be available regarding caseloads, clearance, the nature of cases, and the number of reversals upon appeal. These statistics are still not readily available in many judicial systems. On individual judges data are unfortunately often either not compiled or not disseminated. In

[37] Kelly (2000), p. 11.

addition to increasing accountability of individual courts, this practice also serves as an internal management strategy, allowing the judicial budget to be allocated more efficiently. These statistics may also be combined with suitable case management strategies.

1.15 Ensure Enforcement of Judgments

Clearly court performance depends on a variety of other entities. For instance, where either judgment is not enforced or enforcement is substandard, courts cannot serve their purpose properly. The costs – both monetary and non-monetary – for winning parties can be substantial. Where non-enforcement becomes commonplace, it can lead to a breakdown in the administration of justice and individuals refusing to go to court to pursue legitimate claims. A review of the cooperation structure that exists between the judiciary and the executive may, therefore, be an important feature of judicial reforms, particularly in poorer countries.

1.16 Make More Use of Technology

Greater use of technology in the management of litigation has yielded substantial results in many countries. It has been consistently shown that – where there is commitment – information technology used for case tracking, jurisprudence, and writing decisions can make courts function more efficiently and reduce clearance rates.[38] Countries that have invested in information technology and infrastructure have commonly managed to reduce procedural times, as opposed to those, for instance, that have favoured an increase in the number of judges.[39] A sound system of case tracking enables court officials to ascertain whether procedural requirements have been met, or are still pending at the different stages of a case, which is of fundamental importance in ensuring a case is progressing according to a legally defined timetable, allowing the implementation of quality control techniques.[40] Case tracking and management systems should also generate information on performance as well as aggregate data necessary for a court to effectively manage its caseload.[41]

Shifts towards greater use of technological advances should form part of a broader strategy towards e-governance; where e-governance refers to the use of information technology to achieve efficiency in systematic and routine works in

---

38 Buscaglia and Dakolias (1999), p. 21.

39 Ibid., p. 24.

40 Ibid., p. 21. As Buscaglia and Dakolias note, these time limits are frequently not enforced.

41 USAID (2001), p. 16.

an administration. It is a critical aspect of governance, as the use of technology allows the streamlining of processes, saving money in the long run, and optimizing human resource allocation for more productive jobs for the society. It not only potentially increases efficiency but can also have a substantial impact on transparency and accountability, given that processes are systematized, discretion is reduced and responsibilities are made more easily traceable.

1.17 Use Outreach and the Media

Public surveys frequently reveal that the judiciary is held in low esteem by citizens, often placed at the lower end of public sector institutions.[42] In many developing countries, citizens reveal that they are completely marginalized from and uninterested in the courts.[43] Whilst some of the criticism is warranted, clearly opinion polls do not provide a very accurate instrument whereby to evaluate the performance of the justice system.

The public acquire much of their information on the judiciary second-hand via the media. Generally, they do not have direct contact with the courts themselves. Reporting on court activities is often focused on extraordinary cases, or cases with entertainment value, and is not reflective of the vast majority of cases. It is easy to appreciate then the fact that the goals of the judiciary and those of the media are clearly non-aligned. Though the requirements of judicial independence clearly necessitate caution in outreach measures and a media strategy, courts must find a means to effectively relate to the citizens they serve. Public enlightenment efforts and media strategy have been important components of several judicial reform programmes. Interaction between judges and civil society may not only be of educational value, but can also contribute to a more favourable public perception. Judges should respond through organized institutional programmes to attacks on judicial decisions and egregious media reporting.[44] Communication is a fundamental element in

---

42 Various studies conducted by the Ministry of Justice in France, for instance, have highlighted that the justice system comes last in a ranking of public institutions (available on their website, http://www.justice.gouv.fr/). In Spain, the Higher Council of the Judiciary (*Consejo General del Poder Judicial*) frequently conducts a public perceptions survey on the 'image of the judiciary'. The results are similarly far from flattering (see, for example, Toharia 2000). Some 46 per cent of respondents considered the administration of justice in Spain to function poorly or very poorly. An additional 30 per cent considered it to function only fairly (ibid., p. 96). For a look at the public perception of the state courts in the US, see National Center for State Courts (1999).

43 See Buscaglia et al. (1995) for a survey of some of these studies in Latin America.

44 Dakolias and Thachuk (2000), p. 367.

improving the perception of the administration of justice, and the judiciary should utilize public relation tools.

2. REFORM IN DEVELOPING COUNTRIES

Whilst in many developed countries factors such as growing caseloads, rising costs, longer delays, employee non-feasance and inefficient organizational structures may be the problem, in most developing countries other factors are prevalent that significantly worsen the situation. These include: endemic corruption; politicization and lack of judicial independence; chronic underfunding; inadequate legal training of judges, their staff and lawyers; and divided and conflict-ridden societies where access is effectively denied to many sectors of society. The reality of legal systems in numerous parts of the world is that they are seen as almost completely irrelevant to the majority of the population, and citizens facing corruption and chronic inefficiency tend to avoid them in search of other alternatives to resolve disputes.[45]

The aforementioned discussion on possibilities for a reform agenda is still very relevant for developing countries; however, given the realities of many societies, emphasis needs to be shifted to include other factors. It would be imprudent to aim for comprehensiveness here in our suggestions, but we do suggest that *greater emphasis* be placed on the following factors.

2.1 Corruption, Capacity Building and Accountability

Corruption is often a reality of courts in less developed countries. Whilst measures to improve court performance in wealthier nations often concentrate on raising efficiency levels in the administration of justice, reform measures in developing countries should move beyond focusing purely on efficiency and capacity building to include accountability and integrity building tools.

There is a clear overlap between measures to improve court capacity and those to improve accountability, given that factors that further efficiency in the administration generally reduce opportunities for improbity. It is imprudent, however, for reforms to concentrate solely on the capacity or efficiency enhancing aspect, neglecting means to further judicial integrity and accountability.

Common capacity enhancing measures include the following:

---

45 Ibid. See also Buscaglia (2004).

Increasing pay Judges and their staff still receive very low salaries in some countries, in some instances not even reaching a 'living wage'. Where judges cannot make ends meet, it is clear that courts will not be manned with appropriately qualified or motivated individuals. Moreover, judges who are poorly paid are generally not held in high regard by citizens and court users.

Improving court infrastructure Court infrastructure remains a problem in many countries. The range of problems is vast, but often includes dilapidated buildings, electricity power shortages, leaking roofs, poor location, and a general lack of facilities. Given these failings, it is clear why international donor agencies often concentrate on this factor.

Increasing the court budget Principle 7 of the United Nations Basic Principles on the Independence of the Judiciary is that 'It is the duty of each Member State to provide adequate resources to enable the judiciary to properly perform its functions.' It is axiomatic that courts should avail of sufficient resources to conduct their work in a just, effective and efficient manner. As we identified above, however, poor management of resources within the judiciary may in some instances be more of a problem than the shortage of resources that are allocated to the courts.

Instituting training activities for judges Training is one of the areas where international donor institutions get most involved. Activities range from legal training to managerial and practical skills, including computer literacy, case and court management, quality and productivity and leadership skills. Long-term results can only be achieved where training activities are institutionalized and sustainable over lengthy periods of time.

Introducing or improving records and case management systems Case filing, tracking and management are important for reasons well beyond court efficiency, extending to the heart of judicial effectiveness, democracy and the rule of law. Information is necessary for courts to deliver timely justice, and control and monitor their operations. Moreover, it is necessary for the furtherance of transparency and the rule of law, as well as monitoring judicial entities.

These measures, however, are not sufficient to make a big impact in an environment where corruption and ethical lassitude are commonplace. Greater attention needs to be given to means to further accountability and integrity. Any proposals for judicial capacity building and accountability must be developed by, or in consultation with, the judges themselves but input should be sought from other key groups including prosecutors, justice ministries and bar associations.

Tackling corruption is notoriously difficult in any public body, but it is more difficult in judiciaries, where court operations are shielded by guarantees of judicial independence. To fight corruption, it is necessary to understand how these networks function. Corrupt exchanges are intricately linked to a broad web of reciprocities, which can be perfectly legal in nature. Consequently, corrupt networks have the ability to sanction with both legal and illegal measures. Sometimes these measures are tied to organizational, economic, social or political issues, giving corrupt parties a plethora of options to sanction those who refuse to conform. To shift a society from high-level to low-level corruption, it is therefore necessary to address measures in each of the above spheres of human activity. It is necessary to understand the mechanisms of corrupt exchanges.[46] A comprehensive and coordinated approach is necessary. The history of reform teaches us that tackling just one aspect of the justice system, such as the courts, is not enough; other areas need to be tackled, such as the police, prisons and other administrative bodies active in the entire justice system. Moreover, since the nature of corruption in the courts may be closely tied to socio-economic and political factors, judicial sector reforms should form only one component of a national good governance programme, given that all pillars of society are necessary to effectuate real and sustainable change. Attempts to clean up the judiciary without addressing other economic, legal, social and political factors are unlikely to be successful.

Among the most important accountability and integrity building measures within the courts are the following:

Introducing a code of conduct Numerous countries have made attempts to improve ethical standards of judges by introducing a code of conduct. Following the establishment of a code, judges should receive training based on its provisions when they are appointed, and if necessary at regular intervals thereafter. Moreover, transparency and publication of a code are important to ensure that those who appear before judges – as well as the media – are informed about the standards of conduct they are entitled to receive from judges.

Training in judicial ethics Introducing a code of conduct is only the first and probably the easiest step. Training in judicial ethics is an essential component of a comprehensive programme to strengthen judicial integrity. Such training may be part of university education, post-graduate training at a judicial institute, or part of continuing professional education. It should not be restricted to

---

46 Fitzpatrick (2003).

judges but should include other court staff as well. Senior judges may informally offer ethics guidance and lead by example. An official ethics body, sometimes a sub-committee to a judicial service commission with the mandate to monitor compliance with the code of conduct and to instil discipline in case of violations, may offer advice on specific ethical problems. Moreover, the disciplinary body will contribute to the implementation and evolution of the ethical standards through the publication and regular reporting of their reasoned decisions. The judiciary needs a mechanism to interpret the code and to keep a record of those interpretations that will be available for those seeking guidance.

Performance indicators[47] Public sector organizations and actors have traditionally resented the idea of their performance being monitored, and this is especially the case for the judiciary, which has often hidden behind arguments of judicial independence. Establishing performance-monitoring standards and indicators for judges, court staff and courts can become an extremely effective way of enhancing both the efficiency and accountability of judicial systems. Performance monitoring requires first and foremost a definition of what is to be measured.[48] Secondly, the means of measuring must be determined. One must argue against an over-reliance on quantifiable criteria. Performance monitoring must be directly linked to training programmes, so that the system does not only demand improvements but also provides for the necessary tools to bring about behavioural change.[49] As with other measures, indicators must be developed by or in close consultation with the judiciary itself.

Reinforcing disciplinary structures[50] Judicial discipline is a most complex matter and the range of mechanisms employed differs greatly; they include elections, criminal prosecutions, commissions, collegial supervision, the media, and civil society.[51] The judiciary must clearly be primarily in charge of disciplinary matters, availing of well-established internal supervisory structures. In the pursuit of accountability, judicial independence is and should always be the primary factor that influences measures, given its importance as an institutional support for the furtherance of the rule of law.

---

47 Performance indicators were discussed at length above. See Chapter 3, Section 8.

48 This may include factors such as judicial efficiency, integrity, quality of and access to justice, transparency and public confidence.

49 Hammergren (2002), p. 22.

50 Disciplining judges was discussed at length above. See Chapter 3, Section 10.

51 Dakolias and Thachuk (2000).

Instituting or improving a public complaints system Feedback from court users is a *sine qua non* for promoting better court management and better court performance. Where the public can voice eventual complaints against all actors in the justice sector, levels of efficiency and probity can be increased. Moreover, whilst increasing the efficacy of a public complaints system may actually in the short term increase the likelihood of scandal and reproach directed at judges and the courts, in the long term it serves as a fundamental democratic tool, both increasing citizen participation and deterring unwanted behaviour. The establishment of a credible and effective complaints system must be well known to court users.

Improving transparency in legal proceedings One factor is transparency in court and judicial procedures, which affords citizens the possibility of supervising their courts. Open court proceedings for interested citizens, the media and civil society are an important safeguard against malfeasance or the appearance of malfeasance. Public commentary on matters such as the efficacy, integrity and fairness of proceedings and outcomes is important and should not be unduly restricted by legislation, judicial orders or the application of contempt-of-court offences.[52]

Whistleblower protection It is important for countries to institute proper systems of whistleblower protection. The basis of whistleblower protection is that it should offer an environment conducive to reporting malfeasance by reducing the costs of blowing the whistle. Though whistleblower protection can reduce the costs of reporting undesirable behaviour, those that report generally receive no financial gain from doing so. The reasons for reporting, therefore, should be ethical. Difficult decisions need to be made regarding, *inter alia*, if and when whistleblowers can remain anonymous and penalties for erroneous, mischievous or strategic complaints. Another consideration is whether employees who have blown the whistle must later prove that they have been discriminated against, or whether the burden of proof should be reversed to show that whistleblowing was not a factor in decisions affecting the official's employment. For example, if a judge or court employee who had reported unethical behaviour were at a later date to find himself transferred to a court where nobody wanted to work, would he have to prove it was on account of his former actions in reporting improbity, or would those who made the decision have the burden of showing that his whistleblowing had nothing to do with their actions?

---

[52] See United Nations Office on Drugs and Crime (2004), p. 114.

2.2 Judicial Independence

Judicial independence, in essence, refers to the ability of a judge to decide a matter free of pressures, bias and inducements. Taken at an institutional level, the independence of the judiciary captures the tenet that the judicial body as a whole must be able to conduct its affairs independently of the legislative and executive arms of government. This, in particular, refers to the judiciary's constitutional role as guardian of the rule of law, reviewing the actions of the other two arms of government for constitutional and legislative compliance. Though judicial systems vary from one country to the next, societies governed by democratic principles universally aim at creating and enforcing laws in the public and private spheres objectively, and independently, without the arbitrary use of influence and power.[53] Moreover, the issue of judicial independence has many subcomponents.[54] Substantive independence refers to making and exercising official duties subject to no other authority than the law. Personal independence refers to adequately secured judicial terms of office, salary and tenure. Collective independence refers to judicial participation in the central administration of the courts, and internal independence refers to independence from judicial superiors and colleagues.

The principle of judicial independence is frequently violated in many developing countries. Many means are subtle and may involve tampering with the judicial budget, but some are quite blatant, and may come in the form of appointments along loyalty lines, perks and benefits, bribery, and disciplining members of the judiciary that do not fall into line.[55] This list is not exhaustive but suggestive of some of these means:

Court infrastructure Where court infrastructure is insufficient, court capacity is seriously hampered. This not only interferes with the efficiency of court operations, but actually may be a sign of executive interference, particularly where this is done as a means to affect the standing of the judiciary in the eyes of the citizenry. It may be a means to intentionally keep the judiciary weak.

Judicial budget The judicial budget is a potential means for interfering with the independence of the judiciary. This is recognized by Principle 7 of The United Nations Basic Principles on the Independence of the Judiciary, which states that 'It is the duty of each Member State to provide adequate resources to enable the judiciary to properly perform its functions.' The judicial budget

53 Dakolias and Thachuk (2000), p. 353.
54 Ibid., pp. 361–2.
55 See also Pope (2000), Chapter 8.

may be consistently too small to meet the needs of the court, or held back as a means to try 'to keep the judiciary in line'. On some occasions, where the judiciary is chronically under-funded, it may even need to seek additional resources, such as office space, furniture, photocopying facilities, and so on, from the private sector, further hampering its ability to operate impartially and independently.

Remuneration Many judicial systems have recognized the importance of remuneration as a means to attract talented and honest members to the judiciary. In Singapore, for instance, a judge's salary is reportedly 90 per cent of that of lawyers of similar experience in the top law firms.[56] In many other countries, judges are given what is often considered a type of honesty premium, which may also be reflective of the responsibilities that accompany their work. Where judges and members of the judicial administration are poorly paid, it is very difficult to attract honest and talented employees. Moreover, it affects the standing of the judiciary in the eyes of the citizens. Where the judiciary is chronically under-funded and salaries hardly constitute a living wage, it becomes increasingly easy to bribe judges and judicial staff. Further, where judges and their staff are viewed as corrupt and treated accordingly, this can lead to a self-perpetuating phenomenon, whereby the perception of improbity, malfeasance and unprofessionalism actually supports their occurrence.

Appointments The appointment process is a clear pathway in many instances for the executive to gain adverse influence within the judiciary, by appointing as many of its supporters or sympathizers as it views possible. For this reason judicial reformers need to give special attention to the appointment process to ensure that mere partisans of the executive are not offered positions that bias the quality, capacity and integrity of the judiciary. Though it is not possible to identify which selection process works best, some fundamentals are emerging:[57]

1. Transparency is of utmost importance. This can be achieved, for example, by advertising judicial vacancies widely, and publicizing candidate's names and their backgrounds, as well as the selection process and criteria. Moreover public comments on candidates' qualifications can be invited and responsibility for the process divided between two separate bodies.

[56] Langseth (2004).
[57] See USAID (2002), pp. 17–18. See also Langseth (2005).

2. Composition of the judicial council can be improved by including actors to dilute the influence of any political entity. We recommend that lawyers, law professors and lower-level judges should participate, and representative members should be chosen by the sectors they represent.
3. Merit-based selection should be put in place. Candidates hereby are evaluated according to their background and tested for their knowledge, abilities and physiological fitness. In some instances, candidates may attend a six-month course at a judicial academy and its graduates receive preference over external competitors for openings. The cost factor provides a significant constraint, particularly when one considers that some of these candidates may not become judges.
4. A judiciary that reflects the diversity of its country is more likely to acquire public confidence and support, important for judicial credibility.

Judicial council The composition of a judicial council is of obvious importance to the notion of judicial independence. It is clear that the majority of the members should come from within the judiciary itself. Nominated members must be of proven integrity and should be subject to background testing.

Benefits Some benefits may come in the form of honours or rankings or promotion, but others may be more blatant, in the form of cars, housing or privileges to children.[58] Those who do not play ball may find themselves posted to unattractive locations, where infrastructure is poor and they do not receive the same privileges as in other areas; this is another familiar means of interference.

Use of the media The media may be an important tool to improve accountability in all arms of government, but they are also a tool of interference, particularly by the executive and wealthy citizens. Strategic use of the media to influence the image of the judiciary in the eyes of the public can greatly affect the perceived accessibility of the courts to ordinary citizens, as well as discredit verdicts and greatly damage the rule of law.

Initiating improper investigations The executive may also use its influence to initiate improper proceedings against members of the judiciary as a means to bring others into line.

Direct interference in specific cases In some countries, it is still common for local and national politicians to induce prosecutors and judges to stop

---

58 See Pope (2000), Chapter 8.

investigations and cases. In some instances, judicial staff may be induced to lose files or cause delays.[59]

Threats and bribery Directly threatening a judge who continues with a case is common in countries where wealthier citizens and politicians are able to get away with it and judges are not afforded adequate protection. Bribery, in addition to being the classical case of corruption, is also the classical form of interference. It is most likely to occur where corruption is considered a norm and ethical standards are low and where corruption goes undetected and unpunished.

As we emphasized above, reform proposals must be developed by, or in close consultation with, the judges themselves in order to protect judicial independence – with input from other key groups including prosecutors, justice ministries and bar associations. Integrity training and accountability structures must always be designed so as not to encroach upon judicial independence, with the general goal of aligning the interests of the judiciary as a whole with those of the citizenry. Self-regulation structures should be developed where they are an option. History teaches us that introducing proper systems of accountability is a slow process, and sustainable processes are themselves best guarded by tradition.

2.3 Shifting Decisions towards the Political Process and the Market

As indicated in Chapter 2, societies generally avail of three means to allocate resources. The first is the market. Within the market, societies' needs and wants are satisfied according to the laws of supply and demand. Freedom of contract, according to which individuals decide of their own accord to enter into the voluntary exchange of goods and services, is at the heart of market transactions. The second is the political process. There are essentially two basic activities. The first activity is that of legislator or regulator, according to which the rules of economic behaviour are defined by the state. The second concerns the state as economic agent, producing goods and services, either in a direct or an indirect fashion. The third means of allocating resources is the adjudicative process, that is, the courts.

---

[59] In 1997 in Guatemala City 1061 case files were lost in 7 of the 11 trial courts alone. As a result of this, many escaped prosecution and other accused remained in jail without a trial. In 1998, following the opening of a first court of clerks office that year with a new records management system, only one case file went missing, and the responsible party was located and prosecuted. See USAID (2002), p. 32.

Clearly in a country of well-paid, professional, and highly educated judges and staff, who avail of substantial economic resources and technological advances, courts are better able to meet the demands placed upon them than in countries where these elements are lacking. The economic costs of attempting to upgrade the courts' resources and man the courts with highly educated staff may, however, be intangible. For this reason countries may consider a greater shift in responsibilities to the two other processes of allocating resources.

Societies may consider creating more precise rules (laws) within the political process and fewer general standards. The distinguishing property of a rule is that it attempts to specify outcomes before a particular case arises.[60] Conversion to a system of rules refers to advances in the law that try to make most or nearly all legal decisions under the governing provision prior to actual cases.[61] A list specifying hazardous substances that may not be released into the water would constitute a rule; a standard may only prohibit the discharge of hazardous substances, leaving the determination of what is hazardous to officials and adjudication.[62] A law that states that no one should drive his car above 100 kilometers per hour is a rule. A law that states that one should drive at a reasonable speed is a standard. Rules are more costly to create than standards, given that the institution responsible (for example, the legislature or government agency) must research and gather enough information before making it law, whereas standards are more costly than rules for individuals to interpret and for adjudicators to apply.[63]

The point we are making is that a greater emphasis on rules may help to accommodate for some of the structural weaknesses inherent in courts; the degree to which a shift toward more rules is necessary depends on local realities within a country. Greater shifts towards rules involve higher investments by the political process, but the legislature and/or agencies may be better equipped to draw on technical expertise than courts and may have specialized knowledge. More precise rules have three advantages: (1) they allow for countries to economize on human capital and court expenditure; (2) they can lead to a reduction in corruption, as judgments become easier to monitor; (3) they may lead to a higher rate of settlement, as there is less uncertainty regarding the likely outcome of adjudications.

However, designing a rule for every eventuality is wasteful. The desirability of a rule over a standard depends on the frequency with which a certain decision occurs. Contingencies that frequently arise are best decided by rules.

---

60 Kaplow (1992, 1999); Sunstein (1995).
61 Sunstein (1995), p. 961.
62 Kaplow (1999), p. 508.
63 Kaplow (1992).

Rules may be simple or complex. Compare, as Diver (1983) suggests, the following two rules:

1. No person may pilot a commercial plane after her 60th birthday.
2. No person may pilot a commercial airplane if she falls within one of the following categories – high blood pressure, high prescription on corrective lenses, and so on.

Both of the above are rules. The first is a general rule, the latter more precise. The advantage of the latter is that it allows for greater inclusiveness, that is, a more accurate picture of actual persons that are still able to pilot a plane. The greater the degree of precision however, the greater are the costs of formulating legal commands.[64] In addition to greater formulation costs there are also greater costs of implementation (enforcement and adjudication costs) and greater accessibility costs; that is, the law becomes more difficult for citizens to understand and to comply with. There are, therefore, important trade-offs between general and complex rules. Moreover, a standard may be converted into a rule through use of precedent,[65] or through constant agency practice.[66] Precedent, however, bears similarities to capital stock that depreciates over time, indicating that when not in use it becomes less rule-like.[67]

We have identified that the seriousness of resource limitations depends on the realities of a particular country and that the economic costs of attempting to upgrade courts' resources and man them with highly educated staff may make these endeavours intangible. It may, then, be advisable to shift some responsibilities from the courts towards the political process. But why stop here? This framework would suggest taking the argument a step further: why should the result be a mere shift in responsibilities from courts to the political process and not also a shift away from reliance on courts towards the market? This would involve the possibility, *inter alia*, of greater deregulation vis-à-vis developed countries. It is ironic that it is precisely in many developing countries where courts do not work well that they are over-burdened with numerous regulations which increase their workload.[68]

[64] Kaplow (1999), p. 503.

[65] Ott and Schäfer (1993); Kaplow (1992), p. 564.

[66] Sunstein (1995).

[67] Kaplow (1999), p. 512.

[68] We have identified that there is a natural limitation in court size as well as the court's resources vis-à-vis the market and the political process. This should not be confused, however, with cases of serious under-funding and lack of resources. Where courts cannot cope with caseloads, for whatever reason, it should not be surprising for them to drop cases for procedural reasons or engage in other undesirable measures to control their workloads.

Moreover, it may involve employing different liability rules from those found in developed countries. As Coase (1960) identified in his seminal work on 'The problem of social cost', the costs of liability must be weighed against the benefits of an activity for a society. In his words: 'The world must have factories, smelters, oil refineries, noisy machinery and blasting, even at the expense of some inconvenience to those in the vicinity and the plaintiff may be required to accept some not unreasonable discomfort for the general good.'[69] And it is the general good associated with the activity that is key here. Clearly where growth is a priority, as it must be in many developing countries, standards should not be the same.

---

69 Coase (1960), p. 11.

References

Abel, Richard L. (2003), *English Lawyers between Market and State: The Politics of Professionalism*, Oxford: Oxford University Press.

Akerlof, George A. (1970), 'The market for lemons: quality uncertainty and the market mechanism', *Quarterly Journal of Economics*, **84**, 488–500.

American Bar Association Central European and Eurasian Law Initiative (ABA/CEELI) (2001), *Judicial Reform Index*: *Manual for JRI Assessors*, available at http://www.abanet.org/ceeli/publications/jri/home.html.

Andrews, Neil (2005), 'The new English Civil Procedure Rules (1998)', in C.H. van Rhee (ed.), *European Traditions in Civil Procedure*, Antwerp and Oxford: Intersentia, pp. 161–81.

Arrow, Kenneth J. (1950), 'A difficulty in the concept of social welfare', *Journal of Political Economy*, **58** (4), 328–46.

Arrow, Kenneth J, Robert H. Mnookin, Lee Ross, Amos Tversky and Robert Wilson (eds) (1995), *Barriers to Conflict Resolution*, New York: W.W. Norton & Company.

Arruñada, Benito (1993), 'The economics of notaries', *European Journal of Law and Economics*, **33** (3), 5–37.

Ashenfelter, Orley (1987), 'Arbitration behavior', *American Economic Review: Papers and Proceedings*, **77**, 342–6.

Ashenfelter, Orley and David E. Bloom (1993), 'Lawyers as agents of the Devil in a Prisoner's Dilemma game', NBER Working Paper No. 4447.

Ashenfelter, Orley, Theodore Eisenberg and Stewart J. Schwab (1995), 'Politics and the judiciary: the influence of judicial background on case outcomes', *Journal of Legal Studies*, **24** (2), 257–82.

Atkins, Burton (1990), 'Interventions and power in judicial hierarchies: appellate courts in England and the United States', *Law & Society Review*, **24**, 71–103.

Bar Council (2001), '"Competition in Professions": The Bar's Consultation Paper in response to the OFT Report', London.

Bar Gill, Oren (2006), 'The evolution and persistence of optimism in litigation', *Journal of Law, Economics and Organization,* 22, 490–507.

Bebchuk, Lucian A. (1988), 'Suing solely to extract a settlement offer', *Journal of Legal Studies*, **17**, 437–50.

Bebchuk, Lucian A. (1996), 'A new theory concerning the credibility and success of threats to sue', *Journal of Legal Studies*, **25**, 1–25.

Bebchuk, Lucian A. and Howard Chang (1999), 'The effect of offer-of-settlement rules on the terms of settlement', *Journal of Legal Studies*, **28**, 489–513.

Becker, Gary S. (1996), *Accounting for Tastes*, Cambridge, MA: Harvard University Press.

Becker, Gary S. and Kevin M. Murphy (1992), 'The division of labour, coordination costs, and knowledge', *Quarterly Journal of Economics*, **107** (4), 1137–60.

Becker, Gary S. and Kevin M. Murphy (2000), *Social Economics: Market Behavior in a Social Environment*, Cambridge, MA: Belknap Press.

Bell, John (2001), *French Legal Cultures*, Cambridge, UK: Cambridge University Press.

Bell, John (2006), *Judiciaries within Europe: A Comparative Review*, Cambridge, UK: Cambridge University Press.

Benson, Bruce L. (2000), 'Arbitration', in Boudewijn Bouckaert and Gerrit De Geest (eds), *Encyclopedia of Law and Economics*, Vol. 5, Cheltenham, UK and Northampton, MA, USA: Edward Elgar, pp. 159–93.

Bentham, Jeremy (1776), 'A Fragment on Government: being an examination of what is delivered, on the subject of Government in General in the introduction of Sir William Blackstone's Commentaries', London: T. Payne.

Bernstein, Lisa (1992), 'Opting out of the legal system: extralegal contractual relations in the diamond industry', *Journal of Legal Studies*, **21**, 115–57.

Blankenburg, Erhard (1991), 'Legal cultures compared', in Erhard Blankenburg, Jacques Commaille and Marc Galanter, *Disputes and Litigation*, Oñati: Oñati International Institute for the Sociology of Law, pp. 11–22.

Blankenburg, Erhard (1994), 'The infrastructure of avoiding civil litigation: comparing cultures of legal behavior in the Netherlands and West Germany', *Law and Society Review*, **28** (4), 789–808.

Blankenburg, Erhard (1996), 'Changes in political regimes and continuity of the rule of law in Germany', in Herbert Jacob, Erhard Blankenberg, Herbert M. Kritzer, D. Marie Provine and Joseph Sanders, *Courts, Law and Politics in Comparative Perspective*, New Haven and London: Yale University Press, pp. 249–313.

Bowers, James W. (2000), 'Security interest, creditors' priorities and bankruptcy,' in Boudewijn Bouckaert and Gerrit De Geest (eds), *Encyclopedia of Law and Economics*, Vol. 2, Cheltenham, UK and Northampton, MA, USA: Edward Elgar, pp. 90–127.

Brealey, Richard A. and Julien R. Franks (2005), 'The organisational structure of legal firms; a discussion of the recommendations of the 2004 review of the regulatory framework for legal services in England and Wales', report prepared for the Department for Constitutional Affairs.

Buscaglia, Edgardo (2004), 'Justice and the poor: formal vs. informal dispute resolution mechanisms: a government-based approach', paper presented at International Workshop on Law and Economic Development, Hamburg University.

Buscaglia, Edgardo and Maria Dakolias (1999), 'Comparative international study of court performance indicators: a descriptive and analytical account', Washington, DC: World Bank.

Buscaglia, Edgardo and Paul B. Stephan (2005), 'An empirical assessment of the impact of formal versus informal dispute resolution on poverty: a governance-based approach', *International Review of Law and Economics*, **25**, 89–106.

Buscaglia, Edgardo, Maria Dakolias and William Ratliff (1995), *Judicial Reform in Latin America: A Framework for National Development,* Palo Alto: Hoover Institution on War, Stanford University.

Cabrillo, Francisco (1994), 'Industrialización y derecho de daños en la España del siglo XIX', *Revista de Historia Económica*, **12**, 591–609.

Cabrillo, Francisco (2007), 'Law and economic development, common law versus civil law', in J. Casas and P. Schwartz (eds), *Problems of Democracy*, Cheltenham, UK and Northampton, MA, USA: Edward Elgar.

Cabrillo, Francisco and Santos Pastor (2001), *Reforma Judicial y Economía de Mercado*, Madrid: Círculo de Empresarios.

Cadiet, Loïc (1999), 'Civil justice reform: access, cost, and delay: the French perspective', in A.A.S. Zuckerman (ed.), *Civil Justice in Crisis: Comparative Perspectives of Civil Procedure*, Oxford and New York: Oxford University Press, pp. 291–346.

Calabresi, Guido (1970), *The Costs of Accidents*, New Haven: Yale University Press.

Cappelletti, Mauro (1989), *The Judicial Process in Comparative Perspective*, Oxford: Clarendon Press.

Carrington, P.D. (2004), 'Asbestos litigation in the United States: delay in court and premature adjudication', in C.H. van Rhee (ed.), *The Law's Delay: Essays on Undue Delay in Civil Litigation*, Antwerp, Oxford and New York: Intersentia, pp. 69–82.

Castán Tobeñas, José (1967), *Derecho Civil Español, Común y Foral*, Madrid: Editorial Reus.

Chiarloni, Sergio (1999), 'Civil justice: an Italian perspective', in A.A.S. Zuckerman (ed), *Civil Justice in Crisis: Comparative Perspectives of Civil Procedure*, Oxford and New York: Oxford University Press, pp. 263–90.

Círculo de Empresarios (2003), '*Justicia, economía y empresa*', mimeo, Madrid.

Coase, Ronald H. (1960), 'The problem of social cost', *Journal of Law and Economics*, **3**, 1–44; reprinted in Ronald H. Coase, *The Firm, the Market and the Law* (1988), Chicago: University of Chicago Press, pp. 95–156.

Cole, Bill (2007), *Trends in the Solicitors' Profession Annual Statistical Report 2006*, London: Strategic Research Unit, The Law Society.
Coleman, James (1990), *Foundations of Social Theory,* Cambridge, MA: Belknap Press.
Condorcet, Marquis de (1785 [1972]), 'Essai sur l'application de l'analyse à la probabilité des decisions rendues à la pluralité de voix', New York: Chelsea Publishing Company.
Consejo General del Poder Judicial (2006), *Memoria Anual*, Madrid: Consejo General del Poder Judicial.
Cooper Alexander, Janet, (2000), *An introduction to class action procedure in the United States*, published online at the http://www.law.duke.edu/grouplit/papers/classactionalexander.pdf, from Conference, Debates over Group Litigation in Comparative Perspective, Duke University and University of Geneva, Geneva, Switzerland, 21–22 July.
Cooter, Robert (1996), 'The theory of market modernization of law', *International Review of Law and Economics*, **16**, 141–72.
Cooter, Robert D. and Daniel L. Rubinfeld (1989), 'Economic analysis of legal disputes and their resolution', *Journal of Economic Literature*, **27**, 1067–97.
Cooter, Robert D. and Daniel L. Rubinfeld (1994), 'An economic model of legal discovery', *Journal of Legal Studies*, **23**, 435–63.
Curran, Barbara A. and Clara N. Carson (1994), *The Lawyer Statistical Report: The U.S. Legal Profession in the 1990s*, Chicago: American Bar Foundation.
Curran, Barbara A. and Clara N. Carson (2004), *The Lawyer Statistical Report: The Legal Profession in 2000*, Chicago: American Bar Foundation.
Curran, Barbara A., Katherine J. Rosich, Clara N. Carson and Mark C. Puccetti (1985), *The Lawyer Statistical Report: A Statistical Profile of the U.S. Legal Profession*, Chicago: American Bar Foundation.
Dakolias, Maria and Kim Thachuk (2000), 'Attacking corruption in the judiciary: a critical process for judicial reform', *Wisconsin International Law Journal*, **18** (2), 353–406.
Damaska, Mirjan R. (1986), *The Faces of Justice and State Authority: A Comparative Approach to the Legal Process*, New Haven, CT: Yale University Press.
Daughety, Andrew F. (2000), 'Settlement', in Boudewijn Bouckaert and Gerrit De Geest (eds), *Encyclopedia of Law and Economics*, Cheltenham, UK and Northampton, MA, USA: Edward Elgar, Vol. 5, pp. 95–158.
Davies, Stephen (2005), 'The economic implications of partnership restrictions in the legal services sector and their possible removal', report prepared for the Department for Constitutional Affairs.
Davis, William (2002), 'The role of court administration in strengthening

judicial independence and impartiality', in USAID, *Guidance for Promoting Judicial Independence and Impartiality*, Washington, DC: Office of Democracy and Governance.

Dayton, Kim (1991), 'The myth of alternative dispute resolution in the Federal Courts', *Iowa Law Review,* **76**, 889.

de Castro, Federico (1984), *Derecho civil de España*, Madrid: Civitas.

Department for Constitutional Affairs (2004a), *Judicial Statistics Annual Report 2004,* London.

Department for Constitutional Affairs (2004b), 'Increasing diversity in the judiciary', Consultation Paper CP 25/04, London.

Department for Constitutional Affairs (2005), *Step Up to a Judicial Career: A Guide to Career Opportunities as a Judge*, London, available at http://www.dca.gov.uk/publications/reports_reviews/judicial career05.pdf.

Devlin, Lord (1976), 'Judges and lawmakers', *Modern Law Review*, **39**, 1–16.

Dicey, Albert V. (1885 [1915]), *Introduction to the Study of the Law of the Constitution*, 8th edn, London: Macmillan.

Diver, Colin S. (1983), 'The optimal precision of administrative rules', *Yale Law Journal*, **93**, 65–109.

Dymond, Glenn (2006), *The Appellate Jurisdiction of the House of Lords,* House of Lords Library, Parliament Library Note, London.

Edelman, Paul H. (2002), 'On legal interpretations of the Condorcet Jury Theorem', *Journal of Legal Studies*, **31**, 327–49.

Eisenberg, Theodore (2005), 'Judge–jury agreement in criminal cases: a partial replication of Kalven and Zeisel's *The American Jury*', *Journal of Empirical Legal Studies*, **2**, 171–206.

Emons, Winard (1997), 'Credence goods and fraudulent experts', *RAND Journal of Economics*, **28**, 107–19.

Emons, Winard (2003) 'Credence goods: the monopoly case', mimeo.

Emons, Winard and Nuno Garoupa (2004), *The Economics of US-style Contingent Fees and UK-style Conditional Fees*, Discussion paper 0407, Volkswirtschaftliches Institut, Universitat Bern.

Epstein, Richard A. (2004), 'Class actions: the need for a hard second look', Manhattan Institute Civil Justice Report, 4.

European Association of Judges (2002), 'Richtereinkommen im Europäischen Vergleich', mimeo.

Fiss, Owen M. (1984), 'Against settlement', *The Yale Law Journal*, **93** (6), 1073–90.

Fitzpatrick, Sean (2003), *Thinking Strategically about Anti-Corruption Reforms: Addressing the Factors that Increase the Likelihood and Maintenance of Corrupt Exchanges*, Frankfurt am Main: Peter Lang GmbH.

Fix-Fierro, Héctor (2003), *Courts, Justice and Efficiency: A Socio-Legal Study of Economic Rationality in Adjudication*, Oxford and Portland, OR: Hart Publishing.

Fon, Vincy and Francesco Parisi (2004), 'Judicial precedents in civil law systems: a dynamic analysis', George Mason Law & Economics Research Paper No. 04–15.

Friedman, David (2000), *Law's Order: What Economics Has to Do with Law and Why It Matters*, Princeton, NJ: Princeton University Press.

Garoupa, Nuno (2004), 'Regulation of professions in the US and Europe: a comparative analysis', American Law and Economics Association Annual Meetings, Paper 42.

Garoupa, Nuno and Frank H. Stephen (2004), 'Optimal law enforcement with legal aid', *Economica*, **71**, 493–500.

Gazal, Oren (1998), 'The economics of standard form contracts', mimeo.

Gessner, Volkmar (ed.) (1996), *Foreign Courts: Civil Litigation in Foreign Legal Cultures*, Aldershot, UK: Ashgate.

Giménez, Ignacio Díes-Picazo (1999), 'Civil justice in Spain: present and future – access, cost, and duration', in A.A.S. Zuckerman (ed.), *Civil Justice in Crisis: Comparative Perspectives of Civil Procedure*, Oxford and New York: Oxford University Press, pp. 385–412.

Gottwald, Peter (1999), 'Civil justice reform: German perspective', in A.A.S. Zuckerman (ed.), *Civil Justice in Crisis: Comparative Perspectives of Civil Procedure*, Oxford and New York: Oxford University Press, pp. 207–34.

Guarnieri, Carlo and Patrizia Pederzoli (2002), *The Power of Judges*, Oxford: Oxford University Press.

Hadfield, Gillian K. (2000), 'The price of law: how the market for lawyers distorts the justice system', *Michigan Law Review*, **98**, 953–1006.

Haltom, William and Michael McCann (2004), *Distorting the Law: Politics, Media and the Litigation Crisis*, Chicago: University of Chicago Press.

Hammergren, Linn (1999), 'Diagnosing judicial performance: towards a tool to help guide judicial reform programs', working paper prepared for the 9th International Anti-Corruption Conference.

Hammergren, Linn (2002), 'Do judicial councils further judicial reform? Lessons from Latin America', Rule of Law Series 28, Washington, DC: Carnegie Endowment for International Peace.

Hay, Bruce L. and Kathryn E. Spier (1998), 'Settlement of litigation', in Peter Newman (ed.), *The New Palgrave Dictionary of Economics and the Law*, London: Macmillan, Vol. 3, pp. 442–51.

Hayek, F.A. (1973–79), *Law, Legislation, and Liberty*, 3 vols, Chicago: University of Chicago Press.

Hersch, Joni and W. Kip Viscusi (2004), 'Punitive damages: how judges and juries perform', *Journal of Legal Studies*, **33**, 1–36.

Holmes, Oliver Wendell (1992), *The Essential Holmes*, edited by Richard A. Posner, Chicago: University of Chicago Press.

Hommes, Rudolf (1998), 'Institutional reliability and development', in Edmundo Jarquín and Fernando Carrillo (ed.), *Justice Delayed: Judicial Reform in Latin America*, Washington, DC: Inter-American Development Bank.

Horwitz, Morton (1977), *The Transformation of American Law (1780–1860)*, Cambridge, MA: Harvard University Press.

Hovenkamp, Herbert (1983), 'The economics of legal history', *Minnesota Law Review* **67**, 645–97.

Hunter, Margo (1996), 'Improving the jury system: nonunanimous verdicts', Public Law Research Institute Report, UC Hastings.

Irish Competition Authority (2006), *Competition in Professional Services: Solicitors and Barristers*, Dublin: Irish Competition Authority.

Jacob, Herbert (1996), *Courts and Politics in the United States,* in Herbert Jacob, Erhard Blankenberg, Herbert M. Kritzer, D. Marie Provine and Joseph Sanders, *Courts, Law and Politics in Comparative Perspective*, New Haven, CT and London: Yale University Press, pp. 16–80.

Jarquín, Edmundo and Fernando Carrillo (eds) (1998), *Justice Delayed: Judicial Reform in Latin America*, Washington, DC: Inter-American Development Bank.

Johnson, Earl, Jr. (2000), 'Equal access to justice: comparing access to justice in the United States and other industrial democracies', *Fordham International Law Journal*, **24**, 83.

Johnston, Jason Scott and Joel Waldfogel (2002), 'Does repeat play elicit cooperation? Evidence from Federal civil litigation', *Journal of Legal Studies*, **31**, 39.

Kalven, Harry and Hans Zeisel (1966), *The American Jury*, Boston: Little, Brown and Company.

Kaplow, Louis (1992), 'Rules versus standards: an economic analysis', *Duke Law Journal*, **42**, 557–623.

Kaplow, Louis (1994), 'The value of accuracy in adjudication: an economic analysis', *Journal of Legal Studies*, **23** (1), 307–401.

Kaplow, Louis (1999). 'General characteristics of rules', in Boudewijn Bouckaert and Gerrit De Geest (eds), *Encyclopedia of Law and Economics*, Cheltenham, UK and Northampton, MA, USA: Edward Elgar, Vol. 5, pp. 502–28.

Katz, Avery (1987), 'Measuring the demand for litigation: is the English rule really cheaper?', *Journal of Law, Economics, and Organization*, **3**, 143–76.

Katz, Avery (1990), 'The effect of frivolous lawsuits on the settlement of litigation', *International Review of Law and Economics*, **10**, 3–27.

Kelly, F.B. William (2000), 'An independent judiciary: the core of the rule of law', International Centre for Criminal Law Reform and Criminal Justice Policy, Vancouver, Canada, mimeo.

Kilian, Matthias (2003), 'Alternatives to public provision: the role of legal expenses insurance in broadening access to justice: the German experience', *Journal of Law and Society*, **30** (1), 31–48.

Klemperer, Paul (2004), *Auctions: Theory and Practice*, Princeton, NJ: Princeton University Press.

Klerman, Daniel (2006), 'Legal infrastructure, judicial independence and economic development', University of Southern California Law School Paper 43.

Komesar, Neil K. (1994), *Imperfect Alternatives: Choosing Institutions in Law, Economics and Public Policy*, Chicago: Chicago University Press.

Kornhauser, Lewis A. (2000a) 'Appeal and the Supreme Court', in Boudewijn Bouckaert and Gerrit De Geest (eds), *Encyclopedia of Law and Economics*, Cheltenham, UK and Northampton, MA, USA: Edward Elgar, Vol. 5, pp. 45–62.

Kornhauser, Lewis A. (2000b), 'Judicial organization and administration', in Boudewijn Bouckaert and Gerrit De Geest (eds), *Encyclopedia of Law and Economics*, Cheltenham, UK and Northampton, MA, USA: Edward Elgar, Vol. 5, pp. 27–44

Kuijpers, Nicole, Joëlle Noailly and Ben Vollaard (2005), 'Liberalisation of the Dutch notary profession: reviewing its scope and impact', CPB Netherlands Bureau for Economic Policy Analysis, Document 93, The Hague.

Landes, William M. (1971). 'An economic analysis of the courts', *Journal of Law and Economics*, **14**, 61–107.

Landes, William M. and Richard A. Posner (1975), 'The private enforcement of law', *Journal of Legal Studies*, **4**, 1–46.

Landes, William M. and Richard A. Posner (1979). 'Adjudication as a private good', *Journal of Legal Studies*, **8** (2), 236.

Landes, William M. and Richard A. Posner (1987), *The Economic Structure of Tort Law*, Cambridge, MA: Harvard University Press.

Langseth, Petter (2004), '*Strengthening court integrity and capacity: report on a study tour to Singapore*', mimeo.

Langseth, Petter (2005), '*Strengthening judicial integrity and capacity: lessons learned and emerging best practices*', mimeo.

Lieberman, David (1998), 'Sir William Blackstone', in Peter Newman (ed.), *The New Palgrave Dictionary of Economics and the Law,* Vol. 1, London: Macmillan, pp. 164–6.

McEldowney, John (2001), 'Developing the judicial budget: an analysis', paper presented at World Bank Conference, St. Petersburg, Russia, 8–12 July.

Messick, Richard E. (1999), 'Judicial reform and economic development', *The World Bank Research Observer*, **14** (1), 117–36.

Messick, Richard E. (2002), 'Judicial reform: the why, the what, and the how', prepared for conference on Strategies for Modernizing the Judicial Sector in the Arab World, 15–17 March, Marrakech, Morocco.

Miceli, Thomas J. (2004), *The Economic Approach to Law*, Stanford, CA: Stanford University Press.

Miller, Geoffrey P. (1986), 'An economic analysis of Rule 68', *Journal of Legal Studies*, **15**, 93–125.

Miller, Geoffrey P. (1997), 'The legal-economic analysis of comparative civil procedure', *American Journal of Comparative Law*, 45, 905.

Ministère de la Justice (2006), *Les Chiffres-Clés de la Justice*, Paris: Ministry of Justice.

Mnookin, Robert H. (1998) 'Alternative dispute resolution', in Peter Newman (ed.), *The New Palgrave Dictionary of Economics and the Law*, Vol. 1, London: Macmillan, pp. 56–60.

Mnookin, Robert H. and Louis Kornhauser (1979), 'Bargaining in the shadow: the case of divorce', *Yale Law Journal*, **88**, 950–97.

Mnookin, Robert H., Scott R. Peppet and Andrew S. Tulumello (2000), *Beyond Winning: Negotiating to Create Value in Deals and Disputes*, Cambridge, MA: Harvard University Press.

Moorhead, Richard and Pascoe Pleasance (2003), 'Access to justice after universalism: introduction', *Journal of Law and Society*, **30** (1), 1–10.

Mueller, Dennis C. (1979), *Public Choice*, Cambridge, UK: Cambridge University Press.

Murray, Petter L. and Rolf Stürner (2004), *German Civil Justice*, Durham, NC: Carolina Academic Press.

Nahuis, Richard and Joëlle Noailly (2005), 'Competition and quality of the notary profession', CPB Netherlands Bureau for Economic Policy Analysis, Document 94, The Hague.

National Center for State Courts (1999), *How the Public Views the State Courts: A 1999 National Survey*, Williamsburg, VA: NCSC–The Hearst Corporation.

Niskanen, William A. (1971), *Bureaucracy and Representative Government*, Chicago and New York: Aldenine-Atherton.

Noonan, John T. and Kenneth I. Winston (1993), *The Responsible Judge: Readings in Judicial Ethics*, Westport, CT and London: Praeger Publishers.

North, Douglass C. (1990), *Institutions, Institutional Change, and Economic Performance*, Cambridge, UK: Cambridge University Press.

Ogus, Anthony (2002), 'The economic basis of legal culture: networks and monopolization', *Oxford Journal of Legal Studies*, 22, 419–34.

Olson, Walter K. (1991), *The Litigation Explosion: What Happened When America Unleashed the Lawsuit*, New York: Penguin Books.

Ott, Claus and Hans-Bernd Schäfer (1993), 'Emergence and construction of efficient rules in the legal system of German civil law', *International Review of Law and Economics*, **13**, 285–302.

Polinsky, A. Mitchell and Daniel L. Rubinfeld (2003), 'Aligning the interests of lawyers and clients', *American Law and Economic Review*, **5** (1), 165–88.

Pope, Jeremy (2000), *Transparency International Sourcebook – Confronting Corruption: The Elements of a National Integrity System*, Berlin: Transparency International.

Posner, Richard A. (1993), 'What do judges maximize? (the same thing everybody else does)', *Supreme Court Economic Review*, **3**, 2.

Posner, Richard A. (1996), *The Federal Courts: Challenge and Reform*, Cambridge, MA: Harvard University Press.

Posner, Richard A. (1998), *Economic Analysis of Law*, 5th edn, New York: Aspen Law and Business.

Pound, Roscoe (1906), 'The causes of popular dissatisfaction with the administration of justice', *American Bar Association Reporter*, **29**, 395–417.

Pound, Roscoe (1909), 'Liberty of contract', *Yale Law Journal*, **18**, 454–87.

Prakash, Saikrishna and Steven D. Smith (2006), 'How to remove a federal judge', *Yale Law Journal*, **116**, 72.

Priest, George L. (1997), 'Procedural versus substantive controls of mass tort class actions', *Journal of Legal Studies*, **26**, 521–73.

Priest, George L. and Benjamin Klein (1984), 'The selection of disputes for litigation', *Journal of Legal Studies*, **13**, 1–55.

Provine, D. Marie (1996), 'Courts in the political process in France', in Herbert Jacob, Erhard Blankenberg, Herbert M. Kritzer, D. Marie Provine and Joseph Sanders, *Courts, Law and Politics in Comparative Perspective*, New Haven, CT and London: Yale University Press, pp. 177–248.

Ramseyer, J. Mark (1994), 'The puzzling independence of the courts: a comparative approach', *Journal of Legal Studies*, **23**, 721–47.

Revesz, Richard L. (1997), 'Environmental regulation, ideology and the D.C. Circuit', *Vanderbilt Law Review*, **83**, 1717.

Rhode, Deborah L. (2001), 'Access to justice', *Fordham Law Review*, **69**, 1785–1819.

Rhode, Deborah L. (2004), *Access to Justice*, New York: Oxford University Press.

Rickman, Neil, Paul Fenn and Alastair Gray, (1999) 'The reform of legal aid in England and Wales', *Fiscal Studies*, **20** (3), 261–86.

Robbennolt, Jennifer K. (2005), 'Evaluating juries by comparison to judges: a benchmark for judging?', *Florida State University Law Review*, **32**, 469.

Robert, Simon (1993), 'Alternative dispute resolution and civil justice', *The Modern Law Review*, **56**, 452–70.

Roberts, John G. (2007), 'Year-end report on the Federal Judiciary', *The Third Branch*, **39** (1), 1.

Rosen, Sherwin (1992), 'The market for lawyers', *Journal of Law and Economics*, **35** (2), 215–46.

Ross, Lee (1995), 'Reactive devaluation in negotiation and conflict resolution', in Kenneth J. Arrow, Robert H. Mnookin, Lee Ross, Amos Tversky and Robert Wilson (eds), (1995), *Barriers to Conflict Resolution*, New York: W.W. Norton and Company, pp. 26–42.

Rowland, C.K. (1991), 'The Federal District Courts', in John B. Gates and Charles A. Johnson (eds), *The American Courts. A Critical Assessment*, Washington, DC: Congressional Quarterly Inc., pp. 61–85.

Rubin, Paul H. (2000), 'Judge-made law', in Boudewijn Bouckaert and Gerrit De Geest (eds), *Encyclopedia of Law and Economics*, Vol. 4, Cheltenham, UK and Northampton, MA, USA: Edward Elgar, pp. 543–58.

Scalia, Antonin (1997), *A Matter of Interpretation*, Princeton, NJ: Princeton University Press.

Schäfer, Hans-Bernd (1998), 'The significance of a well-functioning civil law in the development process', paper presented at a conference of the Latin American Law and Economics Association, Quito, Ecuador, 15–17 June.

Schäfer, Hans-Bernd (2002), 'Legal rules and standards', German Working Papers in Law and Economics, Paper 2.

Schäfer, Hans-Bernd and Andres Schönenberger (2000), 'Strict liability versus negligence', in Boudewijn Bouckaert and Gerrit De Geest (eds), *Encyclopedia of Law and Economics*, Vol. 3, Cheltenham, UK and Northampton, MA, USA: Edward Elgar, pp. 597–624.

Schneider, Andrea Kupfer (1999), 'Getting along: the evolution of dispute resolution regimes in international trade organizations', *Michigan Journal of International Law*, **20**, 697.

Schwartz, Alan (1981), 'Security interests and bankruptcy priorities: a review of current theories,' *Journal of Legal Studies*, **10**, pp. 1–37.

Schwartz, Gary T. (1981), 'Tort law and the economy in nineteenth-century America: a reinterpretation', *The Yale Law Journal*, **90**, 1717–75.

Schwartz, Warren F. (2005) 'The positive and normative puzzle of decision rules for juries: the example of decision rules for civil litigation in state courts', *Hofstra Law Review*, **34**, 345–9.

Shapiro, Martin (1981) *Courts*, Chicago, IL: The University of Chicago Press.

Shavell, Steven (1982), 'The social versus the private incentive to bring suit in a costly legal system', *Journal of Legal Studies*, **11**, 333–9.

Shavell, Steven (1989), 'Sharing of information prior to settlement or litigation', *RAND Journal of Economics*, **20**, 183–95.

Shavell, Steven (1995a), 'The appeals process as a means of error correction', *Journal of Legal Studies*, **24** (2), 379–426.

Shavell, Steven (1995b), 'Alternative dispute resolution: an economic analysis', *Journal of Legal Studies*, **24**, 1–28.

Shavell, Steven (1997), 'The fundamental divergence between the private and the social', *Journal of Legal Studies*, **26**, 575–612.

Shavell, Steven (1999a), 'The law and economics of judicial systems,' *PremNotes* 26, Washington, DC: World Bank.

Shavell, Steven (1999b), 'The level of litigation: private versus social optimality of suit and of settlement', *International Review of Law and Economics*, **19**, 99–115.

Shavell, Steven (2004), *Foundations of Economic Analysis of Law*, Cambridge, MA: Harvard University Press.

Shavell, Steven (2006) 'The appeals process and adjudicator incentives', *Journal of Legal Studies*, **35**, 1–29.

Silver, Charles (2000), 'Class actions – representative proceedings', in Boudewijn Bouckaert and Gerrit De Geest (eds), *Encyclopedia of Law and Economics*, Vol. 5, Cheltenham, UK and Northampton, MA, USA: Edward Elgar, pp. 194–240.

Smith, Adam (1762–66 [1978]), *Lectures on Jurisprudence*, edited by Ronald L. Meek, David D. Raphael and Peter G. Stein, Oxford and New York: Oxford University Press.

Smith, Adam (1776 [1981]), *An Inquiry into the Nature and Causes of the Wealth of Nations*, edited by R.H. Campbell and A.S. Skinner, 2 vol., Indianapolis: Liberty Fund.

Spier, Kathryn E. (1994), 'Pretrial bargaining and the design of fee-shifting rules', *RAND Journal of Economics*, **25**, 197–214.

Spier, Kathryn E. (forthcoming), 'Economics of litigation', in Steven Durlauf and Larry Blume (eds), *The New Palgrave Dictionary of Economics*, 2nd edn, London and New York: Palgrave Macmillan.

Stephen, Frank (2003), 'An economic perspective on the regulation of legal service markets', Evidence submitted to the Justice 1 Committee's Inquiry into the Regualtion of the Legal Profession.

Stephen, Frank H. and James H. Love (2000), 'Regulation of the legal profession', in Boudewijn Bouckaert and Gerrit De Geest (eds), *Encyclopedia of Law and Economics*, Vol. 5, Cheltenham, UK and Northampton, MA, USA: Edward Elgar, pp. 987–1017.

Stigler, George J. and Gary S. Becker (1977), 'De gustibus non est disputandum', *American Economic Review*, 67, 76–90.

Storme, M. (2004), 'Introductory address', in C.H. van Rhee (ed.), *The Law's Delay: Essays on Undue Delay in Civil Litigation*, Antwerp, Oxford and New York: Intersentia, pp. iii–vi.

Sunstein, Cass R. (1995), 'Problems with rules', *California Law Review*, **83**, 953–1023.

Sunstein, Cass R., David A. Schkade and Lisa Michelle Ellman (2003), 'Ideological voting on Federal Courts of Appeals: a preliminary investigation', University of Chicago Law School, Working Paper 198.

Sunstein, Cass R., Reid Hastie, John W. Payne, David A. Schkade and W. Kip Viscusi (2002), *Punitive Damages: How Juries Decide*, Chicago, IL: University of Chicago Press.

Sutton, John (1991), *Sunk Costs and Market Structure*, Cambridge, MA: MIT Press.

Taruffo, Michele (2001), 'Some remarks on group litigation in comparative perspective', *Duke Journal of Comparative and International Law*, **11**, 405–21.

The Economist (2005a) 'Bills and briefs', 26 May 26.

The Economist (2005b), 'The cost of libel trials', 27October.

The Economist (2007), 'Class actions: if you can't beat them, join them', 17 February.

The Lawyer (2005), *Euro 100*, May, available at: www.thelawyer.com.

The Lawyer (2006), *Global 100*, November, available at: www.thelawyer. com.

Toharia, José Juan (1998), 'Insuficiencias, deficiencias y disfunciones del sistema jurídico-judicial y sus consecuencias sobre la actividad económica y empresarial: la administración de justicia vista por el empresariado español', Madrid: Fundación ICO, mimeo.

Toharia, José Juan (2000), *La Imagen de la Justicia en la Sociedad Española: Séptimo Barómetro de Opinion,* Madrid: Consejo General del Poder Judicial.

Tullock, Gordon (1998), 'Juries', in Peter Newman (ed.), *The New Palgrave Dictionary of Economics and the Law,* Vol. 2, London: Macmillan, pp. 395–400.

United Nations Office on Drugs and Crime (2004), *The Global Programme Against Corruption UN Anti-Corruption Toolkit,* 3rd edn, Vienna.

USAID (2001), *Case Tracking and Management Systems*, Washington, DC: Center for Democracy and Governance, Office of Democracy and Governance, Bureau for Democracy, Conflict, and Humanitarian Assistance, US Agency for International Development.

USAID (2002), *Guidance for Promoting Judicial Independence and Impartiality*, Washington, DC: Center for Democracy and Governance, Office of Democracy and Governance, Bureau for Democracy, Conflict, and Humanitarian Assistance, US Agency for International Development.

van Rhee, C.H. (ed.) (2004), *The Law's Delay: Essays on Undue Delay in Civil Litigation*, Antwerp, Oxford and New York: Intersentia.

van Rhee, C.H. (ed.) (2005), *European Traditions in Civil Procedure*, Antwerp and Oxford: Intersentia.

Velayos, M.I. (2004), 'Measures to accelerate Spanish civil procedure (1881–2003)', in C.H. van Rhee (ed.), *The Law's Delay: Essays on Undue Delay in Civil Litigation*, Antwerp, Oxford and New York: Intersentia, pp. 315–34.

Viscusi, W. Kip (ed.) (2002), *Regulation Through Litigation*, Washington, DC: AEI–Brookings Joint Center for Regulatory Studies.

Waldfogel, Joel (1998) 'Reconciling asymmetric information and divergent expectations theories of litigation', *Journal of Law and Economics*, **41** (2), 451–76.

Walter, Gerhard (2001), 'Mass tort litigation in Germany and Switzerland', *Duke Journal of Comparative and International Law*, **11**, 369–79.

Wijffels, Alain (2005), 'Concilation and other types of alternative dispute settlement', in C.H. van Rhee (ed.), *European Traditions in Civil Procedure*, Antwerp and Oxford: Intersentia, pp. 197–205.

Wilkins, David B. (1992), 'Who should regulate lawyers?', *Harvard Law Review*, **105**, 799–887.

Wilson, Robert (1996), 'Signaling in negotiations', in Richard J. Zeckhauser, Ralph L. Keeney and James K. Sebenius (eds), *Wise Choices: Games, Decisions, and Negotiations*, Cambridge, MA: Harvard Business School Press, pp. 400–416.

Wolfensohn, James D. (1999), 'A proposal for a comprehensive development framework', mimeo.

Woolf, Lord (1995), *Access to Justice: Interim Report to the Lord Chancellor on the Civil Justice System in England and Wales*, London: HMSO.

Woolf, Lord (1996), *Access to Justice: Final Report to the Lord Chancellor on the Civil Justice System in England and Wales*, London: HMSO.

Woolf, Lord (1997), 'Civil justice in the United Kingdom', *American Journal of Comparative Law*, **45** (4), 709–36.

World Bank (2002), *Initiatives in Legal and Judicial Reform*, Legal Vice Presidency, Washington, DC, mimeo.

World Bank (2005), 'Legal modernization initiative: justice sector action plan' (draft), mimeo.

Yuille, Lua Kamal (2004), 'No one's perfect (not even close): reevaluating access to justice in the United States and Western Europe', *Columbia Journal of Transnational Law*, **42**, 863.

Zuckerman, A.A.S. (ed.) (1999), *Civil Justice in Crisis: Comparative Perspectives of Civil Procedure*, Oxford and New York: Oxford University Press.

Zuckerman, A.A.S. (2003), *Civil Procedure*, London: LexisNexis UK.

Index